Theology Made Practical

Theology Made Practical
New Studies on John Calvin and His Legacy

Joel R. Beeke
David W. Hall
Michael A. G. Haykin

Reformation Heritage Books
Grand Rapids, Michigan

Theology Made Practical
© 2017 by Joel R. Beeke, David W. Hall, and Michael A. G. Haykin

All rights reserved. No part of this book may be used or reproduced in any manner whatsoever without written permission except in the case of brief quotations embodied in critical articles and reviews. Direct your requests to the publisher at the following addresses:

Reformation Heritage Books
2965 Leonard St. NE
Grand Rapids, MI 49525
616-977-0889 / Fax 616-285-3246
orders@heritagebooks.org
www.heritagebooks.org

Printed in the United States of America
18 19 20 21 22 21/11 10 9 8 7 6 5 4 3 2

Library of Congress Cataloging-in-Publication Data

Names: Beeke, Joel R., 1952- | Hall, David W., 1955- | Haykin, Michael A. G.
Title: Theology made practical : new studies on John Calvin and his legacy /
    Joel R. Beeke, David W. Hall, Michael A.G. Haykin.
Description: Grand Rapids, MI : Reformation Heritage Books, 2017. | Includes
    bibliographical references.
Identifiers: LCCN 2017036618 (print) | LCCN 2017037048 (ebook) | ISBN
    9781601785374 (epub) | ISBN 9781601785367 (pbk. : alk. paper)
Subjects: LCSH: Calvin, Jean, 1509-1564.
Classification: LCC BX9418 (ebook) | LCC BX9418 .T445 2017 (print) | DDC
    284/.2092—dc23
LC record available at https://lccn.loc.gov/2017036618

For additional Reformed literature, request a free book list from Reformation Heritage Books at the above regular or e-mail address.

With heartfelt appreciation to
Steve Renkema
faithful, kind, conscientious, and patient friend,
lover of Christ, and
the world's greatest bookstore manager.
—Joel R. Beeke

With sincere thanks to the fine young pastors who
would make Calvin smile and who have worked with me
as fellow-laborers and friends:
**Marc Harrington, Joel Smit, Ben Thomas,
David Barry, and Mic Knox**.
—David W. Hall

To
Steve Wellum
with deep appreciation for a
beloved friend, esteemed colleague,
and faithful theologian.
—Michael A. G. Haykin

Contents

Abbreviations ix

Preface xi

Part 1: Calvin's Biography

1. The Young Calvin: Preparation for a Life of Ministry
   Michael A. G. Haykin 3
2. Practical Lessons from the Life of Idelette Calvin
   Joel R. Beeke 21

Part 2: Calvin's Systematic Theology

3. "Uttering the Praises of the Father, of the Son, and of the Spirit":
   John Calvin on the Divine Triunity—*Michael A. G. Haykin* 35
4. Calvin on Similarities and Differences of Election
   and Reprobation—*Joel R. Beeke* 49
5. Calvin on the Holy Spirit—*Joel R. Beeke* 63
6. Explicit and Implicit Appendixes to Calvin's View of
   Justification by Faith—*David W. Hall* 89

Part 3: Calvin's Pastoral and Political Theology

7. Calvin's Experiential Preaching—*Joel R. Beeke* 109
8. "A Sacrifice Well Pleasing to God": John Calvin and the
   Missionary Endeavor of the Church—*Michael A. G. Haykin* 131
9. Calvin on Principles of Government—*David W. Hall* 143
10. Calvin on Welfare: Diaconal Ministry in Geneva and
    Beyond—*David W. Hall* 165
11. Christian Marriage in the Twenty-First Century: Listening to
    Calvin on the Purpose of Marriage—*Michael A. G. Haykin* 177

Part 4: Calvin's Legacy

12. Calvin's Circle of Friends: Propelling an Enduring
    Movement—*David W. Hall* 193
13. Calvin as a Calvinist—*Joel R. Beeke*.......................... 211
14. Calvinism and Revival—*Michael A. G. Haykin* 233

Afterword 247

Abbreviations

Calvin, *Commentary*	John Calvin, *Commentaries* (Calvin Translation Society; repr., Grand Rapids: Baker, 2003). Cited by Scripture reference.
Calvin, *Institutes*	John Calvin, *Institutes of the Christian Religion*, ed. John T. McNeill, trans. Ford Lewis Battles, The Library of Christian Classics XX–XXI (Philadelphia: Westminster, 1960). Cited by book.chapter.section.
Calvin, *Institutes* (1536)	John Calvin, *Institutes of the Christian Religion: 1536 Edition*, trans. and annot. Ford Lewis Battles, rev. ed. (Grand Rapids: The H. H. Meeter Center for Calvin Studies/Eerdmans, 1986).
Calvin, *Predestination*	John Calvin, *Concerning the Eternal Predestination of God*, trans. J. K. S. Reid (London: James Clarke, 1961).
Calvin, *Tracts and Letters*	John Calvin, *Tracts and Letters*, trans. Henry Beveridge and Jules Bonnet respectively (1844–1851, 1858; combined repr., Edinburgh: Banner of Truth, 2009).
CNTC	*Calvin's New Testament Commentaries*, ed. David W. Torrance and Thomas F. Torrance (Grand Rapids: Eerdmans, 1959–1972).
CO	John Calvin, *Opera quae supersunt omnia*, ed. Guilielmus Baum, Eduardus Cunitz, and Eduardus Reuss, in *CR*, vols. 29–87.
CR	*Corpus Reformatorum* (Brunsvigae: Schwetschke, 1863–1900).

Preface

Writing in either 1777 or 1778 in a yet-unpublished manuscript, the English Baptist author Andrew Fuller (1754–1815) referred to John Calvin (1509–1564) as "that morning star of the Reformation."[1] While not every author who has written on Calvin since Fuller would describe the Reformer in like terms, there is no doubt that anyone who has written about the Reformation since Fuller's day has recognized the preeminent role Calvin played in sixteenth-century life and thought. Even in Calvin's own day his preeminence was recognized, as the Lutheran theologian Philip Melanchthon (1497–1560) bore witness when he dubbed Calvin "the theologian."[2] The essays in this book, some of them initially written for the quincentennial of the Reformer's birth in 2009, are being published with this recognition in mind.

By outlining the early life of Calvin prior to his going to Geneva in 1536, the first essay by Michael Haykin sets the stage for the various analyses of Calvin's thought that follow. Haykin especially highlights the conversion of Calvin, for, contrary to the thinking of some recent Reformed historians and theologians, conversion was a critical concept for the Reformers, Calvin included. Calvin's first round of ministry in Geneva, beginning in 1536, ended two years later when he and his coworker Guillaume Farel were expelled from the city and Calvin made his way to Strasbourg. There, he married Idelette de Bure and in her found a helper—to use the biblical phrase from Genesis 2— who became vital to his second round of ministry back at Geneva in the 1540s. Idelette would die in 1549 before seeing the triumph of much of Calvin's visionary agenda for the Reformation in Geneva in the late 1550s and

---

1. Andrew Fuller, "Thoughts on the Power of Men to Do the Will of God" (unpublished ms., 1777/1778), James P. Boyce Centennial Library archives, The Southern Baptist Theological Seminary, Louisville, Ky., 3.

2. As quoted in I. John Hesselink, "Calvin's Theology," in Donald K. McKim, ed., *The Cambridge Companion to John Calvin* (Cambridge: Cambridge University Press, 2004), 74.

xii

Preface

early 1560s. But her married life with Calvin is nonetheless important for any reflection on Calvin's life and thought. Joel Beeke in the next essay helpfully points out various lessons we can learn from the life and death of Idelette.

In the second section of this book are four essays that deal with Calvin's theology. First, there is a chapter on Calvin's Trinitarianism by Michael Haykin. It is often said that Calvin's theology, as it first appeared in his first edition of *The Institutes of the Christian Religion* (1536), did not essentially change. Yet this is not exactly true if we look at his thoughts about the Trinity. Calvin was initially loath to use the terminology of classical Trinitarian thought that had been hammered out in the Arian crisis of the fourth century. After confronting errors regarding the persons of the Godhead later in his ministry, Calvin saw the wisdom of using the Trinitarian grammar of the ancient church. The next three essays deal with critical areas of Calvin's thought: two by Joel Beeke that treat respectively Calvin's doctrine of election and reprobation and his perspective on the Holy Spirit, and one by David Hall that considers Calvin on justification. In the essay on election and predestination, Beeke shows that Calvin's "theocentric causality" in saving and condemning sinners does not undermine human responsibility. After considering Beeke's next essay, it should be clear to the reader that Calvin rightly merits the title "the theologian of the Holy Spirit" bestowed on him by the Presbyterian theologian B. B. Warfield. Here Beeke looks at the extensive writing Calvin did on the Spirit's work in relationship to the Scriptures, union with Christ, faith, salvation and sanctification, as well as assurance of salvation and the *charismata*. In his essay on Calvin's theology, David Hall first summarizes Calvin's understanding of the nature of justification—it is both being "reckoned righteous in God's judgment" and "accepted on account of his [that is, Christ's] righteousness." For Calvin, justification always led to sanctification, and thus Hall investigates how this theological concept impacted Calvin's thinking on various theological loci such as Christian liberty, prayer, the church and the state, and the last things.

Part 3 of this volume looks at five areas of Calvin's pastoral and political theology. For all the Reformers, the preaching of the Scriptures was a key mark of a true church. Calvin himself stated, "Whenever we see the Word of God purely preached and heard, and the sacraments administered according to Christ's institution, it is not to be doubted, a church of God exists."[3] The

---

3. As quoted in Sam Chan, *Preaching as the Word of God: Answering an Old Question with Speech-Act Theory* (Eugene, Ore.: Pickwick Publications, 2016), 71.

Preface xiii

Reformation, coming as it did hard on the heels of the invention of the printing press in the fifteenth century, turned back to the biblical emphasis on words, both preached and written, as the primary vehicle for cultivating faith and spirituality. Preaching was thus central for Calvin in arousing and perfecting faith, as Joel Beeke shows in the first essay in this section. The centrality of the pulpit for Calvin is well recognized, but not his commitment to the missionary endeavor given by Christ to the church. The essay by Michael Haykin seeks to rectify this lacuna by looking at Calvin's thought about and actual involvement in missions.

It has been argued that if Calvin had not lived, the political shape of the West would be quite different. David Hall's essay on Calvin's political thought endorses this idea, for, as he notes at the beginning of his paper, "seldom have so few words [as those of Calvin on politics in his *Institutes*] had such political impact." Hall shows that Calvin did not regard politics as a necessary evil, but as an area in which human beings can nobly serve their Creator. The Reformation critique of the medieval view that alms-giving was a virtue that earned merit in the sight of a holy God meant that the Reformers had to approach the issue of poverty through a different avenue. The Genevan church did so through the Bourse Francaise, a diaconal ministry, which David Hall discusses in his essay "Calvin on Welfare." The care of the poor was so important to Calvin that he once remarked, "Do we want to show that there is reformation among us? We must begin at this point, that is, there must be pastors who bear purely the doctrine of salvation, and then deacons who have the care of the poor."[4] The final paper in this section, by Michael Haykin, looks at Calvin's thinking about marriage. Like his political theology, Calvin's views on marriage helped to lay the groundwork for marriage in Western Protestantism that has persisted as a major cultural determinant down to the 1960s.

The final set of essays in part 4 looks at Calvin's legacy. Obviously an entire volume could be written on this subject; therefore, these three essays look at representative areas of impact: in the lives of Calvin's sixteenth-century friends (David Hall); in those who have been called Calvinists, most notably the Puritans of the seventeenth century (Joel Beeke); and in the reviving of Calvin's theological descendants, the Calvinistic Baptists, in the long eighteenth century (Michael Haykin).

---

4. As quoted in Elsie A. McKee, *John Calvin on the Diaconate and Liturgical Almsgiving* (Geneva: Librarie Droz, 1984), 184.

As authors, we wish to thank our gracious wives and families for encouraging us and bearing with us in our studies of Calvin and his thought and legacy over the years. Their kindness to us is beyond our ability to repay. We are also thankful for the expert assistance of Annette Gysen and Paul Smalley as editors, Gary den Hollander as proofreader, Linda den Hollander as typesetter, and Amy Zevenbergen as cover designer.

We trust that reading these essays will reveal that Calvin's thought has been, and still is, a dynamic wellspring of fruitfulness and flourishing in numerous areas of the Christian life. More than 450 years since Calvin experienced the beatific vision, his thinking about God and His Word still possesses what our culture passionately longs for—true relevancy.

PART 1:
Calvin's Biography

—1—

The Young Calvin: Preparation
for a Life of Ministry

Michael A. G. Haykin

In the 1534 treatise *Psychopannychia*, John Calvin's earliest publication after his conversion, the French theologian reflected on what life is like without a saving knowledge of the living God.[1] While his comments are not autobiographical in form, they can be interpreted, as Heiko Oberman has pointed out, as a commentary on his life prior to his conversion:

> Do you want to know what the death of the soul is? It is to be without God, to be deserted by God, to be abandoned to yourself.... Since there is no light outside of God who lights our darkness, when he withdraws his light then our soul is certainly blind and buried in darkness; our soul is mute because it cannot confess, and call out to embrace God. The soul is deaf because it cannot hear his voice. The soul is crippled since it does not have a hold on...God.[2]

It is not surprising that Calvin would have veiled his experience in this way, for of all the Reformers, he was the most reluctant to discuss details of his life in works destined for public consumption. As he told Cardinal Jacopo Sadoleto (1477–1547), "I am not eager to speak about myself."[3] He

---

1. For help with obtaining a couple of the sources for this chapter, I am indebted to Dr. Monte Shanks and Dr. Ian Clary.

2. As quoted in Heiko A. Oberman, "*Subita Conversio*: The Conversion of John Calvin," in *Reformiertes Erbe: Festschrift für Gottfried W. Locher zu seinem 80. Geburtstag*, ed. Heiko A. Oberman, Ernst Saxer, Alfred Schindler, and Heinzpeter Stucki, trans. Heiko Oberman, *Zwingliana* 19 (Zürich: Theologischer Verlag, 1993), 2:295n4. For a translation of *Psychopannychia*, see Calvin, *Tracts and Letters*, 3:413–90. For Beveridge's rendering of the passage that Oberman has translated, see *Tracts and Letters*, 3:454–55. For the Latin behind this translation, see *CO*, 5:204–205. For a study of *Psychopannychia*, see George H. Tavard, *The Starting Point of Calvin's Theology* (Grand Rapids: Eerdmans, 2000). Also see Bernard Cottret, *Calvin: A Biography*, trans. M. Wallace McDonald (Grand Rapids: Eerdmans, 2000), 77–82.

3. *De me non libenter loquor*. Calvin makes this remark in his *Reply to Sadoleto*, in *CO*, 5:389.

4   Theology Made Practical

had, as Heiko Oberman aptly puts it, a "dislike of self-disclosure."[4] Calvin himself has provided only two major sources for details about his life before his conversion, and they should be used with caution since they are not explicitly autobiographical[5]—namely, sections from his *Reply to Sadoleto* (1539) and from the preface to his commentary on the Psalms (1557).[6] Calvin's occasional remarks here and there in his works, some of which are noted below, help fill in some of the gaps of his early life, as does the biography by his friend and ministerial colleague Theodore Beza (1519–1605). Beza wrote two lives of his friend and mentor. The first saw the light of day in 1564, three months after Calvin's death.[7] The following year, one of Beza's fellow pastors, Nicolas Colladon, published a considerably enlarged life of Calvin that built on the work of Beza but incorporated new material.[8] Ten years later, after Colladon had left Geneva in 1571 for Lausanne, Beza issued a revision of his own biography that made liberal use of the material in Colladon's work.[9]

---

4. Heiko Oberman, *Initia Calvini: The Matrix of Calvin's Reformation* (Amsterdam: Koninklijke Nederlandse Akademie van Wetenschappen, 1991), 7. This article can also be found in *Calvinus Sacrae Scripturae Professor: Calvin as Confessor of Holy Scripture*, ed. Wilhelm H. Neuser (Grand Rapids: Eerdmans, 1990), 113–54.

5. Thus, Richard Stauffer, "Les discours à la première personnes dans les sermons de Calvin," in *Regards contemporains sur Jean Calvin. Actes du colloque Calvin Strasbourg 1964* (Paris: Presses Universitaires de France, 1965), 206.

6. For the relevant portion of the *Reply to Sadoleto*, I have used the translation by J. K. S. Reid in *John Calvin: Writings of Pastoral Piety*, ed. and trans. Elsie Anne McKee (New York/ Mahwah, N.J.: Paulist Press, 2001), 41–49. Subsequent references to the *Reply to Sadoleto* are cited as *Reply to Sadoleto* with the page number in McKee's volume. For the Latin, see *CO*, 5:385–416. For more detail on this work, see John C. Olin, ed., *A Reformation Debate: John Calvin and Jacopo Sadoleto* (1966; repr., Grand Rapids: Baker, 1976). For the preface to Calvin's commentary on the Psalms, I have used the translation of Joseph Haroutunian with Louise Pettibone Smith, *Calvin: Commentaries*, Library of Christian Classics, vol. 23 (Philadelphia: Westminster, n.d.), 51–57. For an older translation, see James Anderson, trans., *Commentary on the Book of Psalms* (repr., Grand Rapids: Baker, 1996), 1:xxxv–xlix. My quotations from and references to Haroutunian's and Smith's translation are henceforth cited as "Calvin, preface," along with the relevant page number. There are Latin and French versions of the preface for both of them, see *CO*, 9:13–36.

7. *CO*, 21:21–50.

8. *CO*, 21:51–118.

9. *CO*, 21:119–72. This third edition of the life of Calvin has been used in this chapter. For an accessible translation of this version, see Theodore Beza, *The Life of John Calvin*, in *Banner of Truth* no. 227–228 (August/September 1982): 9–68. This translation is essentially that of Calvin, *Tracts and Letters*, 1:xvii–c. Quotations are from the *Banner of Truth* magazine translation and are cited as Beza, *Life of John Calvin*.

"Intended…for Theology"

John Calvin[10] was born on July 10, 1509, in Noyon, Picardy, in northeastern France, to Gérard Cauvin (d. 1531) and his wife Jeanne, née le Franc (d. 1515), both of whom Beza described as "widely respected and in comfortable circumstances."[11] From town clerk, Calvin's father had risen to occupy the position of a financial administrator in the cathedral of Noyon. Jeanne, whom Calvin does not appear to have ever mentioned in print,[12] died when he was a boy of six. It may be, as some historians have argued, that Calvin's mother was steeped in the medieval Roman Catholic devotion to relics, for in his biting treatise on relics, he recalls kissing a reputed fragment of the hand of Anna, the mother of Mary, at the Church of Ourscamp, not far from Noyon, where his mother may have taken him.[13] In addition to John, there were an older brother, Charles (d. 1537); two younger brothers, Antoine (d. 1573) and François, who died as a child; and two half sisters, daughters of Gérard by his second wife.[14]

Given Gérard's close ties to the church, it is not surprising that he initially desired John to study for the priesthood. Gérard also directed Charles into the priesthood, though the latter left it in 1536.[15] "My father," Calvin recalled in the late 1550s, "intended me as a young boy for theology."[16] So it was that in 1523[17] young Calvin set off for Paris to study for a master of arts degree that would eventually lead to theological studies and the priesthood. Because of his father's connection with the church, Calvin was able to finance his studies from various church benefices he had been given in childhood and in his early teens—one of the abuses of the medieval church.

---

10. The French form of Calvin's name was Jean Cauvin. It became Calvin via the latinized form for his surname, Calvinus.

11. Beza, *Life of John Calvin*, 11. For more details of the background of Calvin's family, see Cottret, *Calvin: A Biography*, 8–12.

12. Allan Menzies, "The Career and Personality of Calvin," in *A Study of Calvin and Other Papers* (London: Macmillan and Co., 1918), 129.

13. Cottret, *Calvin: A Biography*, 10. Cf., though, Menzies, "Career and Personality of Calvin," 129. For the recollection, see John Calvin, *An Admonition, showing the Advantages which Christendom might derive from an Inventory of Relics*, in *Tracts and Letters*, 1:329.

14. Richard Stauffer, "Calvin," in Menna Prestwich, ed., *International Calvinism 1541–1715* (Oxford: Clarendon Press, 1985), 16; "Notice littéraire," in *CO*, 21:14.

15. Cottret, *Calvin: A Biography*, 11.

16. Calvin, preface, 51.

17. For the date, see Ford Lewis Battles, "Calvin's Humanistic Education," in *Interpreting John Calvin*, ed. Robert Benedetto (Grand Rapids: Baker, 1996), 48; and Cottret, *Calvin: A Biography*, 11.

6   Theology Made Practical

In Paris he initially studied for three months at the Collège de la Marche, where he improved his skill in Latin under the superb tutelage of Mathurin Cordier (1479–1564). Calvin later recognized his debt to Cordier when in 1550 he dedicated his commentary on Paul's letters to the Thessalonians to his old teacher:

> It was under your guidance that I entered on a course of studies, and made progress at least to the extent of being some benefit to the Church of God. When my father sent me as a boy to Paris I had done only the rudiments of Latin. For a short time, however, you were an instructor sent to me by God to teach me the true method of learning, so that I might afterwards be a little more proficient.... It was my desire to testify to posterity that, if they derive any profit from my writings, they should know that to some extent you are responsible for them.[18]

After this brief time of what might be viewed as preparatory studies at the Collège de la Marche, Calvin went on to the formidable Collège de Montaigu. This institution, founded in 1314 and revived in the late fifteenth century after a period of decline, was well known for both its theological conservatism and severe discipline. Overall, the Collège de Montaigu was marked by a "narrow-minded and hair-splitting orthodoxy" that resulted in violent opposition to and persecution of nascent French Protestantism.[19] The mode of life inculcated within the college walls is well depicted in a description by the Dutch humanist Erasmus (1466–1536) who, reflecting on a stay there in 1495, recalled the place as "filthy, bleak, inhospitable, reeking with the foulest smells, [and] clotted with dirt." He went on: "I carried nothing away from there except a body poisoned with infected humors!"[20] It is noteworthy that another key figure of this era, the Counter-Reformation

---

18. *CNTC*, 8:331. On Cordier, see Battles, "Calvin's Humanistic Education," 52–53; and Cottret, *Calvin: A Biography*, 12–16.

19. Alexandre Ganoczy, "Calvin's Life," trans. David L. Foxgrover and James Schmitt, in Donald K. McKim, ed., *The Cambridge Companion to John Calvin* (Cambridge: Cambridge University Press, 2004), 4.

20. As quoted in Hans Hillerbrand, *The Division of Christendom: Christianity in the Sixteenth Century* (Louisville: Westminster, 2007), 296; and Cottret, *Calvin: A Biography*, 17. On the college, see also Battles, "Calvin's Humanistic Education," 48–49; Alister E. McGrath, *A Life of John Calvin: A Study in the Shaping of Western Culture* (Oxford: Blackwell, 1990), 27–31; and Cottret, *Calvin: A Biography*, 16–20.

The Young Calvin: Preparation for a Life of Ministry   7

leader Ignatius Loyola (1491–1556), equally renowned as Calvin for his disciplined life, studied at this college, though just after the Frenchman.[21]

Much has been written about the philosophical and theological influences that shaped Calvin during his time at Montaigu,[22] but the truth is that there are no documents from Calvin during this period that can accurately pinpoint the exact nature of these influences. Was Stoicism one of them, as Alexandre Ganoczy has suggested? Calvin's first book was a commentary on a treatise by the Stoic philosopher Seneca (c. 4 BC–AD 65), and in the sixteenth century Seneca was viewed as a Stoic with a distinct sympathy for Christianity.[23] Or was the Augustinian theology of Gregory of Rimini (d. 1358) a major influence, as Alister E. McGrath has posited?[24] As Oberman has noted, however, Calvin never mentioned Gregory, and, as even McGrath concedes, in "the end…we do not know with any certainty precisely what Calvin studied while at Montaigu; we do not know under whom he studied (with the obvious exception of Cordier), or what lectures he attended; we do not even know what books he read."[25] Such uncertainty about the ideas and books that shaped Calvin during a formative period does not mean Calvin is not indebted intellectually to elements of the medieval world, but it does mean that claims about such influences need to be made with great circumspection.[26]

French historian Richard Stauffer has noted that during Calvin's time in Paris, he must have been aware, to some degree, of the presence of

---

21. Battles, "Calvin's Humanistic Education," 49. Cf. Hillerbrand's recent remark about Calvin: "His temperament seems to suggest kinship with none other than Ignatius of Loyola. The second generation of the Reformation called for men of this type, brilliant, determined, cool." *Division of Christendom*, 314.

22. See Oberman, Initia Calvini, 10–19, for an overview of these studies and a response to this method of inquiry.

23. Alexandre Ganoczy, *The Young Calvin*, trans. David Foxgrover and Wade Provo (Philadelphia: Westminster, 1987); T. H. L. Parker, *John Calvin: A Biography* (Philadelphia: Westminster, 1975), 28. On Calvin's Seneca commentary, see below. See also the response of Oberman, Initia Calvini, 13–14, to this suggestion of the influence of Stoicism over the young Calvin.

24. McGrath, *Life of John Calvin*, 37–47 passim.

25. McGrath, *Life of John Calvin*, 36.

26. For a succinct summary of the theologians of the patristic and medieval era to whom the mature Calvin was indebted, see Stauffer, "Calvin," 29. As Stauffer notes, "While Calvin was nurtured on the Bible, his reading of it was enriched by his astonishing knowledge of the great authors of the Christian tradition." For more detail, see Ford Lewis Battles, "The Sources of Calvin's Seneca Commentary," in *Interpreting John Calvin*, 65–89; Anthony N. S. Lane, *John Calvin: Student of the Church Fathers* (Grand Rapids: Baker, 1999); and Jean-François Gilmont, *John Calvin and the Printed Book*, trans. Karin Maag, Sixteenth Century Essays and Studies 72 (Kirksville, Mo.: Truman State University Press, 2005), 156–66.

8   Theology Made Practical

evangelicals in France. Evangelicals were martyred in 1525; for instance, Jean Châtelain, an Augustinian monk, was burned in January at Metz, and a Franciscan who had embraced Lutheran ideas, possibly Pierre de Sébiville, suffered and died by burning at Grenoble. In August 1526, Jacques Pauvan was killed in Paris at the Place-de-Gréve.[27] In addition to the evangelical witness of martyrs, Marguerite d'Angoulême (1492–1549), sister of the king of France and the most powerful woman in France after the queen mother, published a book in 1524 in which she took a decided stand for the Lutheran doctrine of justification by faith alone.[28] But there is no evidence that at this point Calvin had even a modicum of interest in joining the cause of reform.

"Called Back…to Learn Law"

Having obtained his arts degree in 1528, Calvin was ready to begin his formal training in theology, but it was not to be. Although his father had intended John to become a priest like his older brother, suddenly he changed his mind and instructed his son to go into law and move to Orléans to study at what was then the preeminent French university for legal studies. Calvin later described this sudden change in his life thus: "When he [his father] saw that the science of law made those who cultivate it wealthy, he was led to change his mind by the hope of material gain for me. So it happened that I was called back from the study of philosophy to learn law."[29]

Calvin studied at Orléans from 1528 to 1529 and then transferred to Bourges for two more years of legal studies from 1529 to 1531. The central reason for this move was that the famous Italian jurist Andrea Alciati (1492–1550) came to Bourges.[30] The legal knowledge Calvin obtained during this period of concentrated study gave him an abiding interest in the nature of law and justice, the tools to create institutions in Geneva that would serve the advance of the gospel, and a mastery of how to read texts in light of their

---

27. Philip Edgcumbe Hughes, *Lefèvre: Pioneer of Ecclesiastical Renewal in France* (Grand Rapids: Eerdmans, 1984), 147–50.

28. Stauffer, "Calvin," 16. Similarly, John T. McNeill, *The History and Character of Calvinism* (1954; repr., Oxford: Oxford University Press, 1967), 109. On Marguerite d'Angoulême, see George Saintsbury, "Marguerite de Valois," *Encyclopedia Britannica*, 11th ed. (New York: Encyclopedia Britannica, 1910), 17:706.

29. Calvin, preface, 51–52. See also Beza, *Life of John Calvin*, 11.

30. For details about these two law schools and the teachers there under whom Calvin studied, see Battles, "Calvin's Humanistic Education," 49–50, 55–58; and Cottret, *Calvin: A Biography*, 20–24.

The Young Calvin: Preparation for a Life of Ministry

literary and linguistic contexts.[31] What is also especially important about his shift into law was that one of his tutors at both Orléans and Bourges was German scholar Melchior Wolmar (1497–1560), who was committed to the evangelical perspective of Martin Luther (1483–1546).[32] At Bourges Wolmar began teaching Calvin Greek, which would open up for the future Reformer the riches of the New Testament.[33] It is noteworthy that a number of Calvin's contemporaries regarded the study of Greek with deep misgivings. As one writer put it: "We must avoid [Greek] at all costs, for this language gives birth to heresies. Especially beware of the New Testament in Greek; it is a book full of thorns and prickles!"[34] In 1530 the Faculty of Theology in Paris went as far as to condemn the idea that one cannot understand Scripture well without a knowledge of the original languages in which they were given.[35] Calvin, on the other hand, would come to consider the study of Greek essential for anyone who desired to be a herald of the gospel.[36] Simon Grynaeus (1493–1541), the winsome professor of Greek at the University of Basel, would personally help Calvin deepen his grasp of Greek when Calvin resided in Basel from 1535 to 1536.[37]

To what extent Wolmar may have shared his faith with Calvin is not known.[38] When Calvin noted his debt to Wolmar for the rudiments of Greek in the dedicatory preface of his commentary on 2 Corinthians, he made no

---

31. G. R. Potter and M. Greengrass, *John Calvin* (New York: St. Martin's Press, 1983), 4; McGrath, *Life of John Calvin*, 59; Oberman, Initia Calvini, 38; and Randall C. Zachman, *John Calvin as Teacher, Pastor, and Theologian: The Shape of His Writings and Thought* (Grand Rapids: Baker, 2006), 16–17.

32. On Wolmar, see Battles, "Calvin's Humanistic Education," 57–58; and Helmut Feld, "Volmar (Rufus), Melchior," *Biographisch-Bibliographisches Kirchenlexikon*, ed. Friedrich Wilhelm Bautz and Traugott Bautz (Herzberg: Verlag Traugott Bautz, 1997), 12:1588–91.

33. See also Menzies, "Career and Personality of Calvin," 136–37.

34. As quoted in Parker, *John Calvin: A Biography*, 21.

35. McGrath, *Life of John Calvin*, 62.

36. See John D. Currid, *Calvin and the Biblical Languages* (Fearn, Ross-shire, Scotland: Christian Focus, 2006).

37. On Grynaeus, see Alexander Gordon, "Grynaeus, Simon," in *Encyclopedia Britannica*, 11:642. On Calvin's relationship with him, see also Cornelis Augustijn, Christoph Burger, and Frans P. van Stam, "Calvin in the Light of the Early Letters," in *Calvinus Praeceptor Ecclesiae: Papers of the International Congress on Calvin Research*, ed. Herman J. Selderhuis (Geneva: Librairie Droz S.A., 2004), 145–47.

38. See the brief discussion by Danièle Fischer, "Nouvelles réflexions sur la conversion de Calvin," *Etudes théologiques et religieuses* 58 (1983): 216–17, regarding Wolmar's possible influence on Calvin's religious development.

10   Theology Made Practical

mention of theological matters.[39] In fact, there is clear evidence to show that at that time Calvin was still seriously committed to the Roman Church.[40] There was a deeply conservative streak in Calvin's character. As he admitted in his reply to Sadoleto, "It was with the greatest difficulty I was induced to confess that I had all my life long been in ignorance and error."[41]

Following his law studies, Calvin returned to Paris, where he learned that his father was seriously ill. He hurried to Noyon to be with him during his final days. His father had run afoul of Roman Catholic authorities two years earlier, in November 1528, when he refused to give the local bishop the accounting books for the cathedral. It is not clear whether he was guilty of a misdemeanor or whether his pride was piqued at the questioning of his integrity.[42] He was excommunicated, and thus died unreconciled to the Roman Church.[43] Whether this impacted Calvin's thinking about the Roman Church and its discipline is unknown.

The year following Gérard's death saw Calvin's first publication, his commentary on Seneca's *De Clementia*.[44] This publication, which Calvin funded out of his own pocket,[45] is a clear indication that his intellectual roots are in Renaissance humanism, with its watchcry, in its desire to rejuvenate certain aspects of medieval civilization, of *ad fontes*—"back to the sources" of Western culture in the ancient Graeco-Roman world.[46] Allan Menzies notes that Calvin's knowledge of the classics is abundantly evident in this first venture into the world of print culture: Calvin "shows himself acquainted with the whole of Greek and Latin classical literature, citing 155 Latin authors and 22 Greek, and citing them with understanding."[47] In the providence of God, this Renaissance passion for seeking wisdom from the past would provide

---

39. "The first time my father sent me to study civil law, it was at your instigation and under your tuition that I also took up the study of Greek, of which you were at that time a most distinguished teacher.... My indebtedness to you for this is still great for you gave me a good grounding in the rudiments of the language and that was of great help to me later on." *CNTC*, 10:1.

40. Cottret, *Calvin: A Biography*, 24; Ganoczy, "Calvin's Life," 5.

41. Calvin, *Reply to Sadoleto*, 48.

42. Hillerbrand, *Division of Christendom*, 296.

43. Cottret, *Calvin: A Biography*, 24.

44. *CO*, 5:1–162.

45. John Calvin to Francois Daniel, May 23, 1532, in *Tracts and Letters*, 4:31. See also Calvin to Francois Daniel, 1532, in *Tracts and Letters*, 4:32.

46. See Alister E. McGrath, *The Intellectual Origins of the European Reformation*, 2nd ed. (Oxford: Blackwell, 2004), 125–30.

47. Menzies, "Career and Personality of Calvin," 137.

The Young Calvin: Preparation for a Life of Ministry

invaluable direction to humanist scholars like Calvin who came to accept evangelical convictions: the source of church renewal could be found only at the fountainhead of the Christian faith, the Holy Scripture. As Calvin later noted, the teaching of the Reformers went back to Christianity's "source and, as it were, clearing away the dregs, restored it to its original purity."[48]

Calvin's footsteps between the publication of his humanist treatise in April 1532 and his moving back to Paris in the late autumn of 1533 are not easy to trace. He did go back to Orléans to receive his law degree. And at some point in 1533, the greatest of all changes took place in his life when, in his words, the "Lord shone upon [him] with the brightness of [His] Spirit,"[49] and he joined the ranks of the Reformers.

"A Taste and Knowledge of True Piety"

The date of Calvin's conversion is among the most disputed topics of Reformation scholarship. When did it take place? T. H. L. Parker has argued for 1529/1530, a date accepted by a number of other scholars, among them James I. Packer.[50] Traditionally, though, the date that has been given is 1533, which rightly commands strong scholarly support.[51] Although we do not possess irrefutable data to determine the time of Calvin's conversion, there are two extended discussions from Calvin himself about the nature of his conversion—intimations in his *Reply to Sadoleto* and his 1557 preface to his *Commentary on the Psalms*—and of these the latter is the most important.[52] In it, after mentioning his father's desire that he become a lawyer, Calvin states concerning God's work in his life:

> God, by the secret leading of his providence, turned my course another way [than the study of law]. First, when I was too firmly addicted to the superstitions of the Papacy to be drawn easily out of such a deep mire, by a sudden conversion God subdued and made

---

48. Calvin, *Reply to Sadoleto*, 48.

49. Calvin, *Reply to Sadoleto*, 44.

50. Parker, *John Calvin: A Biography*, 22, 162–65; James I. Packer, "John Calvin and Reformed Europe," in *Great Leaders of the Christian Church*, ed. John D. Woodbridge (Chicago: Moody, 1988), 206, 210.

51. Menzies, "Career and Personality of Calvin," 143; François Wendel, *Calvin: Origins and Development of His Religious Thought*, trans. Philip Mairet (1963; repr., Durham, N.C.: Labyrinth Press, 1987), 37–45; and Stauffer, "Calvin," 18; Oberman, "*Subita Conversio*," 283 and n17.

52. Parker, *John Calvin: A Biography*, 162.

12   Theology Made Practical

teachable [*domta et rangea à docilité*] my mind, already more rigid than suited my age. Having therefore received a taste and knowledge of true piety, I burned with such a desire to carry my study further, that although I did not drop other subjects, I had no zeal for them. In less than a year, all who were looking for a purer doctrine began to come to learn from me, although I was a novice and a beginner.[53]

Six aspects of this concisely worded theological reflection on God's saving work in his life beg for comment.

First, Calvin is indeed recounting the historical circumstances by which God brought him from a state of spiritual death to a living faith in Him. Alexandre Ganoczy, though, has denied that this text should be read primarily as a historical narrative of Calvin's conversion. Rather, it must be viewed as a theological reflection from the vantage point of Calvin's mature theological thought. For example, Calvin's assertion that he underwent a "sudden conversion" is a statement made for theological reasons to emphasize conversion as a divine miracle. Ganoczy believes that the primary sources for Calvin's life from the 1530s bear this out and reveal that Calvin's movement away from the Roman Church was "a gradual spiritual development."[54] Undoubtedly, Calvin's account of his conversion is not free from theological interpretation, and, as Ganoczy has argued, Calvin here included details of his conversion to help explain his call to be a minister of the Word in Geneva. But none of this lessens the historicity of his conversion account.[55] Moreover, it is telling that Calvin embeds the story of his conversion within a larger block of text that details historical events and recounts how it was that he became involved in the Genevan Reformation.

Second, Calvin remembered that, prior to his conversion, he was "too firmly addicted to the superstitions of the Papacy to be drawn easily out of such a deep mire." Calvin did not specify which superstitions he had in mind, but by comparing them to a bog, he was indicating that liberation

---

53. Calvin, preface, 52, altered. For the original Latin and French, see *CO*, 9:21–22. This translation is from the French version primarily, though in what follows I have also referred to the Latin version.

54. Ganoczy, *Young Calvin*, 252–66; and Ganoczy, "Calvin's Life," 9–10. Similarly, James A. de Jong, "An Anatomy of All Parts of the Soul: Insights into Calvin's Spirituality from His Psalms Commentary," in Neuser, *Calvinus Sacrae Scripturae Professor*, 3–4 and n7; Gilmont, *John Calvin and the Printed Book*, 9–10; McGrath, *Intellectual Origins*, 55–56.

55. See Fischer, "Nouvelles réflexions sur la conversion de Calvin," 203–7; and Cottret, *Calvin: A Biography*, 68–70.

The Young Calvin: Preparation for a Life of Ministry

from these distortions of Christian truth and "the matrix of late medieval religion" could only have taken place through an outside agency.[56] Calvin made no mention of the human instruments through whom he may have heard the gospel: possibly Wolmar; his cousin Pierre Olivétain (1506–1538), who translated the New Testament into French and whom Beza wrongly saw as the key figure through whom Calvin became "acquainted with the reformed faith";[57] or the early Protestant martyr Étienne de la Forge, with whom Calvin lodged while in Paris.[58] Nor did he make any mention of human writings that he must have read, works by Martin Luther, for instance.[59] But this is typical of Calvin and the Reformed faith: an emphasis on the absolute sovereignty of God in salvation. Calvin could thus state in his treatise *The Eternal Election of God* (1562): "It is not within our power to convert ourselves from our evil life, unless God changes us and cleanses us by his Holy Spirit."[60] Or as he put it in his *Reply to Sadoleto*, referring to the way he came to realize that salvation was by grace alone: "You, O Lord, shone upon me with the brightness of Your Spirit."[61]

Third, the Latin behind the word "sudden," in the phrase "sudden conversion," is *subita*, which can mean "unexpected" or "unpremeditated," and this is probably the better translation. In other words, Calvin's conversion was not ultimately the result of his wish or intention.[62] Alister E. McGrath puts it well when he writes that this word "resonates with overtones of

---

56. McGrath, *Life of John Calvin*, 70. For a summary of what Reformed authors like Calvin considered to be distortions of Christianity, see Graeme Murdock, *Beyond Calvin: The Intellectual, Political and Cultural World of Europe's Reformed Churches, c. 1540–1620* (New York: Palgrave Macmillan, 2004), 8–15.

57. Beza, *Life of John Calvin*, 11–12. On Beza's error in this regard, see Menzies, "Career and Personality of Calvin," 140–41.

58. De la Forge was a Waldensian merchant from Piedmont. See McNeill, *History and Character of Calvinism*, 109; O. R. Johnston, "Calvin the Man," in *Able Ministers of the New Testament: Papers Read at the Puritan and Reformed Studies Conference, December 1964* ([London]: Puritan Reformed Studies Conference, 1964), 22; and James Leo Garrett Jr., introduction to *Calvin and the Reformed Tradition*, ed. Leo Garrett Jr. (Nashville, Tenn.: Broadman Press, 1980), 24.

59. For Luther's influence on Calvin, see McNeill, *History and Character of Calvinism*, 109–10; and Ganoczy, *Young Calvin*, 137–45. Zachman believes that Calvin's "sudden conversion to teachableness" was "most likely through the writings of Martin Luther." Zachman, *John Calvin as Teacher*, 17–19.

60. *CO*, 8:113. See also the similar statements in his commentary on Jeremiah: *CO*, 38:466, 671.

61. *Reply to Sadoleto*, 44. See McNeill, *History and Character of Calvinism*, 118.

62. Parker, *John Calvin: A Biography*, 163–64.

14   Theology Made Practical

the unexpected, the unpredictable, the uncontrollable."[63] One of Calvin's natural characteristics was a resistance to change, as he indicated in this text. But God broke into his life, and, as this passage intimates, brought to pass a completely unexpected upheaval that caused him to change his views of God and salvation and led him to embrace evangelical doctrine as the truth. What led him to hesitate and refuse to listen to evangelical authors, as he made clear in his *Reply to Sadoleto*, was "reverence for the church": "But when once I opened my ears and allowed myself to be taught, I perceived that this fear of derogating from the majesty of the church was groundless. For they reminded me how great the difference is between schism from the church, and studying to correct the faults by which the church herself is contaminated. They spoke nobly of the church and showed the greatest desire to cultivate unity."[64]

For Calvin, then, conversion meant the formation of a teachable heart. As he asserted, "God subdued and made teachable (*domta et rangea à docilité*) my mind, already more rigid than suited my age." The verb "subdued" was associated with the taming of wild animals, specifically horses that needed bridle and bit to be ridden and directed.[65] It is a frequent metaphor in Calvin's writings, an indication of the importance Calvin placed on teachableness and submissiveness to the will of God as being central to the nature of biblical Christianity, especially among those who aspire to be ministers of the Word. In Calvin's words, taken from his comments on 1 Corinthians 14:31, "No one will ever be a good teacher, if he does not show that he himself is teachable, and always ready to learn."[66]

Fifth, as François Wendel has noted, conversion meant for Calvin "a total change of orientation" in his studies. In Calvin's words, having had "a taste and knowledge of true piety, I burned with such a desire to carry my study further, that although I did not drop other subjects, I had no zeal for them." He had lost his passion for the sort of studies that had culminated

---

63. McGrath, *Life of John Calvin*, 72. McGrath's favoring Ganoczy's nonhistorical interpretation of this passage in the preface does not affect the point he is making about this term.

64. Calvin, preface, 48.

65. J. I. Packer, "Calvin: A Servant of the Word," in *Able Ministers of the New Testament*, 42; Parker, *John Calvin: A Biography*, 163; Oberman, *Initia Calvini*, 7–8n3; Oberman, "*Subita Conversio*," 290.

66. As quoted in Randall C. Zachman, "The Conciliating Theology of John Calvin: Dialogue among Friends," in *Conciliation and Confession: The Struggle for Unity in the Age of Reform, 1415–1648*, ed. Howard P. Louthan and Randall C. Zachman (Notre Dame, Ind.: University of Notre Dame Press, 2004), 94–95.

The Young Calvin: Preparation for a Life of Ministry

in his commentary on Seneca's *De Clementia*. Rather, it was the study of Scripture and evangelical theology that henceforth gripped his heart.[67] Allan Menzies captured the depth of the change when he stated that Calvin now "no longer writes as a Humanist, but as one who is guided by the Word, and who feels the cry newly arising from the blood of the martyrs being spilt around him."[68]

Finally, the language that Calvin used to describe the affective impact of his conversion is noteworthy. There is a strong tradition of thought about Calvin that depicts him as cold and unemotional. But this account of his conversion—especially his statement about burning with desire (*enflammé*) to grow in his knowledge of God—indicates the exact opposite and that he had an unusually ardent nature. In fact, as James A. de Jong has noted in a study of Calvin's piety as found in his commentary of the Psalms, Calvin's observations on this portion of Holy Scripture help dispel the "stubborn perception of Calvin as cold, rationalistic, vindictive, and aloof." Instead, one finds an "experiential believer of considerable depth and warmth."[69] Calvin's conversion consisted not merely in enlightenment. It entailed nothing less than an "unreserved, wholehearted commitment to the living God."[70] This ardent commitment finds expression in Calvin's crest, which pictures a heart upon an open, outstretched hand with a motto underneath that reads *cor meum tibi offero Domine prompte et sincere* (My heart I give you, Lord, eagerly and earnestly).[71]

"All Who Were Looking for a Purer Doctrine"

According to Calvin, within a year of his conversion, his gift for teaching was recognized and sought by those hankering for "a purer doctrine" than

---

67. Wendel, *Calvin*, 44–45. See also Harro Höpfl, *The Christian Polity of John Calvin* (Cambridge: Cambridge University Press, 1982), 19. And among the books he certainly read were some by Luther: see Calvin's *Second Defence of the Pious and Orthodox Faith concerning the Sacraments, in answer to The Calumnies of Joachim Westphal*, in *Tracts and Letters*, 2:253.

68. Menzies, "Career and Personality of Calvin," 145.

69. De Jong, "An Anatomy of All Parts of the Soul," 4. I owe this reference to J. Nigel Westhead, "Calvin and Experimental Knowledge of God," in *Adorning the Doctrine: Papers Read at the 1995 Westminster Conference* ([London]: The Westminster Conference, 1995), 16.

70. McNeill, *History and Character of Calvinism*, 116.

71. On this crest, see H. J. Selderhuis, "Calvin as an Asylum Seeker," in Wilhelm H. Neuser, Herman J. Selderhuis, and Willem van't Spijker, eds., *Calvin's Books: Festschrift Dedicated to Peter De Klerk on the Occasion of His Seventieth Birthday* (Heerenveen: Uitgeverij J.J. Groen en Zoon BV, 1997), 286.

16   Theology Made Practical

that of Rome.[72] He was not a complete novice to teaching. For instance, he had already been involved in giving a series of lectures on Seneca in the late summer or early fall of 1533.[73] He now found himself part of a movement in France that had been seeking reform within Roman Catholicism since the early 1520s. At the heart of this reform movement was the biblical scholar Jacques Lefèvre d'Etaples (c. 1455–1536).[74]

By the 1520s, Lefèvre was famous throughout Western Europe for the depth of his learning—many believed him to be equal to that paragon of humanist scholarship, Erasmus. He had spent his early career immersed in Aristotelianism and medieval mysticism, but after the publication of his commentary on the Pauline correspondence in 1512, he was increasingly known as a theologian, even though he had never had any formal theological education.[75] Scholars are divided over whether Lefèvre anticipated the Lutheran doctrine of justification by faith alone—Philip Edgcumbe Hughes says yes; others, like Richard Stauffer, say no[76]—but what is clear is that Lefèvre was deeply appreciative of Luther's early writings. And in Lefèvre's later works, especially those after 1518, the French scholar completely rejected the cult of the saints and other aspects of what he regarded as corrupt worship present in medieval Catholicism.[77] In Beza's words, Lefèvre began the "revival of pure religion."[78] And though some of Lefèvre's disciples would so embrace the scholar's critique of medieval piety as to break with Rome—men like Calvin's close friend Guillaume Farel (1489–1565)—others, including Lefèvre himself, did not see this issue as a just cause for separation. Nonetheless, Calvin's doctrinal convictions concerning true worship—one of the central

---

72. Augustijn, Burger, and Stam, "Calvin in the Light of the Early Letters," 144.

73. See Oberman, *Initia Calvini*, 36n119, for an eyewitness report of these lectures. See also Augustijn, Burger, and Stam, "Calvin in the Light of the Early Letters," 141.

74. For an excellent study of Lefèvre, see Hughes, *Lefèvre: Pioneer*. For an overview of his career, see Eugene F. Rice Jr., introduction to *The Prefatory Epistles of Jacques Lefèvre d'Etaples and Related Texts*, ed. Eugene F. Rice Jr. (New York: Columbia University Press, 1972), xi–xxv. For Calvin's relationship to Lefèvre, see Hermann Dörries, "Calvin und Lefèvre," *Zeitschrift für Kirchengeschichte* 44 (1925): 544–81.

75. Rice Jr., introduction, xiv. For a discussion of the theological themes in this commentary, see Hughes, *Lefèvre: Pioneer*, 69–99 passim.

76. Hughes, *Lefèvre: Pioneer*, 74–78; Richard Stauffer, "Lefèvre d'Etaples: artisan ou spectateur de la Réforme," *Bulletin de la Société de l'Historie du Protestantisme français* 113 (1967): 405–23.

77. See Carlos M. N. Eire, *War against the Idols: The Reformation of Worship from Erasmus to Calvin* (Cambridge: Cambridge University Press, 1986), 168–94.

78. As quoted in Eire, *War against the Idols*, 193.

The Young Calvin: Preparation for a Life of Ministry

issues of the Reformation—are certainly rooted in Lefèvre's radical critique of late medieval piety.[79]

The 1520s had seen episodes of persecution of this reform movement, some of it extremely violent (previously mentioned was the martyrdom of Jacques Pauvan, one of Lefèvre's disciples). Another period of persecution commenced on November 1, 1533, following an address by the rector of the University of Paris, Nicolas Cop, who was one of Calvin's friends.[80] The address, by no means radical by later Protestant standards (while it does contain mild overtones of Lutheranism, there is also an invocation of the Virgin Mary), rattled enough of the Faculty of Theology in Paris for them to issue a condemnation of it and of Cop. Cop quickly left Paris for Basel, and in the wake of his address, arrests of those sympathetic to Lutheran ideas began. Calvin, who was associated with Cop, also fled. Beza noted that Calvin's rooms were searched at the time and various papers seized, an indication that he was indeed in danger of arrest.[81] Nearly thirty years later, in 1562, reflecting on this persecution in a sermon on 2 Samuel in 1562, Calvin admitted that he was terrified and in such distress that he could have wished to have been dead to have escaped the agony of the time.[82]

He found safety in Angoulême with a friend, Louis du Tillet, who possessed a fabulous library of several thousand volumes. Calvin probably used these works in the spring of 1534 to do some of the research that culminated in his *Psychopannychia*—a response to the Anabaptist theory of soul sleep—which he either wrote or finished in Orléans later in the year, though publication of this work was delayed until 1542.[83] Beza noted that Calvin also found the time to visit Lefèvre during this period. According to Beza,

---

79. Eire, *War against the Idols*, 186.

80. For this address, see Calvin, *Institutes* (1536), 364–72. According to Beza, Calvin wrote the address for Cop. *Life of John Calvin*, 13. This seems unlikely. See the discussion of the address and the question of Calvin's role in writing it by McGrath, *Life of John Calvin*, 64–66; and Cottret, *Calvin: A Biography*, 73–76. For a recent defense of Calvin as the author, see Joseph N. Tylenda, "Calvin's First Reformed Sermon? Nicholas Cop's Discourse— 1 November 1533," in Richard C. Gamble, *Calvin's Early Writings and Ministry*, Articles on Calvin and Calvinism (New York: Garland, 1992), 2:120–38. This article first appeared in the *Westminster Theological Journal* 38, no. 3 (1975–1976): 300–318. Augustijn, Burger, and Stam also support the case for Calvin's authorship. "Calvin in the Light of the Early Letters," 143.

81. Beza, *Life of John Calvin*, 13.

82. As quoted in Oberman, *Initia Calvini*, 27–28n84.

83. McGrath, *Life of John Calvin*, 72. Du Tillet acted as Calvin's patron until 1537. His subsequent return to the Roman Catholic Church severed the bond between him and Calvin. See Tavard, *Starting Point*, 140–41; and Gilmont, *John Calvin and the Printed Book*, 20.

18   Theology Made Practical

Lefèvre "was delighted with young Calvin, and predicted that he would prove a distinguished instrument in restoring the kingdom of heaven in France."[84] Another trip in this year of travel took Calvin to Noyon, his birthplace. Cathedral records indicate that on May 4 Calvin personally resigned one of his benefices. Presumably he gave the others up at the same time. Curiously, Beza makes no mention of this event, but it probably signaled Calvin's final break with Rome and his full-blooded commitment to the Reformation.[85] Calvin spent the months immediately following this May journey in transit: he journeyed to Nérac, where Marguerite d'Angoulême held court and was ever favorable to evangelical views; he went back to Paris at great risk to meet Michael Servetus (1511–1553), who failed to keep the appointment; and he spent some time in Orléans.

"Christ's Road Is a Thorny One"
That fall, as he was working on the finishing touches of *Psychopannychia*, an event took place that would push Calvin's wandering beyond the realm of France. During the late evening October 17 and the early morning October 18, posters (*placards*) were set up in various prominent places in Paris, Rouen, Orléans, and other French towns, denouncing the Mass as an abomination before God. Driving the theological perspective of the man behind the posters, Antoine Marcourt, a pastor in Neuchâtel, was the soteriology of the book of Hebrews: What need was there for the priestly mediation of the Mass when Christ offered himself up on the cross to the Father once for all (Heb. 7:27)? A poster was even placed on the door of King Francis I's bedchamber![86] Francis was furious. Evangelical theology was now seen as a positive danger to the state.[87] Less than four weeks later, over two hundred had been arrested, twenty-four of whom would be burned as heretics. Among the latter was Calvin's Parisian landlord, Étienne de la Forge.

So it was that Calvin made the decision to leave France. He found refuge, like Cop had, in the Swiss town of Basel, where he arrived in January 1535. Other French evangelicals were there, including Farel and Pierre Viret (1511–1571), who was Swiss born like Farel and would later, along with Farel,

---

84. Beza, *Life of John Calvin*, 14.
85. Johnston, "Calvin the Man," 23; Stauffer, "Calvin," 18; and McGrath, *Life of John Calvin*, 73–74.
86. Cottret, *Calvin: A Biography*, 82–88; and Tavard, *Starting Point*, 13–17.
87. McGrath, *Life of John Calvin*, 74.

be numbered among Calvin's closest friends and colleagues. Powerful testimony to what Calvin called the "holy bond of friendship" between these three men can be found in his dedication to them of his commentary on Titus: "I think there has never been in ordinary life a circle of friends so heartily bound to each other as we have been in our ministry. With both of you I discharged here [that is, Geneva] the office of pastor, and so far from there being any appearance of rivalry, I always seemed to be of one mind with you."[88]

Calvin also would have had time to reflect on what had taken place in France and its implications for Christian discipleship. Years later he could look back and see what God was doing in his life during this time. Some words from his exposition of Matthew 8:19 ("a certain scribe came, and said unto him, Master, I will follow thee whithersoever thou goest,") in his commentary on the Synoptic Gospels well express those later thoughts about God's work in his life in the days following his conversion:

> We realize that he was a scribe, a man accustomed to a quiet and easy existence, treated with respect, who would be no match for hard words or hard times, for persecution, or the cross. He wishes to follow Christ, but he imagines to himself a soft and pleasant path, lodging with all good things provided—while Christ's road is a thorny one for his disciples; it leads through endless pains to a cross.... So we should learn that, in his person, we are all being told not to make wild and irresponsible claims to be Christ's disciples, without taking any thought for the cross and the hardships.... This is the basic training which admits us to his school, denying ourselves and lifting up our cross.[89]

Calvin was learning in the school of Christ that if he would serve the Master wholeheartedly, he must walk a "thorny" road. In modern parlance, the French scholar was being taught the cost of discipleship and thus being prepared for his life's work in Geneva.

---

88. *CNTC*, 10:347.
89. *CNTC*, 1:254.

—2—

Practical Lessons from the Life of Idelette Calvin

Joel R. Beeke

John Calvin was devoted to Scripture and the church.[1] He emphasized God's sovereignty and Christian living in his preaching and writing, and he was surrounded by many loyal Christian friends. Not surprisingly, he also had a happy marriage. Yet finding a suitable marriage partner had proved to be a daunting task for Calvin. Many of his well-meaning friends and family members had attempted to play matchmaker for him, and each time Calvin had been disappointed. In time, he nearly resigned himself to celibacy.[2] When Calvin's friend Guillaume Farel wrote to tell him of yet another possible life mate, Calvin responded: "I do not belong to that foolish group of lovers, who are willing to cover even the shortcomings of a woman with kisses, as soon as they have fallen for her external appearance. The only beauty that charms me is that she is virtuous, obedient, not arrogant, thrifty, and patient, and that I can expect her to care for my health."[3] When Calvin finally married Idelette van Buren, he found in her the one thing needful for which he was looking: a sincere and obedient heart of piety toward God. For Calvin and Idelette, such piety was key to braving the difficulties and challenges of married life.

While we know little of Calvin and Idelette's home life, from all indications it was serene and godly despite its many tragedies and hardships. As we examine Idelette's life with Calvin, let us focus on several lessons that we can learn from her godly example. For in their relationship we see what can be called the blueprint for Christian marriage. It is the pattern of holy living that Colossians 3:12–13 says includes "kindness, humbleness of mind,

---

1. This article was first delivered as an address on October 31, 2009, at the seventeenth Annual Audubon Bible Church Reformation Celebration, Laurel, Mississippi.

2. Calvin, *Tracts and Letters*, 4:191.

3. Machiel A. van den Berg, *Friends of Calvin*, trans. Reinder Bruinsma (Grand Rapids: Eerdmans, 2009), 125 (cf. Calvin, *Tracts and Letters*, 4:141).

22   Theology Made Practical

meekness, longsuffering; forbearing one another, and forgiving one another."
These ingredients, which permeated John and Idelette's marriage, still offer
us a variety of helpful ways to enrich and bless our marriages.

Courtship

Calvin's duties as a pastor and Reformer were too much for his health. He
contracted so many diseases under his heavy load that his friends persuaded
him that he needed a helpmeet to relieve some of the burdens of domestic
life. Calvin had several students living with him, a few retirees (pensioners),
and a surly housekeeper and her son. Calvin's good friend Farel attempted
twice to find Calvin a spouse who would match his biblical ideal.

Eventually Martin Bucer suggested the widow Idelette van Buren (possibly from Buren in the Dutch province of Gelderland) as a suitable candidate.
By this time, Calvin was ready to remain single for the rest of his life. After
contemplating Bucer's suggestion, however, Calvin realized that Idelette
indeed appeared to have the character that he sought.

Idelette was a young widow with two young children. Her husband, Jean
Stordeur, a cabinetmaker from Liège (one of "those cities of the Netherlands
in which the awakening had been most remarkable," D'Aubigne writes),[4]
had contracted the plague in 1540, a little more than a year after Calvin's
arrival there, and died within a few days. The Stordeurs lived in Strasbourg,
which was a refuge for Christians fleeing Roman Catholic persecution. They
were Anabaptists, who were rejected by Roman Catholics, Lutherans, and
the Reformers alike. It is possible that Idelette was the daughter of a famous
Anabaptist, Lambert van Buren, who was convicted of heresy in 1533, had
his property confiscated, and was banished from Liège.[5]

In addition to not believing in infant baptism, the Anabaptists embraced
several teachings that differed from those of the Reformed faith. For example, the Anabaptists believed they should not participate in government
or fight in wars. They also believed they should never swear an oath, even
in court. In some cases, Anabaptists tried to separate themselves from the
world by establishing their own communities. Though Jean and Idelette
did not belong to the radical wing of the Anabaptists, generally speaking,

---

4. J. H. Merle D'Aubigne, *History of the Reformation in Europe in the Time of Calvin*
(repr., Harrisonburg, Va.: Sprinkle, 2000), 6:508.

5. D'Aubigne, *History of the Reformation*, 6:508; cf. Philip Schaff, *History of the Christian
Church* (repr., Grand Rapids: Eerdmans, 1985), 8:415.

the Anabaptists were radical compared with other faith expressions of the Reformation. Some Anabaptists stressed spiritual life at the expense of Scripture and sound doctrine. Others took radical measures to promote their beliefs, even to the point of violence. Interestingly, Calvin helped suppress Anabaptism by his writings and by supporting the imprisonment and banishment of some of its more radical members.[6]

When Calvin and Farel were expelled from Geneva in 1538, Calvin began preaching in the French church in Strasbourg, where Jean and Idelette attended services. How curious they must have been to hear Calvin, who was already well known for writing the *Institutes of the Christian Religion*. Convinced of the Reformed truth, Jean and Idelette soon left the Anabaptists and joined Calvin's church. There they acquired a love for Scripture and its central place in worship. They also enjoyed the clear preaching, pastoral care, and warm friendship of their leader.[7]

At this time Idelette was already exhibiting a strong commitment to Christ and a teachable spirit. Instead of resenting Calvin's stern policy against the Anabaptists, she read the *Institutes* and learned to appreciate Calvin's devotion to the Word of God. She and her husband attended many of Calvin's daily Bible lectures. They were also very hospitable to Calvin. He enjoyed their friendship and considered them, as they called themselves, his disciples. He admired "the simplicity and sanctity of their lives."[8]

Jean Stordeur's death was a profound blow to Idelette. Not only did she miss her dear husband, with whom she was united in so many ways, but, as a widow, she had no way to support herself and her children. Shortly after Stordeur's death, Bucer asked Calvin, "What about the gentle Idelette?" Though Calvin had formerly thought of Idelette as a dear sister in Christ, he now began to reconsider that relationship. While working hard to expand the *Institutes* from six chapters to seventeen, he must have periodically heard the echo, *Why not Idelette?* After all, the woman was godly, kind, and intelligent. Though she was a few years older than Calvin, she was strikingly young and attractive. Machiel van den Berg noted that "the extroverted Farel expressed his astonishment that she was such a pretty woman!"[9] Ultimately,

---

6. Willem Balke, *Calvin and the Anabaptist Radicals*, trans. William J. Heynen (Grand Rapids: Eerdmans, 1981).

7. J. H. Alexander, *Ladies of the Reformation: Short Biographies of Distinguished Ladies of the Sixteenth Century* (repr., New York: Westminster, 2002), 88.

8. Alexander, *Ladies of the Reformation*, 89.

9. Van den Berg, *Friends of Calvin*, 129.

24 Theology Made Practical

though, it was the evident fruit of Colossians 3:12–13 in Idelette's life that most impressed Calvin, who pursued godliness in every aspect of his life.

Calvin had enjoyed Idelette's hospitality both before and after her first husband had died. Those visits increased when Calvin formally began to court Idelette. A few months later, on August 17, 1540, Calvin married Idelette, taking her and her children (a son and a daughter) into his home. Friends came from near and far to attend Calvin's wedding.[10]

One of the first lessons we can learn from Calvin's new wife is the importance of having a full allegiance and humble submission to the Scriptures as well as a teachable and hospitable spirit. Too often today people are governed more by tradition than by Scripture. They do not study the Word for themselves or seek to learn and grow under the faithful expositional ministry of the Word. What about you? Are you humbly submitting to the Scriptures? Do you demonstrate a teachable spirit? Are you hospitable and warm to others?

Character

Idelette was quiet, unassuming, and cheerful, yet sober.[11] Theodore Beza, Calvin's first reliable biographer, called her a most choice woman—"a serious-minded woman of good character."[12] Although she was petite and suffered from poor health, Idelette devoted all her strength to educating her children.[13] Idelette's faithfulness within the hardships she faced indicated her meekness and humility. These responses did not mean that she was weak or fearful, however. Following Christ on the path of suffering takes great strength and courage, and Idelette submitted patiently to God's various providences.

To make room for Idelette and her children in his little home in Strasbourg, Calvin had to let two of his renters go. Letting these sources of revenue go was a significant sacrifice for Calvin, considering his meager salary, but he appears to have made it gladly. Only weeks after he was married, he wrote to Farel about how pleased he was with his new wife. As van den Berg writes, Calvin "clearly found marriage a special experience of joy." Van den Berg goes on to say that their "marriage was more than simply a rational

---

10. D'Aubigne, *History of the Reformation*, 6:509.

11. Schaff, *History of the Christian Church*, 8:416. Farel recalled her disposition as "grave."

12. Theodore Beza, *The Life of John Calvin* (Darlington, U.K.: Evangelical Press, 1997), 35; cf. Edna Gerstner, *Idelette* (Morgan, Pa.: Soli Deo Gloria, 1992).

13. Schaff, *History of the Christian Church*, 8:415.

Practical Lessons from the Life of Idelette Calvin 25

agreement; it became a true and solid bond of love and loyalty. The quiet and patient Idelette was an exceptionally suitable friend-in-marriage."[14]

Shortly after he married Idelette, Calvin went to Regensburg to attend a theological debate. While he was gone, the plague hit Strasbourg. One of Calvin's closest friends, Claude Feray, died from it. Calvin worried about Idelette, who took refuge outside the city. He wrote, "Day and night my wife is in my thoughts, now that she is deprived of my counsel and must do without her husband."[15] Eventually Calvin could not endure the worry anymore; he left the debate early to return to Idelette.

Idelette and Calvin stayed in Strasbourg for less than a year before Calvin was called back to Geneva to continue his great work as a Reformer. The stress of this decision weighed heavily on him. Calvin's letters from this period indicate that he was happy in Strasbourg and did not wish to return to Geneva. He wrote to Farel, "I dread throwing myself into that whirlpool I found so dangerous."[16] While we have no account of Idelette's thoughts and feelings at that time, the couple decided to move to Geneva in response to the will of God. Idelette's daughter, Judith, accompanied them, while her son remained in Strasbourg with relatives.

The second lesson we learn from Idelette is that true spiritual growth and resignation to God's will are nearly always inseparable. When is the last time that you patiently submitted to God's will even when you did not feel like doing it? How did you feel after you placed your will under God's will by the Spirit's grace?

While the Genevan city council provided a beautiful parsonage for Idelette and Calvin at the top of the Rue de Chanoines—it had a little garden and a magnificent view of Lake Leman and the Jura Mountains on one side and the Alps on the other—Calvin received a salary of only about two hundred dollars per year, twelve measures of corn, and two casks of wine. Though the resources at her disposal were modest, Idelette gladly opened up her home to numerous refugees and frequently extended hospitality to Calvin's friends, such as Farel, Beza, and Viret, who all highly respected her.

Idelette was a wonderful wife and companion for Geneva's most prominent pastor. When Calvin's work as a pastor, writer, and civil servant threatened his health, Idelette proved to be a much-needed confidant,

---

14. Van den Berg, *Friends of Calvin*, 130.
15. Van den Berg, *Friends of Calvin*, 131.
16. Alexander, *Ladies of the Reformation*, 91.

26   Theology Made Practical

counselor, and sounding board. She tended to his downcast spirit and his fragile health and visited the sick in his place. She also went out of her way to assure Calvin that she respected him for remaining true to God and Scripture, no matter the cost. Idelette was willing to share with him whatever burdens he carried and assured him that he should never be tempted to shrink from his duties for the sake of her ease and comfort. She was deeply committed to Calvin's ministry as a preacher and teacher as well as to his organization of a form of church-state government founded on the principles of Scripture.[17]

After Idelette's death in 1549, Calvin wrote to a friend, "I have been bereaved of the best companion of my life, of one who, had it been so ordered, would not only have been the willing sharer of my exile and poverty, but even of my death. During her life she was the faithful helper of my ministry. From her I never experienced the slightest hindrance."[18]

Another lesson a Christian woman can learn from Idelette is that a marriage will be greatly blessed if the wife is committed to being a faithful helpmeet for her husband and if her goals, vision, and passion are similar to his. Do not marry someone you are not committed to helping or someone whose vision and goals differ from your own. Such a marriage will only cause division later on.

Perhaps the crucial point of Calvin and Idelette's marriage is that God's wisdom shines brightest in poor earthen vessels. A woman Calvin considered marrying before Idelette was wealthy. Although she could have provided a substantial dowry, she did not speak his native French. Instead, she spoke German, which Calvin did not know well. Can you imagine trying to carry out the world-changing, church-shaping task of providing spiritual direction for the people of God during one of the most challenging times in history with a spouse who did not speak your language? When we seek God's will first for our lives, we obtain the blessing, says Colossians 3:24. Calvin and Idelette did not seek riches, status, or worldly gain for themselves. They are a beautiful example of believers who united as spouses to do God's work in a magnificent way.

Learn from what Idelette had to offer Calvin that when you look for a spouse for life, do not let wealth or the lack of it be a significant issue. Rather,

---

17. Alexander, *Ladies of the Reformation*, 91–92.
18. Schaff, *History of the Christian Church*, 8:419.

Practical Lessons from the Life of Idelette Calvin

focus on this question: Are both of us deeply committed to using our talents to provide spiritual direction and health for the church and kingdom of God?

Trials and Perseverance

Soon after their return to Geneva, Idelette prematurely gave birth to a little boy they named Jacques. The baby died a month later in August 1542. "The Lord has certainly inflicted a severe and bitter wound by the death of our infant son," Calvin wrote to Viret. "But He is Himself a Father and knows what is necessary for His children."[19] In the same letter, Calvin noted that Idelette was too grief-stricken to write, though she was submitting to God in her affliction. She had also nearly lost her life in the delivery of their baby. Calvin wrote to Viret that she had been in "extreme danger."

Idelette recovered, but sorrow followed upon sorrow. Two years later she gave birth to a daughter on May 30. Calvin wrote to Farel, "My little daughter labors under a continual fever," and days later she too died.[20] Sometime later a third child was stillborn. In the midst of Calvin's overwhelming duties and pressures, the grief of losing children was most profound, particularly for Idelette. Yet she and Calvin pressed on, submitting to the Lord and putting their trust in Him.

Here is yet another lesson we can learn from Idelette. Her life, which included considerable suffering, shows us the beauty of submitting to God in grief rather than denying or rebelling against it. Her submission teaches us that genuine Christianity bows under God, trusting Him as the greatest friend, even when He seems to be our greatest enemy. The end result of such trust is what the Puritans called the "rare jewel of Christian contentment." We might all ask for a greater portion of this Christlike submission.

Insult was then heaped upon sorrow as some Roman Catholics wrote that since sterility in marriage was a reproach and a judgment, the childless condition of Calvin and Idelette must be God's judgment against Calvin.[21] One writer, Baudouin, even wrote, "He married Idelette by whom he had no children, though she was in the prime of life, that the name of this infamous man might not be propagated."[22]

---

19. Alexander, *Ladies of the Reformation*, 93.
20. Calvin, *Tracts and Letters*, 4:420.
21. Schaff, *History of the Christian Church*, 8:418–19.
22. Alexander, *Ladies of the Reformation*, 93.

Calvin later said the profound affliction of his childlessness was lifted only by meditating on God's Word and through prayer. He wrote privately to his close friend Pierre Viret that he also found comfort in knowing that he had "myriads of sons throughout the Christian world."[23]

Just as Idelette, together with her husband, took refuge in God's Word and in prayer in their time of need, we ought to find relief in the midst of life's trials by turning in prayer to the Word-based means of grace. Have you, too, discovered that the Bible is an amazing book of comfort, and that prayer gives us solace quite unlike anything else?

More heartbreak followed. Around this time the plague struck people all over Geneva. It spread all over Europe, displacing hundreds of thousands of people from their cities and homes. In a letter from Calvin to his father in April 1541, we learn that Calvin sent Idelette and the children to Strasbourg for safety. The separation from Idelette was unbearable. Though Calvin was deeply anxious about his wife's safety,[24] he was also unwavering in his confidence in Christ. We should learn from this that nothing on earth bound Idelette and Calvin together as strongly as their bond of love anchored in Christ.

Learn from Idelette, together with her husband, that love for truth that is grounded in unwavering confidence in Christ is what holds a marriage together even in times of prolonged absence and great suffering. We need to cultivate loving trust in each other in good times, when we are not under trials or absent from each other, so that we have much on hand to draw from when the trials and absences do impact our lives.

In 1545, hundreds of persecuted Waldensians took refuge in Geneva. Idelette was at Calvin's side during that time, working hard to provide lodging and employment for them. They were so tireless in their devotion to the immigrants that some Genevans accused them of being more helpful to strangers than to friends.

Learn from Idelette not to expect everyone to praise you, even when you are doing good. Criticism is an unavoidable reality of life. Learn to accept it, to turn it over to God, and to walk forward with biblical integrity and humility.

John and Idelette Calvin experienced joyous times as well as many heartaches. In our day, when so many psychologists and therapists promise

---

23. Alexander, *Ladies of the Reformation*, 93.
24. Schaff, *History of the Christian Church*, 8:421.

help for marriages, it is tempting to dismiss Scripture as insufficient for telling us what married life should be. Yet Calvin and Idelette offer a striking example of how a Scripture-based, Christ-centered marriage can function in the midst of challenging circumstances. Losing children and friends, uprooting from one community to another, facing an incredibly demanding schedule, and adjusting to a new marriage are just some of the trials that faced this couple. Yet, they were blessed with a peaceful and joyous marriage and family life.

Calvin and Idelette attributed the success of their marriage to the grace of God. God was their source of forgiveness, compassion, mercy, tenderheartedness, patience, and contentment through all their difficulties. By God's grace, these gifts and principles do not change with the times but remain stable in Christ for believers who pursue God-glorifying marriages. When we live by these principles in union with Christ, our marriages can know a joy that far exceeds worldly happiness.

Learn from Idelette, together with her husband, that patterning our marriage after Ephesians 5:21–33, then giving God the glory for any success and joy we encounter in marriage, is a sure way to increase our joy until the day we are finally wedded forever to Jesus Christ, the perfect Bridegroom, in the glory of heaven.

Idelette's Death

Idelette's health steadily worsened during her nine years with Calvin. She suffered from fever during the last three years of her life. By March 1549, she was bedridden. At that same time, Calvin was being hounded by powerful enemies in Geneva, not knowing that they would be defeated in six years' time. For the moment, it seemed that everything in his life was crashing down upon him. The city appeared to be rejecting him, his reforms were failing, and his precious wife was dying. Yet, through it all, God sustained His servant.

Idelette's last earthly concern was for her children. Calvin promised to treat them as his own, to which she replied, "I have already commended them to the Lord, but I know well that thou wilt not abandon those whom I have confided in the Lord."[25]

---

25. James I. Good, *Famous Women of the Reformed Church* (repr., Birmingham, Ala.: Solid Ground Christian Books, 2002), 29.

Theology Made Practical

"This greatness of soul," Calvin later wrote, "will influence me more powerfully than a hundred commendations would have done."[26]

At the close of her earthly life, Idelette prayed, "O God of Abraham and of all our fathers, the faithful in all generations have trusted in Thee, and none have ever been confounded. I also will hope."[27] She passed on to glory April 5, 1549. Calvin was at her side, speaking to her of the happiness they had enjoyed for nine years and about the joy she would soon have in "exchanging an abode on earth for her Father's house above."[28]

Learn from Idelette that those who, by grace, live well, usually die well. Idelette had a sweet, submissive death, despite the pain that preceded it. When we surrender everything to God, both in life and in death, we will not only worry less in this life but we will also not be confounded even when difficulties loom before us. Our comfort in Christ and His salvation is good for both life and death and for all eternity.

Calvin's letters shortly after Idelette's death expressed his grief over losing his dearest companion—a rare woman, he said, who was without equal. Even on her deathbed, "she was never troublesome to me," he wrote.[29] That made Calvin's sorrow even more profound. This trial shows us that submitting ourselves to the will of God does not excuse us from hardship.

Calvin was only forty when Idelette died. Like Hezekiah, he would have fifteen years added to his life, but they would be years without his precious wife. He wrote to his friends that he could scarcely continue with his work, yet he steeled himself to do so. Calvin's enemies charged him with being heartless for working so diligently, but he was anything but heartless. He wrote to a friend:

> I do what I can that I may not be altogether consumed with grief. I have been bereaved of the best companion of my life; she was the faithful helper of my ministry.... My friends leave nothing undone to lighten, in some degree, the sorrow of my soul.... May the Lord Jesus confirm you by His Spirit, and me also under this great affliction, which certainly would have crushed me had not He whose

---

26. Alexander, *Ladies of the Reformation*, 97.
27. Good, *Famous Women of the Reformed Church*, 29.
28. Alexander, *Ladies of the Reformation*, 97.
29. Schaff, *History of the Christian Church*, 8:419.

Practical Lessons from the Life of Idelette Calvin 31

office it is to raise up the prostrate, to strengthen the weak, and to revive the faint, extended help to me from heaven.[30]

Conclusion

Our culture has a cynical view of marriage and promiscuity; a recent report on the rising rate of divorce shows that it is highest among people ages twenty-five to thirty-five. The biblical view of marriage is quite different. Scripture teaches us that sin has deeply disfigured God's intentions for marriage, but Christ has lovingly restored it. True joy in marriage results when a husband strives to love his wife the way Christ loves the church and when the wife strives to respect her husband the way the church respects Jesus Christ. John and Idelette Calvin knew that joy. One of the most amazing things about their relationship is that they exuded joy even in the most traumatic circumstances. They knew what it meant to rejoice in God in the midst of persecution. They found joy in the fear of God as they strove to glorify Him. They found joy in their salvation, joy in their fidelity to each other, joy in each other's love and companionship, and joy in service to their neighbor. In short, Idelette was a genuine, joyous helpmate to her husband.

Learn from Idelette, together with her husband, that true joy is not found in living for one's self; it is found only in serving God first, serving our spouse second, and serving ourselves third. That is the essence of the blueprint for a truly joyous marriage and joyous life that Paul has outlined for us in Colossians 3:12–17.

---

30. Alexander, *Ladies of the Reformation*, 97.

PART 2:
Calvin's Systematic Theology

—3—

"Uttering the Praises of the Father, of the Son, and of the Spirit": John Calvin on the Divine Triunity

Michael A. G. Haykin

> It is impossible to praise God without also uttering the praises of the Father, of the Son, and of the Spirit.
> —John Calvin, *Commentary* on Isaiah 6:2

In a masterful study of the unfolding of early Christian thought, Jaroslav Pelikan, the doyen of twentieth-century patristic studies, noted that the "climax of the doctrinal development of the early church was the dogma of the Trinity."[1] The textual expression of that climax is undoubtedly the Niceno-Constantinopolitan Creed that was issued at the Council of Constantinople (381), in which Jesus Christ is unequivocally declared to be "true God" and "of one being (*homoousios*) with the Father," and the Holy Spirit is described as the "Lord and Giver of life," who "together with the Father and the Son is worshipped and glorified." The original Nicene Creed, issued by the Council of Nicaea in 325, had made a similar statement about the Son and His deity, but had said only this about the Holy Spirit: "[We believe] in the Holy Spirit." When the deity of the Spirit was subsequently questioned in the 360s and 370s, it was necessary to expand the Nicene Creed to include a statement about the deity of the Holy Spirit. In the end this expansion involved the drafting of a new creedal statement at the Council of Constantinople.[2]

---

1. Jaroslav Pelikan, *The Christian Tradition: Vol. 1: The Emergence of the Catholic Tradition (100–600)* (Chicago: University of Chicago Press, 1971), 172. For help in locating sources for this paper, I am indebted to Dr. David Puckett of The Southern Baptist Theological Seminary and my one-time assistant at the Andrew Fuller Center for Baptist Studies, Dr. Steve Weaver.

2. For the text of these two creeds, see J. N. D. Kelly, *Early Christian Creeds*, 2nd ed. (London: Longmans, Green, 1960), 215–16, 297–98. See also Johannes Roldanus, *The Church in the Age of Constantine: The Theological Challenges* (New York: Routledge, 2006), 123–26.

36 Theology Made Practical

Although some historians have argued that these fourth-century creedal statements represent the apex of the Hellenization of the church's teaching, in which fourth-century Christianity traded the vitality of the New Testament church's experience of God for a cold, abstract philosophical formula, nothing could be further from the truth.[3] The Nicene and Niceno-Constantinopolitan Creeds helped to sum up a long process of reflection that had its origins in the Christian communities of the first century. The New Testament itself provides clear warrant for the direction that theological reflection on the nature of God took in fourth-century Christian orthodoxy. As Douglas Ottati, an American professor of theology, once put it, "Trinitarian theology continues a biblically initiated exploration."[4] Or, in the words of the early twentieth-century American Presbyterian theologian Benjamin B. Warfield, the "doctrine of the Trinity lies in Scripture in solution; when it is crystallized from its solvent it does not cease to be scriptural, but only comes into clearer view."[5]

The Servetus Affair

Apart from the controversy between the Greek East and the Latin West over the *filioque*, the Niceno-Constantinopolitan creed essentially closed the door on debates about the Trinity for the next millennium. With the upheaval caused by the Reformers' questions about salvation, worship, and the source of authority, however, it is not surprising that some would broach questions about Trinitarian matters long thought settled. On three distinct occasions, for instance, John Calvin found himself embroiled in controversy about the triune nature of God. One is all too well known—namely, the controversy with Spanish humanist and physician Michael Servetus (1511–1553), whose execution in Geneva on October 27, 1553, has defined, for many, Calvin's character as a theocratic tyrant.[6] Servetus had been incessant in his rejection

---

3. Stephen M. Hildebrand identifies Edwin Hatch and Adolf von Harnack as two of the scholars who argued along these lines. See Stephen M. Hildebrand, *The Trinitarian Theology of Basil of Caesarea: A Synthesis of Greek Thought and Biblical Truth* (Washington, D.C.: Catholic University of America Press, 2007), 7.

4. Douglas Ottati, "Being Trinitarian: The Shape of Saving Faith," *The Christian Century* 112, no. 32 (November 8, 1995): 1045.

5. Benjamin B. Warfield, "The Biblical Doctrine of the Trinity," in Benjamin B. Warfield, *Biblical and Theological Studies*, ed. Samuel G. Craig (Philadelphia: Presbyterian and Reformed, 1952), 22.

6. Bruce Gordon, *Calvin* (New Haven, Conn.: Yale University Press, 2009), 217. On Calvin's controversy with Servetus, see Eric Kayam, "The Case of Michael Servetus: The

John Calvin on the Divine Triunity

of the ontological deity of Christ and in his anti-Trinitarian campaigning, even daring to call the blessed Trinity a "hell's dog with three heads, [a] devilish phantom," and "an illusion of Satan."[7]

He also appears to have been obsessed with coming to Geneva to finally confront the man he regarded as the archenemy of the true Reformation.[8] For his part, Calvin viewed Servetus as a dangerous heretic. Yet while the French Reformer did play a role in Servetus's condemnation, Calvin's Geneva was not a theocracy by any stretch of the imagination.[9] Moreover, at the time of Servetus's execution, Calvin did not have the political power to sentence anyone to death, and those who condemned Servetus in this regard were actually Calvin's opponents, who used the occasion to assert their authority over the French Reformer.[10] Nevertheless, as Sebastian Castellio (1515–1563), a one-time coworker of Calvin who later became one of his most ardent opponents, observed in a work he wrote against Calvin's 1554 defense of the heretic's execution: "To kill a man is not to protect a doctrine, but it is to kill a man. When the Genevans killed Servetus, they did not defend a doctrine, they killed a man. To protect a doctrine is not the magistrate's affair (what has the sword to do with doctrine?) but the teacher's.... But when Servetus fought with reasons and writings, he should have been repulsed by reasons and writings."[11]

Background and Unfolding of the Case," *Mid-America Journal of Theology* 8, no. 2 (Fall 1992): 117–46; Gordon, *Calvin*, 217–32; Jean-Luc Mouton, *Calvin* ([Paris]: Éditions Gallimard, 2009), 302–42; and Christoph Strohm, "Calvin and Religious Tolerance," trans. David Dichelle, in Martin Ernst Hirzel and Martin Sallmann, eds., *John Calvin's Impact on Church and Society, 1509–2009* (Grand Rapids: Eerdmans, 2009), 176–79.

7. As quoted in Kayam, "Case of Michael Servetus," 123.

8. Gordon, *Calvin*, 218–19.

9. On Geneva not being a theocracy, see Mark J. Larson, *Calvin's Doctrine of the State* (Eugene, Ore.: Wipf & Stock, 2009), 1–19.

10. James I. Packer, "John Calvin and Reformed Europe," in John D. Woodbridge, ed., *Great Leaders of the Christian Church* (Chicago: Moody, 1988), 212–13; and Gordon, *Calvin*, 217–29.

11. *Contra libellum Calvini in quo ostendere conatur haereticos jure gladii coercendos esse* (Holland, 1612). This work was published in 1612, but Castellio actually wrote it in 1554 as a response to Calvin's *Defensio orthodoxae fidei de sacra Trinitate* (1554), his justification of the execution of Servetus. For the quote, I am indebted to Marian Hillar, "Sebastian Castellio and the Struggle for Freedom of Conscience," in *Essays in the Philosophy of Humanism*, ed. D. R. Finch and M. Hillar (n.p.: n.p., 2002), 10:31–56, http://www.socinian.org/files/castellio .pdf; and Timothy George, "Calvin's Biggest Mistake: Why He Assented to the Execution of Michael Servetus," *Christianity Today* 53, no. 9 (September 2009): 32. For an overview of Castellio's views on religious tolerance, see Strohm, "Calvin and Religious Tolerance," 187–88.

38   Theology Made Practical

The Controversy with Pierre Caroli

Two decades before this controversy with Servetus, though, the shoe had been on the other foot, as Calvin, along with his close friends Guillaume Farel (1489–1565) and Pierre Viret (1511–1571), had been charged with Arianism by Pierre Caroli (c. 1480–c. 1547). Like Farel, Caroli had come from the circle of reform associated with Jacques Lefèvre d'Étaples (c. 1455–1536), but, unlike Farel, Caroli never decisively committed himself to the theological agenda of the Reformation. A one-time professor of theology at the Sorbonne, Caroli had fled France in the 1530s after embracing Protestantism. He eventually made his way to Lausanne, where he was appointed the main preacher in the city. Caroli was theologically unstable, though, and returned to the Roman Church in the summer of 1537, only to leave that communion for Protestantism once again in 1539. Warfield has rightly described him as "one of the most frivolous characters brought to the surface by the upheaval of the Reformation."[12]

Caroli found ammunition for his charge against Calvin and his friends in that Farel, in his *Sommaire et brève declaration* (1525), the first work in French to set forth the essential aspects of the Reformed faith, omitted any clear reference to the Trinity, as did the confession of faith drawn up in 1536 for the church in Geneva.[13] The emptiness of Caroli's accusation is immediately apparent, however, when one considers that in the first edition of Calvin's *Institutes*—published in Basel in March 1536 and available to Caroli before he made his accusation—the French Reformer had set forth a decisive rejection of Arianism and a clear affirmation of his faith in the Trinity:

> Persons who are not contentious or stubborn see the Father, Son, and Holy Spirit to be one God. For the Father is God; the Son is God; and the Spirit is God: and there can be only one God.

---

12. Benjamin B. Warfield, "Calvin's Doctrine of the Trinity," in Benjamin B. Warfield, *Calvin and Augustine*, ed. Samuel G. Craig (Philadelphia: Presbyterian and Reformed, 1980), 204. For an extremely thorough overview of the so-called Caroli affair, see Karl Barth, *The Theology of John Calvin*, trans. Geoffrey W. Bromiley (Grand Rapids: Eerdmans, 1995), 309–45. For the course of the affair, see also Warfield, "Calvin's Doctrine of the Trinity," 204–12; Richard C. Gamble, "Calvin's Controversies," in Donald K. McKim, ed., *The Cambridge Companion to John Calvin* (Cambridge: Cambridge University Press, 2004), 199; and Gordon, *Calvin*, 72–75.

13. Guillaume Farel, *Sommaire et brève declaration*, transcribed and ed. Arthur-L. Hofer (Neuchâtel, Switzerland: Éditions "Belle Rivière," 1980), 13–14.

> On the other hand, three are named, three described, three distinguished. One therefore, and three: one God, one essence. Why three? Not three gods, not three essences. To signify both, the ancient orthodox fathers said that there was one *ousia*, three *hypostaseis*, that is, one substance, three subsistences in one substance.[14]

Here Calvin made a solid declaration of the Trinity and was quite happy to express this declaration by means of nonbiblical terms hammered out in the debates about the Trinity in the fourth century—namely *ousia* (being) and *upostasis* (subsistence).

Caroli leveled his accusation against the French Reformers during a disputation with Calvin and Viret at Lausanne on February 17, 1537, over the rectitude of praying for the dead.[15] Calvin's immediate response was to cite a catechism that was used in the church at Geneva, in which there was a brief statement of the triunity of God. It is noteworthy that he did not refer to the passage from his *Institutes* cited above. Caroli refused to consider the catechism to be an adequate expression of Trinitarian faith and demanded that Calvin subscribe then and there to the time-honored Athanasian Creed. Calvin refused to acquiesce to Caroli's demand, for, he explained, he was not prepared to regard any text as authoritative for doctrine unless it had first been tested against the Word of God. At this point, Caroli apparently became incensed and dramatically yelled back that Calvin's explanation was "unbecoming a Christian man."[16] Nearly ten years later, in his pseudonymous *Defence of Guillaume Farel and his colleagues against the calumnies of Pierre Caroli* (1545), Calvin was also somewhat critical of the format of another of the ancient church's creeds, the Nicene, which, as has been noted above, was regarded as the definitive expression of Trinitarianism. Calvin felt that the creed contained needless repetition in clauses like "God of God, light of light, true God of true God." "Why this repetition?" he asked. "Does it add any more emphasis or greater expression? You see, therefore, it is a song, more to be sung, than a suitable rule of faith, in which one redundant syllable is absurd."[17]

---

14. Calvin, *Institutes* (1536), 45. For the rejection of Arianism, see Calvin, *Institutes* (1536), 47–48.

15. Barth, *Theology of John Calvin*, 317–18.

16. Calvin to Kaspar Megander, February 1537, in *Tracts and Letters*, 4:49.

17. *Pro G. Farello et collegis eius adversus Petri Caroli calumnias defensio Nicolai Gallasii*, in *CO*, 7:315–16, author's translation.

40 Theology Made Practical

Not surprisingly, such statements gave substance to Caroli's accusations, and the suspicion that Calvin was unsound regarding Trinitarian doctrine dogged him for years to come.[18] But Calvin was unwilling to have his faith confined to the exact wording of the ancient church's creeds. The touchstone of Scripture was alone requisite in deciding what was orthodox and what was not.[19] Calvin was equally insistent in the course and aftermath of the Caroli affair that he and his colleagues were fully committed to orthodox Trinitarianism. At a synod that was convened in the Franciscan church in Lausanne on May 14, 1537, to settle the Caroli controversy, Viret spoke for Calvin and Farel:

> We confess one God, in one essence of divinity (*sub una divinitatis essentia*), and we hold together the Father with his eternal Word and Spirit. We thus call the Father God in such a way that we proclaim the Son and his Spirit to be the true and eternal God with the Father. We neither confuse the Father with the Word, nor the Word with the Spirit. For we believe the Son to be other than the Father, and again the Spirit to differ from the Son, although there is [only] one [divine] being.[20]

What is noteworthy about this confession is that it is not only an unambiguous rejection of Arianism but it also avoids another bugbear of the ancient church—namely Sabellianism, or modalism.[21]

The Caroli controversy reveals Calvin to have been thoroughly convinced that one must reverently accept the triunity of God as fully biblical but also determined to maintain an independence from the wording of the patristic creeds.[22] In the words of Arie Baars, Calvin "strongly opposes any theology that is characterized by a speculative...inquisitiveness that does not respect the boundaries of Scripture."[23] Thus, in his conflict with Caroli,

---

18. A. Mitchell Hunter, *The Teaching of Calvin: A Modern Interpretation*, 2nd ed. (London: James Clarke, 1950), 42–43; and Bernard Cottret, *Calvin: A Biography*, trans. M. Wallace McDonald (Grand Rapids: Eerdmans/Edinburgh: T&T Clark, 2000), 124–26.

19. Warfield, "Calvin's Doctrine of the Trinity," 207–11; and Hunter, *Teaching of Calvin*, 45–48.

20. *Pro G. Farello...defensio*, in *CO*, 7:312, author's translation.

21. Barth, *Theology of John Calvin*, 324–25.

22. Hunter, *Teaching of Calvin*, 41; Stephen M. Reynolds, "Calvin's View of the Athanasian and Nicene Creeds," *Westminster Theological Journal* 23 (1960–1961): 33–37.

23. Arie Baars, "The Trinity," trans. Gerrit W. Sheeres, in Herman J. Selderhuis, ed., *The Calvin Handbook* (Grand Rapids: Eerdmans, 2009), 246.

John Calvin on the Divine Triunity

Calvin made little use of the patristic way of distinguishing the hypostatic differences within the Trinity— namely, that the Son is eternally begotten of the Father and that the Spirit eternally proceeds from the Father and the Son.[24] But Calvin was determined to uphold the Trinitarianism of the ancient church and showed willingness at times, as the first edition of the *Institutes* shows, to use extrabiblical terms to clarify scriptural truth.[25]

The Battle with the Italian Anti-Trinitarians

Controversies over anti-Trinitarianism in the 1550s, with Michael Servetus earlier in the decade and then with various Italian Protestants in the latter part of the decade, forced Calvin to develop a more explicit and detailed Trinitarianism, which is evident in the final edition of the *Institutes* (1559).[26] An Italian congregation had been meeting for regular worship in Geneva since 1542, but when their minister, Celso Martinengo (1515–1557), died in the summer of 1557, the community was wracked with quarrels over the doctrine of the Trinity. One of the instigators of these theological quarrels was Matteo Gribaldi (c. 1505–1564), who had taught law at the University of Padua before taking up a position at the university in Tübingen.[27] Gribaldi had been in Geneva at the outset of the trial of Servetus and had taken the heretic's side, though his own conviction about the Godhead appears to have been tritheistic.[28] Gribaldi's opposition to orthodox Trinitarianism subsequently had a major influence over a number of the members of the Genevan Italian community, including Giorgio Biandrata (1516–1588),[29] Giovanni Alciati (c. 1515/1520–1573), and Valentino Gentile (c. 1520–1566), from Calabria, who began to voice their views during the course of 1557 and 1558.

---

24. Paul Helm, *Calvin: A Guide for the Perplexed* (London: T&T Clark, 2008), 44.

25. Baars, "The Trinity," 245–46; Helm, *Calvin: A Guide*, 41–44.

26. Helm, *Calvin: A Guide*, 44–45.

27. On Gribaldi, see James T. Dennison Jr. et al., "Trinitarian Confession of the Italian Church of Geneva (1558)," *Kerux* 21, no.1 (May 2006), 3–4 and 4n4; and *Dictionary of Unitarian and Universalist Biography*, s.v. "Matteo Gribaldi," by Peter Hughes, http://uudb.org/articles/matteogribaldi.html.

28. Dennison Jr. et al., "Trinitarian Confession of the Italian Church," 4n4.

29. On Biandrata, see Joseph N. Tylenda, "The Warning That Went Unheeded: John Calvin on Giorgio Biandrata," *Calvin Theological Journal* 12 (April–November 1977): 24–62; and *Dictionary of Unitarian and Universalist Biography*, s.v. "George Biandrata," by Charles A. Howe and Peter Hughes, http://uudb.org/articles/giorgiobiandrata.html.

42 Theology Made Practical

Biandrata, for example, argued that "Jesus never revealed to the world a God other than his Father." In His teaching, Jesus never taught about God being "one essence in three persons," something that Biandrata deemed "clearly incomprehensible."[30] Gentile, on the other hand, argued that there are indeed three persons in the Godhead, but "only the Father is *autotheos*, that is, has his essence (*essentiatus*) from no superior deity, but is God of himself."[31] Neither the Son nor the Spirit are *autotheos*, for the Father poured, as it were, some of His divine being into them and thus deified them.[32]

Calvin responded to these arguments with a number of writings as well as personal meetings with the Italians.[33] From New Testament texts like Romans 9:5, John 1:1 and 20:28, and 2 Corinthians 12:8–9, Calvin could only conclude that Jesus is recognized to be fully God by the New Testament authors.[34] And to Biandrata's argument that "the one essence in three persons was not revealed by Christ," Calvin responded by referring, among other things, to the baptismal command of Matthew 28:19 where Christ "distinctly and undeniably named…[the] three persons of the Father, and of the Son, and of the Holy Spirit."[35] This appeal to Scripture reflected Calvin's conviction that theological reflection about "the one essence and the three persons" is not a waste of time, for the scriptural witness about God clearly proceeds from the presupposition of the Trinity.[36] In fact, at the close of his brief reply to Biandrata, Calvin appealed to the Nicene Creed and the writings of "Athanasius and other ancients," which, according to his reading of their texts, affirmed that though "the Son is distinct from the Father, nevertheless, he is true God, and the same God with him, except in what pertains

---

30. Tylenda, "Warning That Went Unheeded," 52–53.

31. *Impietas Valentini Gentilis detecta et palam traducta, qui Christum non sine sacrilega blasphemia Deum essentiatum esse fingit* (1561), in *CO*, 9:374.

32. Calvin, *Institutes* 1.13.23–26. See also Thomas F. Torrance, "Calvin's Doctrine of the Trinity," *Calvin Theological Journal* 25, no. 2 (November 1990): 180–81; Robert Letham, *The Holy Trinity in Scripture, History, Theology, and Worship* (Phillipsburg, N.J.: P&R, 2004), 256; and Baars, "The Trinity," 250.

33. See, for example, John Calvin, *Ad quaestiones Georgii Blandratae responsum* (1558), in *CO*, 9:321–32; "Confession of Faith Set Forth in the Italian Church of Geneva May 18, 1558," in Dennison Jr. et al., "Trinitarian Confession of the Italian Church," 6–10; and Calvin, *Impietas Valentini Gentilis*, in *CO*, 9:361–420.

34. Calvin, *Ad quaestiones Georgii Blandratae responsum* (1558), in *CO*, 9:327–29.

35. Calvin, *Ad quaestiones Georgii Blandratae responsum* (1558), in *CO*, 9:328. English trans. Tylenda, "Warning That Went Unheeded," 58.

36. Calvin, *Ad quaestiones Georgii Blandratae responsum* (1558), in *CO*, 9:331.

John Calvin on the Divine Triunity

to his person" and that there are "three coeternal [persons] but nevertheless one eternal God."[37]

In May 1558, Calvin helped to draw up a Trinitarian confession of faith for the Italian church in which the errors of Gentile were specifically condemned: "Whatever is attributed" to the Father's "deity, glory and essence, is suitable as much to the Son as to the Holy Spirit."[38] It is noteworthy that in this confession, Calvin used the classical concepts of eternal generation and eternal procession to distinguish the Father from the Son and the Spirit. In his words: "We profess God the Father even to have begotten his Word or Wisdom from eternity, who is his only Son, and the Holy Spirit thus to have proceeded from them both since there is one sole essence of the Father, Son, and Holy Spirit."[39]

In his main response to the arguments of these heterodox Italians— namely, the fifth edition of his *Institutes* (1559)—Calvin employed Scripture to demonstrate the consubstantiality of the Father with both the Son and the Spirit.[40] And because Gentile also argued for his position from the writings of the second-century fathers Irenaeus of Lyons (c. 130–c. 200) and Tertullian (fl. 190–220),[41] Calvin sought to show that neither of these patristic authors, properly interpreted, supported Gentile's position.[42] Calvin was confident that his own Trinitarian perspective was in complete harmony with that of the ancient church.[43]

The Fathers as Conversation Partners

Calvin could be critical of the fathers, but those occasions occur mostly in his exegetical commentaries in relation to the fathers' unwarranted use of biblical texts to support their dogmatic statements.[44] In his 1548 commentary on Colossians, for instance, Calvin noted that the ancient writers during the Arian controversy employed Colossians 1:15 to "insist upon the

---

37. Calvin, *Ad quaestiones Georgii Blandratae responsum* (1558), in *CO*, 9:331–32. English trans. Tylenda, "Warning That Went Unheeded," 61–62.

38. "Confession of Faith Set Forth in the Italian Church of Geneva May 18, 1558," in Dennison Jr. et al., "Trinitarian Confession of the Italian Church," 9.

39. "Confession of Faith Set Forth in the Italian Church of Geneva May 18, 1558," in Dennison Jr. et al., "Trinitarian Confession of the Italian Church," 8.

40. Calvin, *Institutes*, 1.13.23–25.

41. Calvin, *Impietas Valentini Gentilis*, in *CO*, 9:394–96.

42. Calvin, *Institutes*, 1.13.27–28.

43. Calvin, *Institutes*, 1.13.29.

44. Baars, "The Trinity," 247. The expression in the subheading comes from Baars.

44   Theology Made Practical

equality of the Son with the Father" and to assert the Nicene watchword, the consubstantiality (*homoousian*) of the Father and the Son.[45] One of the old writers that Calvin had in mind was John Chrysostom (c. 347–407), the one-time patriarch of Constantinople. According to Calvin, Chrysostom argued that the word "image" speaks of Christ's divine status since "the creature cannot be said to be the image of the Creator." Calvin, though, found this to be a weak argument since Paul can use the word "image" of human beings, as, for example, in 1 Corinthians 11:7, where Paul says man is the "image and glory of God." The word "image," Calvin pointed out, does not refer to Christ's essence but is being used as an epistemological term. Christ is the "image of God because he makes God in a manner visible to us." He can only do so, Calvin averred, because He is the "essential Word of God" and is consubstantial with the Father. Behind this affirmation lies a key principle that Calvin had drawn from his reading of the church fathers: only God can reveal God. Colossians 1:15, therefore, does speak of the Son's *homoousia* with the Father and is "a powerful weapon in opposition to the Arians." Calvin thus arrived at the same place as Chrysostom, but he did so by a more rigorous hermeneutic that paid proper attention to the text. Calvin concluded that this text is a good reminder that "God in himself, that is, in his naked majesty" is invisible to both the physical eye and the eye of human understanding. Only in Christ is God revealed. To seek God elsewhere is to engage in idolatry.[46]

A second example in which Calvin engaged patristic Trinitarian exegesis is his commentary on Hebrews 1:2–3, which the French Reformer wrote the year following his commentary on Colossians. Hebrews 1 was regularly mined in the patristic era for proof of Christ's divinity, and understandably so in light of its high Christology. Following in the train of this exegetical tradition, Calvin deduced the eternal nature of Christ from the fact that He made the world. Since the Father is usually identified as the Creator of the world, this means that there are at least two "persons" involved in this divine work. Since Calvin assumed only God can do such creative work, the Son must be fully divine and share a "unity of essence" with the Father. As persons they are to be distinguished, but as God they have in common "whatever is applied to God alone."[47]

---

45. Calvin, *Commentary*, on Col. 1:15.
46. Calvin, *Commentary*, on Col. 1:15.
47. Calvin, *Commentary*, on Heb. 1:2.

Hebrews 1:3 also speaks of the deity of Christ, though Calvin was careful to note at the outset of his commentary that the reader of Hebrews should not seek to investigate the "hidden majesty of God" by inquiring into the exact way "the Son, who has the same essence with the Father, is a brightness emanating from his light." By describing Christ in this way, the author of Hebrews is not seeking to depict "what likeness the Father bears to the Son," for God is incomprehensible to us. Rather, this description is yet another vital reminder that "God is made known to us in no other way than in Christ."[48]

Hebrews 1:3 also states that Christ is "the very image" of the Father's "substance" (*hupostasis*). By this term, Calvin understood the personal distinctiveness of the Father, not the "essence of the Father." To make the latter point would be redundant, Calvin believed, since both the Father and the Son share the same essence. Calvin was conscious that his interpretation followed in the pathway of patristic exegesis, for Latin exegetes like Hilary of Poitiers (c. 300–c. 368), a staunch opponent of Arianism, made the same point. In other words, Calvin was convinced that this clause declares that anything we know of the Father we find revealed in the person of Christ. While Paul's intention in this text is not to discuss Christ's divine being, which some of the the fathers might not have grasped, Calvin believed this clause refutes "the Arians and the Sabellians." It ascribes to Christ what belongs to God alone—namely, the power to reveal God—and thus the reader is right to infer that "the Son is one God with the Father." At the same time it upholds the distinctiveness of the Father and the Son as persons.[49]

Another key text used by patristic authors like Athanasius (c. 299–373) and Basil of Caesarea (c. 329–79) to prove the deity of the Son and the Spirit was the baptismal formula in Matthew 28:19. Calvin likewise saw in this verse evidence of the triune nature of God.[50] Until the coming of Christ, "the full and clear knowledge" of God's nature remained hidden. While God's old covenant people had some knowledge of the Wisdom and Spirit of God, it was only when the gospel began to be preached that "God was far more clearly revealed in three persons, for then the Father manifested himself in the Son, his lively and distinct image, while Christ, irradiating the world by the full splendor of his Spirit, held out to the knowledge of men both himself

---

48. Calvin, *Commentary*, on Heb. 1:3.
49. Calvin, *Commentary*, on Heb. 1:3.
50. Calvin, *Commentary*, on Matt. 28:19.

46   Theology Made Practical

and the Spirit." Tying this Matthean verse to another Trinitarian text, Titus 3:5, Calvin concluded that there is a good reason for Jesus to mention all three persons of the Godhead since there can be no saving knowledge of God "unless our faith distinctly conceive of three persons in one essence."

Consider some of Calvin's exegetical remarks on Isaiah 6, the commissioning of the prophet.[51] Calvin noted that verse 3 was often cited by the "ancients," that is, the church fathers, when they wished to prove that there are three persons in one essence of the Godhead." On one level Calvin did not disagree with this interpretation. He had no doubt that the angelic worship of God involves all three persons of the Godhead, as "it is impossible to praise God without also uttering the praises of the Father, of the Son, and of the Spirit." But, Calvin argued, there are much stronger passages to prove this article of the Christian faith. And he feared that the use of such "inconclusive" texts as this one would simply embolden the opposition of heretics. Calvin actually did find a good support for Trinitarianism a few verses later, when God asks, "Who will go for us?" Calvin believed that the use of the plural here, as in Genesis 1:26, unquestionably reflects the Father's consultation "with his eternal Wisdom and his eternal Power, that is, with the Son and the Holy Spirit."

Finally, Calvin did not fail to reflect on the Trinitarian implications that the message given to Isaiah to deliver to Israel is twice cited in the New Testament. In the first citation in John 12:37–41, John states that when Isaiah heard these words, he saw the glory of Christ. Then Paul cites this same passage as a word from the Holy Spirit (Acts 28:25–28). From these two New Testament citations of the Isaiah text, Calvin argued, it is evident that "Christ was that God who filled the whole earth with his majesty. Now, Christ is not separate from his Spirit, and therefore Paul had good reason for applying this passage to the Holy Spirit; for although God exhibited to the Prophet the lively image of himself in Christ, still it is certain that whatever he communicated was wholly breathed into him by the power of the Holy Spirit."

A Concluding Word

We see in Calvin's response to Pierre Caroli's charges against him and his friends in the 1530s to his debates with the Italian anti-Trinitarians in the 1550s that the French divine was increasingly conscious of being an heir of

---

51. Calvin, *Commentary*, on Isa. 6.

the patristic formulation of the doctrine of the Trinity. But as a minister of the gospel under the authority of the Word of God alone, he was also determined to refrain from making "any assertion where Scripture is silent."[52] As Calvin read the Scripture, he saw, as had the fathers before him, that it clearly sets forth the oneness of the three—Father, Son, and Holy Spirit. At the same time, though, the restraint of scriptural declaration about the relationships within the immanent Trinity required great circumspection in theological reflection on the Godhead.

Calvin's understanding is best summed up by Greek author Gregory of Nazianzus (c. 330–89), whose observation, the Reformer said, gave him vast delight: "I cannot think on the one without quickly being encircled by the splendor of the three; nor can I discern the three without being straightway carried back to the one."[53]

---

52. Calvin, *Commentary*, on Isa. 6:2.
53. Calvin, *Institutes*, 1.13.17.

—4—

Calvin on Similarities and Differences of Election and Reprobation

Joel R. Beeke

Predestination was not the center of John Calvin's thought, though it reached a new level of preoccupation in his theology due to the influences of Augustine and Martin Bucer and because of the pressures of pastoral concerns and controversy. Calvin presented the cardinal elements of his doctrine of predestination already in 1539 in the second edition of his *Institutes* and in his commentary on Romans, which was published the same year. During his second Genevan stay (1541–1564), predestination became his principal polemical doctrine. The major opponents of his doctrine of predestination were Albert Pighius, Jerome Bolsec, Jean Trolliet, and Sebastian Castellio, who engaged him on this subject from 1542 to 1558. Following these controversies, Calvin augmented his treatment of predestination in the final edition of the *Institutes* (1559).

Through predestination Calvin defended the theological validity of the Reformation's prime doctrine of gratuitous justification apart from meritorious works and enhanced rather than diminished the doctrine of salvation by gracious faith alone. This chapter shows that Calvin's opponents moved him to develop greater clarity on the similarities and differences of election and reprobation, particularly in relation to his often overlooked distinction between proximate and remote causation, which can still be of great help for us today.

Calvin's Opponents

Albert Pighius (c. 1490–1542) was a Dutch humanist and Roman Catholic theologian who studied in Louvain and Paris. He served as a papal privy councilor under Clement VII (1525–1531), after which he returned to the Netherlands to serve as provost at the Church of St. John the Baptist in Utrecht. His writings, which were most influential on predestination,

50 Theology Made Practical

justification, original sin, freedom of the will, and papal infallibility, provoked responses from various Reformers, including Peter Martyr and Calvin.[1] When Pighius reacted in 1542 to Calvin's 1539 *Institutes* with a book titled *De libero hominis arbitrio et devina gratia libri decem* (Ten books on human free choice and divine grace), Calvin responded with his *Defensio doctrinae de servitute arbitrii contra Pighium* in 1543[2] and his *De aeterna Dei praedestinatione* in 1552.[3] The former work Calvin used to attack Pighius's first six books of *De libero hominis arbitrio*, and the latter work responded to Pighius's last four books. As summarized by John Patrick Donnelly, Pighius's chief arguments against Calvin's doctrine of predestination include "that his teaching leads to moral licentiousness, that it implies God desires sin, that it causes men to hate God as an arbitrary tyrant, that it imposes necessity on man's conduct and thereby destroys the notion of responsibility and guilt, and that it virtually denies the goodness of God since the possibility of salvation is open only to a few men."[4]

Calvin's second major opponent on predestination was Jerome Bolsec (c. 1524–1584). A former Carmelite monk, Bolsec left the Roman Catholic Church to study medicine and about 1550 became the personal physician of Jacques de Bourgogne, Lord of Falais, a close friend of Calvin who lived near Geneva. By that time, Bolsec claimed to have become a Reformed Protestant and enjoyed dabbling in theology. He said that he agreed with Calvin in every vital doctrine except predestination, which he often refuted, claiming that Calvin's views made God the author of sin and that therefore Calvinists turned the Christian God into a tyrant and worshiped an idol. Bolsec was imprisoned for his radical assertions and propaganda against Calvin. The Geneva Council, somewhat perplexed by Bolsec's assertions, accepted the proposition of the clergy to ask the advice of the Swiss churches. For Calvin,

---

1. Cf. John Patrick Donnelly, *Calvinism and Scholasticism in Vermigli's Doctrine of Man and Grace* (Leiden: Brill, 1976), 124–37.

2. *CR*, 34:225–404, first translated into English as *The Bondage and Liberation of the Will: A Defense of the Orthodox Doctrine of Human Choice against Pighius*, ed. A. N. S. Lane, trans. G. I. Davies (Grand Rapids: Baker, 1996).

3. *CR*, 36:249–366; English translations include "The Eternal Predestination of God," in *Calvin's Calvinism*, trans. Henry Cole (London: Sovereign Grace Union, 1927), and that of Reid (Calvin, *Predestination*).

4. Donnelly, *Calvinism and Scholasticism*, 137. For Calvin's direct refutation of Pighius on reprobation, see *CR*, 36:313–18 (Calvin, *Predestination*, 120–25). For a summary of Pighius's thought on free will, foreknowledge, and predestination, see A. P. Linsenmann, "Albertus Pighius und sein theologischer Standpunkt," *Theologische Quartalschrift* 48 (1866): 629–44.

Calvin on Election and Reprobation

the Swiss churches responded in a disappointing and mild manner, calling for moderation and reconciliation. Only individual friends such as William Farel, Theodore Beza, and Pierre Viret gave Calvin unequivocal support.[5] By the end of 1551, however, Bolsec's increasingly rash statements against Geneva's clergy and the doctrine of predestination earned him banishment for life from the city. Bolsec found refuge with the Bernese, who expelled him in 1555, after which he returned to the Roman Catholic Church and wrote his grossly fictitious and slanderous biography of Calvin.[6]

Bolsec's arguments were not altogether dissimilar from those of Pighius: First, it was a "pernicious opinion" that God determined the eternal destiny of people before the creation of the world, for none can be regarded by God as among the elect or reprobate apart from belief and unbelief. For Bolsec, belief must precede election, and unbelief must precede reprobation. Second, predestination from eternity makes God both a tyrant and the author of evil. Third, no biblical proof can be given that clearly asserts that God willed, ordered, and determined the fall of Adam by His own counsel. Finally, Bolsec challenged the notion of the hidden will of God as asserted by Calvin.[7]

The Bolsec affair excited few Genevan opponents of Calvin until Jean Trolliet (a former monk who held a grudge against Calvin for hindering his ordination as a Genevan pastor) pressed charges against Calvin's views on predestination in June 1552. Allied with the Perrinist party, Trolliet rebuked Calvin primarily for "(1) relieving men of responsibility by affirming that God had caused Adam to fall, (2) for thereby making God the author of sin, and (3) by virtue of God's causing the fall of Adam, necessarily imposing predestination upon mankind."[8] During the months of debate that ensued, Calvin most likely wrote his *Articles on Predestination* to withstand the onslaught of Trolliet and his Perrinist friends.[9] The Little Council heard both sides with mixed feelings. Through his appeals to Philip Melanchthon and his numerous friendships, Trolliet pressed on until Calvin demanded that justice be carried out under threat of resigning his ministry. On November 9,

---

5. John S. Bray, *Theodore Beza's Doctrine of Predestination* (Nieuwkoop: B. DeGraaf, 1975), 67–68.

6. Cf. Theodore Beza, "Life of Calvin," in *Tracts and Letters*, 1:57–58, 69–70; Williston Walker, *John Calvin: The Organizer of Reformed Protestantism* (repr., New York: G. Putnam's Sons, 1969), 315–20, 346–47.

7. *CR*, 36:149, 157, 161, 179–80.

8. *CR*, 42:171–72.

9. *CR*, 37:713–14.

52 Theology Made Practical

the Little Council finally voted in favor of Calvin and declared that "in [the] future no one should dare to speak against that book [i.e., the *Institutes*] or that doctrine [of predestination]." Nevertheless, when Trolliet finally acquiesced, the Little Council officially declared him to be "a good man and a good citizen."[10]

Finally, for most of his Genevan ministry, Calvin duelled intermittently with Sebastian Castellio, a French humanist scholar and promoter of religious toleration. The author of dialogues on predestination, election, and free will, Castellio waged controversy with Calvin on his doctrine of predestination from 1554 to 1558. Castellio propounded against Calvin that particular election out of a condition of total bondage to sin was false, that the notion of divine hardening was stoical and destroyed morality and piety, and that the denial of God's permissive will made God the author of evil. Calvin responded three times to Castellio in writing.[11]

In summary, Calvin's doctrine of predestination was challenged on three major interrelated fronts by his opponents: the problem of sin and unbelief in relation to predestination; the problem of a divinely decreed fall in conjunction with the particularity of predestination; and the problem of retaining a soteriological theology in the light of reprobation. Essentially, these are the issues that Calvin addressed in his seven polemical works of the period in which he defended sovereign predestination. To each of these issues we will now turn.

Sin and Unbelief in Relation to Predestination

In reaction to his opponents, Calvin increasingly argued for an explicit integration of the doctrines of sin and unbelief into the doctrine of reprobation. God's sovereign decree from eternity is executed in time in a just and equitable manner, Calvin said. Knowing God and ourselves teaches us "what is God's and what is ours."[12] A proper ordering of things teaches us that what belongs to God in every case—hence also in the matter of salvation or

---

10. Cited in Walker, *John Calvin*, 321.

11. *Response a certained calomnies et blasphemes dont quelques malins sefforcent de rendre la doctrine de la predestination de Dieu odieuse*, 1557, in CR, 58:199–206; *Brevis responsio ad diluenda nebulonis cuiusdam calumnias quibus doctrinam de aeterna Dei praedestinatione foedare conatus est*, 1557, in CR, 37:253–66; *Calumniae nebulonis cuiusdam, quibis odio et invidia gravare conatus est doctrinam de occulta Dei providentia*, 1558, in CR, 37:269–318. Cf. H. M. Stuckelberger, "Calvin und Castellio," *Zwingliana* 7 (1939):114–19.

12. Calvin, *Congregation on Eternal Election*, in CR, 36:111.

Calvin on Election and Reprobation

condemnation—is divine glory as the final cause.[13] For Calvin, the fact that divine glory is also the ultimate cause of the decree of reprobation implicitly removes some degree of sharpness from that decree.

Second, Calvin asserted that our natural odiousness toward reprobation can be further minimized when we consider what properly belongs to man—namely, sin. For Calvin, an acknowledgment of the extensive pervasiveness of sin, which permeates the entire life of the natural man, is requisite for understanding why hope for any individual is only possible through predestination. Man's imprisonment to sin is total by nature, Calvin claimed: "There is no salvation for man, save in the mercy of God, because in himself he is desperate and undone."[14] In himself, man is totally given over to evil, full of pollution, and lacks even "a single taste or grain of purity."[15] In fact, "just as a fish is nourished in water so men are confined in sin and iniquity."[16] In looking upon fallen nature, God can see only "complete misery and poverty."[17]

Man's sinfulness, moreover, cannot but yield unbelief. Hence, any spark of true faith must begin from, continue through, and end in God.[18] Thus, election is the only channel of and hope for faith. Election is the source of all saving benefits, apart from which God can never have mercy on grossly sinful man in himself.[19]

Calvin undercut many of his opponents' arguments by concluding: "If all whom the Lord predestines to death are naturally liable to the sentence of death, of what injustice, pray, do they complain?"[20] Simply said, do we not all deserve to be condemned forever on account of sin and unbelief rooted deeply in our corrupt natures? If we truly see what "is ours," is not the miracle of election more staggering than the awesome decree of reprobation? For Calvin, the wonder is that any are redeemed and that not all are reprobated.

Calvin's opponents responded with the following: If all this is true, why did not God decree the miracle of election for all? If there is no separation

---

13. *CR*, 51:277.
14. Calvin, *Predestination*, 121.
15. *CR*, 36:96.
16. *CR*, 33:724.
17. *CR*, 36:95.
18. Calvin, *Predestination*, 158–62.
19. *CR*, 58:40.
20. Calvin, *Institutes*, 2.5.3.

54 Theology Made Practical

among men's works—much less their faith—why did not God determine to save all for the sake of His own glory? In short, why did God reprobate?

Calvin answered that reprobation is of God, is both sovereign and just, does serve to His glory, and, above all, is the will of God. Calvin admitted, though, that even this answer does not probe the depth of the question. Ultimately, there is no fully satisfying answer, for to attempt one is to seek for something higher than the will of God. No such thing exists, however—at least certainly not from the side and perspective of mere man. Hence, why God wills reprobation is not for us to know, for we could not comprehend it even if we did know. Calvin wrote against Pighius:

> Since a man may find the cause of his evil within himself, what is the use of looking round to seek it in heaven?... Though men delude themselves by wandering through obscure immensities, they can never so stupefy themselves as to lose the sense of sin engraved on their hearts. Hence, impiety attempts in vain to absolve the man whom his own conscience condemns. God knowingly and willingly suffers man to fall; the reason may be hidden, but it cannot be unjust.... God wills not iniquity.... In a wonderful and ineffable way, what was done contrary to His will was yet not done without His will, because it would not have been done at all unless He had allowed it. So He permitted it not unwillingly, but willingly.... In sinning, they did what God did not will in order that God through their evil will might do what He willed. If anyone objects that this is beyond his comprehension, I confess it.... Therefore let us be pleased with instructed ignorance rather than with the intemperate and inquisitive intoxication of wanting to know more than God allows.[21]

From our perspective, then, we need to embrace "instructed ignorance" and there leave the matter rest, bearing in mind that we can understand this much: God is at least fully just in reprobating, for the reprobate are all hell-worthy sinners who have no business blaming God for their condemnation when their lives reveal that condemnation is their just desert.[22]

---

21. Calvin, *Predestination*, 122–23.

22. For a chronological/historical development of Calvin's doctrine of reprobation, see Joel R. Beeke, *Debated Issues in Sovereign Predestination: Early Lutheran Predestination, Calvinian Reprobation, and Variations in Genevan Lapsarianism*, Reformed Historical Theology, vol. 42, ed. Herman J. Selderhuis (Göttingen, Germany: Vandenhoeck & Ruprecht, 2017), 83–163.

The Decreed Fall and Particular Reprobation

With regard to the question of how God could decree the fall and the reprobate, Calvin again refused to flinch before his opponents but purposely determined to begin with and end in the Word of God, declaring from the outset that "the inscrutable judgment of God [is] deeper than can be penetrated by man." Unlike Pighius, he resisted the temptation to reduce God to man's level of understanding and asked, "Is there no justice of God, but that which is conceived of by us?"[23] Rather, he asserted fully both the sovereignty of God in decretal reprobation and the responsibility of man in voluntarily falling, despite the irrevocable decree behind his fall. Calvin scripturally exonerated God from being the author of sin while simultaneously positing full blame for all sin at the door of Adam and his descendants. His train of thought runs like this: "Man was so created, and placed in such a condition, that he could have no cause whatever of complaint against his Maker. God foresaw the fall of Adam, and most certainly His suffering him to fall was not contrary to, but according to, His divine will.... Adam could not but fall, according to the foreknowledge and will of God. What then? Is Adam on that account freed from guilt? Certainly not. He fell by his own full free will, and by his own willing act."[24] From here, Calvin reasoned:

And though Adam fell not, nor destroyed himself and his posterity, either *without* the knowledge or *without* the ordaining will of God, yet *that* neither lessens his own fault, nor implicates God in any blame whatsoever. For we must ever carefully bear in mind that Adam, of his own will and accord, deprived himself of that perfect righteousness which he had received from God; and that, of his own accord and will, he gave himself up to the service of sin and Satan, and thus precipitated himself into eternal destruction. Here, however, men will continually offer one uniform *excuse* for Adam—that it was not possible for him to help or *avoid* that which God Himself had *decreed.* But to establish the guilt of Adam for ever, his own *voluntary* transgression is enough, and more than sufficient. Nor, indeed, is the secret counsel of God the *real* and *virtual cause* of sin but manifestly the *will* and *inclination* of man.[25]

---

23. Calvin, "The Eternal Predestination of God," in *Calvin's Calvinism*, 32.
24. Calvin, "The Eternal Predestination of God," in *Calvin's Calvinism*, 92–93.
25. Calvin, "The Eternal Predestination of God," in *Calvin's Calvinism*, 125.

56 Theology Made Practical

Out of this kind of logic, Calvin developed his well-known distinction between God as the *remote* (or ultimate) cause of man's deeds, and man as the *proximate* (or secondary) cause of his own actions. He wrote:

> If then, nothing can prevent a man from acknowledging that the first origin of his ruin was from Adam, and if each man find the *proximate* cause of his ruin in himself, what can prevent our faith from acknowledging afar off, with all sobriety, and adoring, with all humility, that *remote* secret counsel of God by which the fall of man was thus pre-ordained? And what should prevent the same faith from beholding, at the same time, the *proximate* cause within; that the whole human race is individually bound by the guilt and desert of eternal death, as derived from the person of Adam; and that all are in themselves, therefore, subject to death, and to death eternal? Pighius, therefore, has not sundered, shaken, or altered (as he thought he had done) that pre-eminent and most beautiful symmetry with which these *proximate* and *remote* causes divinely harmonize![26]

This distinction between proximate and remote causes (*causae propinquae et remotae)* is of prime importance for Calvin. It assists him in pursuing four major goals.

First, Calvin believed that the proximate/remote distinction crushes several important distinctions propounded by his opponents. Specifically, it answered Castellio's idea that God's "permissive will"[27] did not relate to the origin of evil in any way other than merely permitting it. For Calvin, the proximate/remote distinction showed that to confine God to a role of mere permission was to deprive Him of His rightful role as Judge and Sovereign.[28] Then, too, Calvin argued that the proximate/remote distinction nonplussed Pighius's dichotomizing of the will of God as absolute versus ordained, which necessarily implied events occurring outside the boundary of the divine will. Against Pighius, it allowed him to maintain that there was no ultimate cause for the fall outside of the will of God; besides, no culpability

---

26. Calvin, "The Eternal Predestination of God," in *Calvin's Calvinism*, 91; cf. *Commentary*, on Rom. 9:11, 11:7; and *CR*, 36:346.

27. "*Permission* must not be confused with the term *permissive decree* employed by some Reformed theologians. The permissive decree concerns God's decree and His will. Calvin was contemplating a distinction between *will* and *permission*." Fred Klooster, *Calvin's Doctrine of Predestination* (Grand Rapids: Baker, 1967), 67.

28. Calvin, *Predestination*, 59–61.

tinged the divinely holy and just will at that level since "removing from God all proximate causation of the act [of the fall] at the same time removes from Him all guilt and leaves man alone liable."[29]

Second, by means of the proximate/remote distinction, Calvin not only retains God in full control but also preserves the particularity of His relationship to man. Indeed, the failure to acknowledge the validity of this distinction is precisely where Calvin thought his opponents erred. He wrote that it is not surprising that Pighius "should indiscriminately confuse everything in the judgments of God, when he does not distinguish between causes proximate and remote."[30] Specifically, if God is not acknowledged as the remote cause of the fall, particular reprobation must soon give way, and eventually particular election as well. Furthermore, if particular election is denied, the most solid defense of utterly gratuitous redemption is obliterated; the doctrines of grace are then abandoned for the leaven of human merit, which posits an imaginary salvation that refuses to reckon with the seriousness of sin, the depth of the fall, and, above all, the bondage of the will.

Third, a discrimination of proximate and remote causes is an invaluable asset for Calvin's delicate presentation that balances election and reprobation as equally ultimate in some respects, yet not fully parallel in other respects. As the remote cause of election and reprobation, God's sovereignty by definition demands equal ultimacy; the will of God is just as much the ultimate cause of reprobation as it is of election.[31] Nevertheless, the insertion of a proximate cause of sin, fall, and condemnation allows Calvin to escape the charge of divine arbitrariness and fatalism, for in this sense election and reprobation are by no means parallels. The proximate cause allows for the most important of all nonparallel elements—namely, election is foundationally gratuitous; reprobation, foundationally just. Though human action can never be the proximate cause in divine election since no individual can ever merit God's sovereign choosing, sinful actions certainly do involve themselves as the proximate cause of the condemnation aspect of reprobation, though not of the decretal act itself. Fred Klooster's assessment of Calvin is helpful at this juncture:

---

29. Calvin, *Predestination*, 123–28.

30. Calvin, *Predestination*, 100.

31. Calvin is irrefutably plain that neither sin nor foreknowledge is the ultimate cause of either election or reprobation; all ultimate causation must be the divine will. Calvin, *Institutes*, 3.22.11; 3.23.1, 2, 5, 8, 13–14; *Commentary*, on Rom. 9:14, 18, 22.

58   Theology Made Practical

While God sovereignly passes some by in His decretive will, the ground of His final condemnation of them is their sin and guilt. This sin is our sin; it constitutes the proximate cause of reprobation as far as the unbeliever's condemnation is concerned. It is important to observe, however, that sin is not the ground or the proximate cause of God's ultimate discrimination between elect and reprobate.... Sin and guilt may be said to be the ground of only one element of reprobation, namely, condemnation; sin is the proximate cause of reprobation only in this sense. Even then, however, it is only the proximate cause. As proximate cause, it is clearly understood by us while the ultimate cause is not. On this proximate cause Calvin did place great emphasis, and concentration upon it makes crystal clear that God is just; the blame for sin and final condemnation is ours, not God's.[32]

In a word, as Calvin said, "none undeservedly perish,"[33] for condemnation, while sovereignly executed, is always hinged to human sin and guilt.[34] Since culpability attaches itself to the proximate cause of any sinful action committed and is so completely absorbed by it, no guilt can or needs to remain for attachment to the remote cause. Hence, God is free of all taint of sin, and man is always the guilty party. Moreover, our consciences confirm this truth, for condemnation is that part of the larger whole of reprobation that we can understand and endorse by the "internal feeling of the heart,"[35]

---

32. Klooster, *Calvin's Doctrine of Predestination*, 76–77.

33. Calvin, *Predestination*, 125.

34. Cf. John Murray, *Calvin on Scripture and Divine Sovereignty* (Philadelphia: Presbyterian and Reformed, 1960), 55–71. Later Reformed theology would take Calvin's implications further by developing the formal distinction in terminology of *negative* and *positive* reprobation—the former characterizing God's act as of the nature of a *praeteritio* (preterition, or passing over) or an *indebitae gratiae negatio* (the denial of unmerited grace); the latter, as *praedamnatio* (predamnation) or *debitae poenae destinatio* (preordaining to merited punishment). Herman Bavinck, *The Doctrine of God*, trans. William Hendriksen (Grand Rapids: Eerdmans, 1951), 398, 403.

35. In this connection, Calvin sometimes prefers to label proximate and remote causes as *evident* and *hidden* causes in order to encourage this heart sense of guilt: "I teach that a man ought to search for the cause of his condemnation in his corrupt nature rather than in the predestination of God.... I expressly state that there are two causes: the one *hidden* in the eternal counsel of God, and the other *manifest* in the sin of man.... Here then, is the very core of the whole question: I say that all the reprobate will be convicted of guilt by their own conscience and that thus their condemnation is righteous, and that they err in neglecting what is quite evident to enter instead into the secret counsel of God which to us is inaccessible." *CR*, 42:379.

which gives a sense of sin and a conviction that the decree of God to perdition necessarily involves "just severity" (*justa severitas*).[36]

Calvin, then, distinguished the decree of reprobation in eternity (of which he often spoke in what later came to be called a supralapsarian manner) from the reality of damnation, which involves just judgment and punishment in time. When he spoke of the reprobate being left or abandoned by God to their own destruction (language that later came to be identified with infralapsarianism), he almost always was referring to what God does in time with the ungodly.[37]

Other nonparallel elements in Calvin's thought on election and reprobation include an accented role of Christ in election, the glorification of different attributes in election and reprobation, and the major accent in preaching and writing being placed on election to coincide with Scripture and pastoral reasons.[38] Parallel elements include that both contribute to divine glory,[39] both lead to destinies that are eternal,[40] and the means of attaining the end results of both are equally decreed, though reprobation is "effected in the 'reverse way' from election."[41] Election is effected by the monergistic work of God, whereas reprobation is synergistic in its outworkings.[42]

Finally, Calvin's proximate/remote discrimination assists him in developing a homogeneous doctrine of reprobation in relation to election. By asserting that ill desert is not the reason for decretal determination while it is the cause for actual condemnation, Calvin underscored the judicial or penal aspect of reprobation even as he maintained the absolutely sovereign will of God.[43] Consequently, the proximate/remote distinction allows Calvin to maintain both that saving faith is not irrational and that it is ultimately "impossible for man to penetrate the relation of God's counsel to human responsibility."[44] Though faith retains its rationality, not all mystery is taken away: God's incomprehensible, sovereign, perfectly just and holy will

---

36. Murray, *Calvin on Scripture and Divine Sovereignty*, 62.

37. Calvin, *Institutes*, 3.22.7; 3.23.3, 8; 3.24.12; and *CR*, 36:266, 270, 298, 313–14.

38. Klooster, *Calvin's Doctrine of Predestination*, 51–52.

39. Calvin, *Predestination*, 35.

40. Murray, *Calvin on Scripture and Divine Sovereignty*, 60–61.

41. Klooster, *Calvin's Doctrine of Predestination*, 77–79.

42. J. V. Fesko, *Diversity within the Reformed Tradtion: Supra- and Infralapsarianism in Calvin, Dort, and Westminster* (Greenville, S.C.: Reformed Academic Press, 2001), 97.

43. Murray, *Calvin on Scripture and Divine Sovereignty*, 63–64.

44. Cornelius Van Til, *The Theology of James Daane* (Philadelphia: Presbyterian and Reformed, 1959), 52.

60   Theology Made Practical

remains the bottom-line answer to contentions about reprobation. According to Calvin, if the doctrine of salvation is rightly presented, declaring that God is God over against man, the full mystery of God's relation to sin cannot be grasped: "But *how* it was ordained by the foreknowledge and decree of God what man's future was without God being implicated as associate in the fault as the author or approver of transgression, is clearly a secret so much excelling the insight of the human mind, that I am not ashamed to confess ignorance."[45] And again:

> For although God did not create the *sins* of men, who but God did create the *natures* of men themselves? which are, in themselves, undoubtedly good, but from which there were destined to proceed evils and sins according to the pleasure of His will, and, in many, such sins as would be visited with eternal punishment. If it be asked, Why did God create such natures? The reply is, Because He willed to create them. Why did He so will? "Who art thou, O man, that repliest against God?"[46]

In short, by asserting the universal agency of God, by repudiating philosophical explanations as to *how* His agency operates, and by recognizing the importance of proximate causes for daily life, Calvin developed a homogeneous doctrine of reprobation in relation to election.[47]

Soteriology and Reprobation

Homogeneous reprobation is essential for homogeneous, salvific election. And when all is said and done, it is this concern for a sound doctrine of salvation that motivated Calvin to be consistent in response to his opponents throughout seven works over the space of seventeen years. Consequently, it is most unfair to say of Calvin's polemical years that they move from a soteriological thrust into theology proper so as to defend reprobation and equal ultimacy.[48]

---

45. Calvin, *Predestination*, 124.
46. Calvin, "The Eternal Predestination of God," in *Calvin's Calvinism*, 70.
47. William Cunningham, *Reformers and Theology of the Reformation* (repr., London: Banner of Truth Trust, 1969).
48. E.g., Heinz Otten, *Calvins theologische Anschauung von der Pradestination* (Munich: Kaiser, 1938), 90, 132–35.

Calvin wanted to exclude works of demerit as the ultimate cause of reprobation in order to consistently exclude meritorious works as the ultimate cause of election. For God to have allowed man to fall only by His permission would be for Him to succumb to human activity on the negative side of salvation—that is, the lack of cooperation. In relation to God's salvific will, such a view would open the "back door" to meritorious works.[49]

For Calvin, reprobation is part and parcel of the predestination decree, and consequently, it stands in tension with, but not in conflict against, election and salvation—neither in its content, nor in its place and importance within theology. Calvin rejected all attempts to deny reprobation as attacks on God's greatness and election. In Calvin, theocentric causality and Christocentric soteriology do not have to slay one another in order for the other to survive. Hence, reprobation is not wrongly placed when conjoined with election under soteriology.[50] Though Calvin has no doctrine that serves as foundational or central for his systematics as a whole, predestination does serve as the heart, touchstone, and organizing principle of his soteriology in an *a posteriori* fashion.[51]

As David Wiley writes, "Predestination was more than the 'crown' or 'capstone' of Calvin's soteriology: it was a foundation stone as necessary for the whole soteriological structure to stand as gratuitous justification itself. This is what Calvin meant when he said that without the doctrine of election half the grace of God disappeared."[52] Wiley then concludes that Calvin distinguished gratuitous justification and predestination as follows: "When looking at the relationship between God and man from the viewpoint of man, gratuitous justification was [Calvin's] key doctrine, for it stated what happened to reconcile God to man; when looking at the relationship from the viewpoint of God, predestination was the key doctrine, for it indicated who [was] justified and what man's role was. Binding them together was the overriding soteriological thrust of Calvin's theology."[53]

---

49. Calvin, *Institutes*, 3.23.2, 7, 8; and *CR*, 36:315; 37:263.

50. Calvin's *placement* of predestination in his theology has long been a hotly contested issue. Most helpful here is Richard Muller, "Predestination and Christology in Sixteenth Century Reformed Theology" (PhD diss., Duke University, 1976), 3–6, 19, 30–31, 47–49, 51–52, 72, 76.

51. Muller, "Predestination and Christology," 436–37.

52. *CR*, 36:261; David Neeld Wiley, "Calvin's Doctine of Predestination: His Principal Soteriological and Polemical Doctrine" (PhD diss., Duke University, 1971), 172.

53. Wiley, "Calvin's Doctine of Predestination," 172.

Conclusion

By means of full-orbed predestination, which embraces both election and reprobation, Calvin defended gratuitous justification and salvation to the glory of God and the humility of the elect. Out of a soteriological compulsion, Calvin embraced the parity of election and reprobation insofar as they are rooted in the decree and will of God. In the relation of election and reprobation, the combination of equal ultimacy from the perspective of divine decree and of nonparallelism from the perspective of grace and justice undergirds a biblical doctrine of soteriology that glorifies God in His triune being and perfections without sacrificing the responsibility of man.

—5—

Calvin on the Holy Spirit

Joel R. Beeke

Although other theologians in the early stages of the Reformed tradition had given significant attention to the doctrine of the Holy Spirit,[1] Presbyterian Benjamin B. Warfield rightly declared John Calvin to be *the* "theologian of the Holy Spirit." Warfield went as far as to say that the "doctrine of the Holy Spirit is a gift from Calvin to the church."[2] These remarks, though, are probably better known than Calvin's actual teaching on the Holy Spirit. There have been several articles discussing Calvin's pneumatology,[3] as well

---

1. See, for example, Willem van 't Spijker, "The Doctrine of the Holy Spirit in Bucer and Calvin" (paper delivered at the International Congress on Calvin Research, 1986), 1.

2. Benjamin B. Warfield, "John Calvin the Theologian," in *Calvin and Augustine* (Philadelphia: Presbyterian and Reformed, 1956), 484–85.

3. Maurice B. Schepers, "The Interior Testimony of the Holy Spirit: A Critique of Calvinist Doctrine," *The Thomist* 29 (1965): 140–76, 295–321, 420–54; J. K. Parratt, "The Witness of the Holy Spirit: Calvin, the Puritans and St. Paul," *Evangelical Quarterly* 41 (1969): 161–68; M. Eugene Osterhaven, "John Calvin: Order and the Holy Spirit," *Reformed Review* 32 (Fall 1978): 23–44; Anthony Lane, "John Calvin: The Witness of the Spirit," in *Faith and Ferment* (London: Westminster Conference Papers, 1982), 1–17; Michael A. Eaton, "John Calvin and the Witness of the Spirit," in *Baptism with the Spirit: The Teaching of Dr. David Martyn Lloyd-Jones* (Leicester, England: InterVarsity, 1989), 41–59; I. John Hesselink, "Calvin, Theologian of the Holy Spirit," in *Calvin's First Catechism: A Commentary* (Louisville: Westminster, 1997), 177–87, 230–33; I. John Hesselink, "Calvin, the Theologian of the Holy Spirit," in *Calvin in Asia Churches* (Seoul: Korean Calvin Society, 2002), 113–28; Stanley M. Burgess, "John Calvin (1509–1564)," in *The Holy Spirit: Medieval Roman Catholic and Reformation Traditions* (Peabody, Mass.: Hendrickson, 1997), 161–71; Eifion Evans, "John Calvin: Theologian of the Holy Spirit," *Reformation & Revival* 10, no. 4 (2001): 83–104; Howard Griffith, "The First Title of the Spirit: Adoption in Calvin's Soteriology," *Evangelical Quarterly* 73, no. 2 (2001): 135–53; Adrian A. Helleman, "John Calvin on the Procession of the Holy Spirit," *One in Christ* 37, no. 4 (2002): 21–36; Paul Chung, "Calvin and the Holy Spirit: A Reconsideration in Light of Spirituality and Social Ethics," *Pneuma* 24, no.1 (Spring 2002): 40–55; Julie Canlis, "Calvin, Osiander and Participation in God," *International Journal of Systematic Theology* 6, no. 2 (April 2004): 169–84; and Yang-en Cheng, "Calvin on the Work of the Spirit and Spiritual Gifts," *Taiwan Journal of Theology* 27 (2005): 173–206.

64 Theology Made Practical

as some work that has appeared in non-English books[4] and unpublished English dissertations,[5] but few thorough, contemporary works on this subject in English have been published.[6] One reason for this lacuna may be the vastness of the subject. Calvin interweaves the work of the Spirit into most chapters of his *Institutes* as well as throughout his commentaries, sermons, and letters. Another reason could be that one cannot find a detailed, systematic treatment of pneumatology in Calvin's *Institutes* or anywhere else in his corpus.[7] This should not be considered surprising as Calvin stresses, in accordance with John 16:14, that the great goal of the Holy Spirit's ministry is to speak of Christ rather than of Himself.

What follows, then, is to be regarded as more introductory than comprehensive. We begin by looking at the personhood and deity of the Holy Spirit in Calvin's theology. A summary of Calvin's thinking on the Spirit in relation to the Scriptures and to Christ follows. We then look at the Spirit's work with regard to the order of salvation (*ordo salutis*)—especially concentrating on faith, justification, and sanctification—as well as the nature of assurance and the application of redemption. Finally, some consideration is given to Calvin's thought about the *charismata*, or gifts of the Spirit.

---

4. The two most important foreign works are in Dutch and German respectively: Simon van der Linde, *De Leer van den Heiligen Geest* (Wageningen: H. Veenman & Zonen, 1943); and Werner Krusche, *Das Wirken des Heiligen Geistes nach Calvin* (Göttingen: Vandenhoeck & Ruprecht, 1957). Both volumes are strongly polemical—van der Linde in opposing Barthianism and Krusche in challenging Emil Brunner and his followers.

5. Jack La-Vere Zerwas, "The Holy Spirit in Calvin" (S.T.M. thesis, Union Theological Seminary, 1947); Jean Abel, "The Ethical Implications of the Doctrine of the Holy Spirit in John Calvin" (PhD diss., Union Theological Seminary, Richmond, 1948); Margaret Virginia Cubine, "John Calvin's Doctrine of the Work of the Holy Spirit Examined in the Light of Some Contemporary Theories of Interpersonal Psychotherapy" (PhD diss., Northwestern University, 1955); and Henry O'Brien, "The Holy Spirit in the Catechetical Writings of John Calvin" (PhD diss., Pontificia Universitas Gregoriana, Facultas Theologiae, Rome, 1991).

6. See Gwyn Walters, *The Sovereign Spirit: The Doctrine of the Holy Spirit in the Writings of John Calvin*, ed. Eifon Evans and Lynn Quigley, Rutherford Studies in Historical Theology (Edinburgh: Rutherford House, 2009). See also the published papers of the sixth colloquium of the North American Calvin Studies Society: *Calvin and the Holy Spirit*, ed. Peter De Klerk (Grand Rapids: Calvin Study Society, 1989). Essays include Jelle Faber, "The Saving Work of the Holy Spirit in Calvin"; John Bolt, "Spiritus Creator: The Use and Abuse of Calvin's Cosmic Pneumatology"; Willem van 't Spijker, "*Extra nos* and *in nobis* by Calvin in a Pneumatological Light"; Richard Gamble, "Word and Spirit in Calvin"; Brian Armstrong, "The Role of the Holy Spirit in Calvin's Teaching on the Ministry"; and Leonard Sweetman Jr., "What Is the Meaning of These Gifts?"

7. The *Institutes* offer only one brief chapter directly on the Holy Spirit (3.1).

Who Is the Holy Spirit?

Calvin's perspective on both the personhood and deity of the Holy Spirit is largely traditional, following the fathers of the ancient church, who held to the full deity of each of the three persons of the Godhead as well as the distinct personhood of each. In arguing for the full divinity of the Spirit, Calvin highlights that the Spirit does what only God can do. Many of the works ascribed to the Son are also attributed to the Spirit. It follows, Calvin maintains, that the Spirit, like the Son, must be fully God. For instance, the Spirit gives spiritual life to dead sinners and raises them from the dead by His own divine power. As such, He must be God.[8] The Holy Spirit must therefore be confessed as the third person of the Trinity, whose deity is totally equal to those of the Father and the Son.

Calvin offers a definition of "person" that is based on Hebrews 1:3: a divine person is "a subsistence in God's essence, which, while related to the others, is distinguished by an incommunicable quality."[9] Calvin was well aware that such theological terms, though needed for the refutation of heresy, have distinct limitations. Drawing on such texts as Ephesians 4:5 and Matthew 28:19, Calvin argues for the importance of maintaining that "in God's essence reside three persons in whom one God is known." As there is only one God, "Word and Spirit are nothing else than the essence of God."[10]

It is vital, however, also to confess, due to the statements of Holy Scripture, that the one God has a "threeness" about Him. Calvin cites the fourth-century Greek theologian Gregory of Nazianzus, who said, "I cannot think of the one without quickly being encircled by the splendor of the three; nor can I discern the three without being straightway carried back to the one."[11] The obvious danger of such an affirmation is so distinguishing the persons as to end up in arguing for three Gods—namely, tritheism. To avoid this problem, Calvin hastens to add that this "splendor of the three" manifests only a distinction in the Trinity, not a division.[12] In his words: "To the Father is attributed the beginning of activity, and the fountain and well-spring of all things; to the Son, wisdom, counsel, and the ordered disposition of all things; but to the Spirit is assigned the power and efficacy

---

8. Calvin, *Institutes*, 1.13.14.
9. Calvin, *Institutes*, 1.13.6.
10. Calvin, *Institutes*, 1.13.6.
11. Calvin, *Institutes*, 1.13.17.
12. Calvin, *Institutes*, 1.13.17.

66   Theology Made Practical

of that activity."[13] There is, therefore, a natural economic order of equality within the Trinity. This order coincides with revelatory and redeeming activity, enabling us to contemplate the Father as the first person, the Son as the second person, and the Spirit as the third person. Calvin says, "For the mind of each human being is naturally inclined to contemplate God first, then the wisdom coming forth from him, and lastly the power whereby he executes the decrees of his plan."[14]

The great danger of discussing the ontological Trinity, Calvin knows, is that well-meaning theologians may produce all kinds of unnecessary words on the subject: "In the one essence of God there is a trinity of persons; you will say in one word what Scripture states, and cut short empty talkativeness."[15] Calvin's great interest is in the practical work of the relational Trinity rather than the theological abstractions of the ontological Trinity. His major goal is to promote practical, experiential Christian living. Thus, in his first catechism (1538) Calvin writes, "When we name Father, Son, and Holy Spirit, we are not fashioning three Gods, but in the simplest unity of God, Scripture and the very experience of godliness disclose to us the Father, his Son, and the Spirit."[16] I. John Hesselink points out that Calvin speaks similarly of the Spirit's divinity in the *Institutes:* "What Scripture attributes to him [the Holy Spirit] we ourselves learn by the sure experience of godliness."[17] Hesselink goes on to say that "Calvin frequently appeals to experience as a secondary sort of confirmation of Scripture, and in this case particularly godliness (or piety)."[18] In a similar vein of thought, B. B. Warfield says of Calvin, "The doctrine of the Trinity did not stand out of relation to his religious consciousness but was a postulate of his profoundest religious emotions; was given, indeed, in his experience of salvation itself."[19]

This focus on the experiential effect of the Spirit's work is central to Calvin's theology. For Calvin, experiencing the work of the Spirit is more important than attempting to describe the essence of the Spirit, since the

---

13. Calvin, *Institutes*, 1.13.18.
14. Calvin, *Institutes*, 1.13.18.
15. Calvin, *Institutes*, 1.13.5.
16. Hesselink, *Catechism* (1538), sec. 20, cited in Hesselink, "Calvin, Theologian of the Holy Spirit," in *Calvin's First Catechism*, 179.
17. Calvin, *Institutes*, 1.13.14.
18. Hesselink, "Calvin, Theologian of the Holy Spirit," in *Calvin's First Catechism*, 179.
19. Warfield, *Calvin and Augustine*, 195.

Calvin on the Holy Spirit

latter remains a mystery we can never fully grasp. Willem van 't Spijker summarizes this well:

> *The Institutes* possesses a unity, but not that of a closed system. It is a unity which always remains open to God, man, and the world. However, this unity is not anthropologically determined. It is rooted in the Spirit, who brings about the encounter between God and man through the real presence of Christ. It can also be said that the presence of the Spirit in almost all *loci* has preserved Calvin's doctrine from petrification.... It is the Spirit who blows through his garden and who makes it alive and blooming.... [His] sound is heard everywhere.[20]

We need to remember, as mentioned above, that Calvin is building upon pneumatological foundations laid in the patristic era, when battles for the deity of the Spirit had to be waged. The deity and the personhood of the Spirit were not central issues of the Reformation, and thus Calvin was free to focus on other areas of pneumatology.

The Spirit and the Scriptures

Calvin confidently, and rightly so, maintains that Holy Scripture is the classroom of the Holy Spirit. The Spirit inspired its words, and as its author, He draws people into the service of God through it and always works in perfect harmony with it.[21] We can summarize what Calvin teaches on these important matters as follows:

---

20. Van 't Spijker, "Doctrine of the Holy Spirit in Bucer and Calvin," 3–4; cf. Calvin, *Institutes*, 1.13.14.

21. Contrary to what John T. McNeill says, I believe that Calvin frequently used the words "God's Word," "the Bible," and "Scripture" as convertible terms; hence, I use them as such in this section of the chapter without entering in that complex debate here. Suffice it to say that at times, Calvin speaks of Jesus Christ and of preaching as "the Word of God," but these usages will not be employed in this chapter. For a sampling of various views on this issue, see Gamble, "Word and Spirit in Calvin," 75–77. For Calvin on the inspiration of Scripture, see chapter 3 of this book; Walters, *The Sovereign Spirit*, 24–34; and I. John Hesselink, "The Holy Spirit in Calvin's Doctrine of Scripture" (Seoul: Kosin University, 2007). For Calvin on inerrancy, see Frederick S. Leahy, "Calvin and the Inerrancy of Scripture," *Reformed Theological Journal* 17 (2001): 44–56.

68 Theology Made Practical

The Internal Testimony or Witness of the Spirit and the Scriptures'
Self-Authenticating Character and Authority

To some who argue that rational proof is necessary to affirm the divine authority of the biblical writers, Calvin responds by appealing to the internal testimony of the Holy Spirit (*testimonium internum Spiritus Sancti*):

> The testimony of the Spirit is more excellent than all reason. For as God alone is a fit witness of himself in his Word, so also the Word will not find acceptance in men's hearts before it is sealed by the inward testimony of the Spirit. The same Spirit, therefore, who spoke through the mouth of the prophets, must penetrate our hearts to persuade us that they faithfully proclaimed what had been divinely commanded.[22]

The believer's confidence in the authority of Scripture finds its confirmation in the Spirit's internal witness, or testimony. This testimony does not establish that authority since the Scriptures are self-authenticating (*autopiston*). Calvin maintains that within Scripture itself there are self-evidencing "proofs" (the *indicia*—that is, statements about Scripture) that assert the credibility of Scripture. Ultimately, though, such proofs have to be considered secondary to the Holy Spirit's illumination of our minds and our consciences that the Scriptures are the words of God. Although these proofs—things like the antiquity of Scripture, the miracles, the fulfilled prophecies, and its preservation—ought not to be lightly dismissed, they only provide confirmation for those who are already believers.[23] In the final analysis, Calvin does not believe that any human argument will convince an unbeliever that the Bible is the word of God. Thus, the Spirit's witness does not relate to evidentiary proofs but to the authority of the Word itself, which is confirmed by the Spirit's witness. Later, Warfield would wrongly reverse this position, as Robert Reymond has noted, because of the American theologian's trust in an "empirical apologetic" that was "based on Thomas Reid's Scottish common sense realism that ruled at Princeton."[24]

---

22. Calvin, *Institutes*, 1.7.4.

23. Calvin, *Institutes*, 1.8.

24. Robert L. Reymond, "Calvin's Doctrine of Holy Scripture," in *A Theological Guide to Calvin's Institutes: Essays and Analysis*, ed. David W. Hall and Peter A. Lillback (Phillipsburg, N.J.: P&R, 2008), 52–53.

Reymond summarizes Calvin's position well when he states that if the Bible needed "anyone or anything other than itself to authenticate and validate its divine character—based on the principle that the validating source is always the higher and final authority (see Heb. 6:13)—it would not be the Word of God because the validating sources would be the higher authority."[25] A key reason Calvin considered the self-authentication of Scripture critical was that it avoids the Roman Catholic error of making Scripture's credibility dependent on the church's decision. Calvin, following Martin Luther, had learned that the believer's ultimate authority in matters of faith and practice has to be the Bible, not the church.[26] In the words of T. H. L. Parker: "All the Church can do is to accept this authority [of the Scriptures] over herself obediently.... She cannot do otherwise than obey it—i.e., regard it as her Lord, because as the Word of her Lord it is the presence of her Lord with her."[27] Ronald Wallace has a similar comment: "For Calvin the Bible is not only the sole source of Church proclamation but also the sole authority that must rule the life of the Church."[28]

For Calvin, it is a basic truism that God reveals Himself through the work of the Holy Spirit. Consequently, the Scripture's authority for belief and behavior rests on its ultimate author, the Holy Spirit, who is described by Scripture as the "Spirit of truth" and as such, truth itself. This Spirit-authored, authoritative book of Scripture is unique to Christianity and to God's people.[29] The Spirit imprints Scripture's divine authority upon the hearts of Christians with the indubitable certainty "that piety requires."[30]

Moreover, Calvin argues, the Spirit graciously takes away the blindness that sin causes in the heart and soul and gives to the new believer eyes to see Scripture for what it is: the divinely breathed-out Word of God. Through the spectacles of Holy Scripture, we see who God is, holy and majestic, and who we are, sinful creatures. Within the realm of faith, we are given a fresh hunger for God and His Word by the Holy Spirit. Calvin understands this

---

25. Reymond, "Calvin's Doctrine of Holy Scripture," in *A Theological Guide to Calvin's Institutes*, 51.

26. Calvin, *Institutes*, 1.7.1–2.

27. Thomas Henry Louis Parker, *The Doctrine of the Knowledge of God: A Study in the Theology of John Calvin* (Grand Rapids: Eerdmans, 1959), 43–44.

28. Ronald S. Wallace, *Calvin's Doctrine of the Word and Sacrament* (Edinburgh: Oliver and Boyd, 1953), 99. Cf. Rupert Eric Davies, *The Problem of Authority in the Continental Reformers: A Study in Luther, Zwingli, and Calvin* (London: Epworth Press, 1946).

29. Forstman, *Word and Spirit*, 15.

30. Calvin, *Institutes*, 1.7.1–2.

70   Theology Made Practical

hunger, which is the Spirit's witness, to be the means of faith, though not the final ground of faith, which is Scripture itself. Here Calvin is in agreement with Louis Berkhof, who writes, "The ground of faith is identical with [Scripture's] contents, and cannot be separated from it. But the testimony of the Spirit is the moving cause of faith. We believe Scripture, not because of, but through the testimony of the Holy Spirit."[31]

The testimony of the Holy Spirit lies at the heart of Calvin's theological system. Without the Spirit's testimony in the heart of the believer, the Word cannot be understood, knowledge cannot be gained, and faith cannot be genuine. On the other hand, apart from the Spirit's testimony, the Word is of no use, knowledge is reduced to opinion, and faith is falsified. But when the believer experiences the testimony of the Holy Spirit, he now knows that Scripture is the living Word of God that lays open his heart before God, calms it with assurances of God's grace in Christ, and spurs him on to live to God's glory. Moreover, the believer knows that the Scriptures are from God with an assurance that is far deeper than any that can be given by the church or human reason.[32]

Prior to Calvin's development of this theological truth, both Luther and Zwingli had alluded to this doctrine of the Spirit's internal witness.[33] It was Calvin, however, who was the first to develop it and show that it involves "a recognition of the evidential value of religious experience."[34] Although much has been written to support Calvin's development of this doctrine, it has been challenged on the grounds that it is subjective and circular. In response to these objections, Hesselink writes:

> In a sense [Calvin's] argument is circular. For how do we know the Bible is the Word of God? Answer: The Spirit tells us so. How do we know it is truly the Spirit who gives us this assurance? Answer: The Bible itself convinces us of this. Yet it should be noted that this kind of argumentation is no invention of the theologians! There are several passages in the New Testament which suggest this approach:

---

31. Louis Berkhof, *Systematic Theology* (Grand Rapids: Eerdmans, 1996), 1:185.

32. Cf. Douglas Schuurman, "Calvin's Doctrine of the *Testimonium Spiritus Sancti*" (paper for Calvin's *Institutes* seminar conducted by Ford Lewis Battles, Calvin Theological Seminary, Grand Rapids, Michigan, fall 1978), 9–10.

33. Hartmann Grisar, *Luther*, trans. E. M. Lamond (London: Kegan Paul, Trench, Trubner & Co., 1915), 4:391–92; and S. M. Jackson, *Huldreich Zwingli, The Reformer of German Switzerland* (New York: G. P. Putnam's Sons, 1901), 42.

34. Walters, *The Sovereign Spirit*, 41.

John 8:13ff.; 1 Corinthians 2:11; Romans 8:16; and 2 Corinthians 3:1–3, for example.[35]

Hesselink notes that the neoorthodox theologian Karl Barth called Calvin's argument a "logical circle," in which the objective Word and the subjective Spirit coalesce. The Bible, which appears to be "objective," is, as Otto Weber further notes, "by its every essence also 'subjective' in the persuasion of its divine origin. When the Spirit internally persuades us of its authority, the "polarity of object and subject is overcome."[36]

John Murray is personally convinced that Calvin could have made the distinction between the objective, intrinsic authority that resides in the Scriptures and the believer's subjective recognition of that authority somewhat clearer. Calvin argues for both the Scriptures' intrinsic authority and the recognition of that authority, but Murray asserts that distinguishing between them would help us reconcile statements of Calvin that emphasize the objective ("The Scripture exhibits as clear evidence of its truth as white and black things do of their color, or sweet and bitter things of their taste"[37]) and the subjective ("[The Scriptures] obtain complete authority with believers only when they are persuaded that they proceed from heaven"[38]).[39] Calvin, however, would respond by emphasizing that these two emphases are seamless, for the Spirit's testimony persuades us of Scripture's authority.[40]

Let me sum up what we can say about Calvin's witness of the Spirit to the Word. First, full conviction of the authority of the Bible can come only through the witness of the Spirit. Though neither rational argument nor the church's testimony should be discounted, Calvin would warn us not to rely too heavily on these sources, for by themselves they can only produce probable conviction of biblical authority. Calvin knew the value of reason and was a lover of the church, but he also knew that to build one's hope on either fosters only instability.

---

35. Hesselink, *Calvin's First Catechism*, 181–82.
36. Hesselink, *Calvin's First Catechism*, 182.
37. Calvin, *Institutes*, 1.7.2.
38. Calvin, *Institutes*, 1.7.1.
39. John Murray, "Calvin and the Authority of Scripture," in *Collected Writings of John Murray* (Edinburgh: Banner of Truth Trust, 1982), 4:183–84. Cf. Derek Naves, "The Internal Witness of the Spirit in the Theology of John Calvin" (unpublished paper, fall 2007), 7–9.
40. Wallace, *Calvin's Doctrine of the Word and Sacrament*, 101–2; and Jack Rogers and Donald McKim, *The Authority and Interpretation of the Bible: An Historical Approach* (San Francisco: Harper & Row, 1979), 104.

72   Theology Made Practical

Second, certainty evolves from paying heed to the witness of the Spirit to Scripture, while uncertainty results from ignoring that witness. We must not look to reason or inner light or to the church for certainty but to the Spirit's witness in our conscience.[41]

Third, embracing the doctrine of the inner witness of the Spirit does not entail a denial of the church's role in recognizing the sacred canon. Not every believer experiences the Spirit's witness with regard to each of the sixty-six books of Scripture in equal measure, as one believer's encounter with a particular book in the canon may differ somewhat from another's. Rather, Calvin maintained that the self-authenticating canon has imposed itself upon the church in such a manner that the Spirit has "opened the eyes of the worldwide church over the ages to discern the limits of the canon."[42]

The Harmony of Word and Spirit

Calvin is absolutely convinced that there is a reciprocal and harmonious relationship between the Word and the Spirit. Apart from the Spirit, the Word is ineffective. And spiritual experience without the Word is meaningless at best and a delusion at worst.[43] The Holy Spirit converts and directs believers by the Word. Here Calvin differs from his spiritual mentor, Luther. Luther so stresses the objective, external Word in his debates with the spiritual radicals of the sixteenth century, men such as the Zwickau Prophets who wanted to discard the Word because they thought they had the Spirit, that there was "the danger of uniting Word and Spirit so completely as to run the risk of identifying them" as one."[44] Calvin, though, rightly maintains that though Word and Spirit are intimately related, they remain distinct from each other. They work in tandem to establish God's kingdom. For example, in explaining the petition "Thy kingdom come" from the Lord's Prayer, Calvin writes that the kingdom comes both by the preaching of the Word and

---

41. Calvin, *Institutes*, 1.7.5.

42. This paragraph is a summary of the thoughts of Lane, "John Calvin: The Witness of the Holy Spirit," 4–5.

43. Calvin, *Institutes*, 1.9. For Calvin's polemics against the Spirit-without-Word theology of some Anabaptists, particularly the Spiritualists among them, see William Klassen, "Anabaptist Hermeneutics: The Letter and the Spirit," *The Mennonite Quarterly Review* 40 (1966): 91; George Hunston Williams, *The Radical Reformation* (Philadelphia: Westminster Press, 1962), 821–28; and Willem Balke, *Calvin and the Anabaptist Radicals* (Grand Rapids: Eerdmans, 1981).

44. I. John Hesselink, "Calvin's Theology," in *The Cambridge Companion to John Calvin*, ed. Donald K. McKim (Cambridge: Cambridge University Press, 2004), 80.

by the secret power of the Spirit: "He would govern us by his Word, but as the voice alone, without the inward influence of the Spirit, does not reach down into the heart, the two must be brought together for the establishment of God's kingdom."[45] Calvin never says the believer is continually being led by some special inner light, as the Quakers would argue in the following century, but he is prepared to admit that the Spirit occasionally works independently from the Word in governing and guiding the believer.[46] Those independent workings, however, never conflict with Holy Scripture but are always in harmony with it.[47]

Ultimately, then, Word and Spirit are bonded together. So Calvin writes:

> By a kind of mutual bond the Lord has joined together the certainty of his Word and of his Spirit so that the perfect religion of the Word may abide in our minds when the Spirit, who causes us to contemplate God's face, shines; and that we in turn may embrace the Spirit with no fear of being deceived when we recognize him in his own image, namely, in the Word.[48]

Richard Gamble has rightly noted that here we see a good example of Calvin's striving for a genuine *via media*; that is, a middle way between false extremes. At one extreme were "rationalistic"-leaning apologists who emphasized the rational evidences of the Word at the expense of the Spirit.[49] At the other extreme were the Roman Catholics, who deemphasized the Word and exaggerated the Spirit's work in the church,[50] and, strange bedmates to be found with them, the Anabaptists, who deemphasized the Word and exaggerated the Spirit's work in the individual.[51] This nexus of Word and Spirit in Calvin has far-reaching consequences for the whole realm of public worship and preaching as well as the various experiential and practical dimensions of Christian living. When the sweet harmony of Word and

---

45. Hesselink, "Calvin's Theology," 81; and Calvin, *Commentary*, on Matt. 6:10.

46. For illustrations of this point, see I. John Hesselink, "Governed and Guided by the Spirit—a Key Issue in Calvin's Doctrine of the Holy Spirit," in *Das Reformierte Erbe, Festschrift für Gottfried W. Locher zu seinem 80. Geburtstag*, ed. H. A. Oberman, Ernst Saxer, et al. (Zurich: Theologischer Verlag, 1992), 161–71.

47. Lane, "John Calvin: The Witness of the Holy Spirit," 5.

48. Calvin, *Institutes*, 1.9.3.

49. Bernard Ramm, *The Witness of the Spirit* (Grand Rapids: Eerdmans, 1960), 12. See Schuurman, "Calvin's Doctrine of the *Testimonium Spiritus Sancti*," 2–7.

50. Calvin, *Institutes*, 4.8.13.

51. Gamble, "Word and Spirit in Calvin," 81–85.

74 Theology Made Practical

Spirit is recognized, then worship, preaching, and personal experience are enriched and empowered in a way that can truly glorify the triune God.[52]

The Spirit and Union and Communion with Christ

Calvin supports the Augustinian impulse that affirmed what scholars have called the *filioque* (literally, "and the Son")—an addition in the Western form of the Niceno-Constantinopolitan Creed that stated that the Spirit proceeds not only from the Father but also from the Son.[53] Thus, Calvin can denominate the Spirit sometimes as the "Spirit of the Father" and sometimes as the "Spirit of the Son."[54] Although in recent days some Western scholars have rejected this doctrine of the double procession of the Spirit (from the Father and the Son), it was the dominant teaching of Western Trinitarianism since Augustine.[55]

It is important to note, however, that here too Calvin is less interested in discussing the ontological relationship between the Son and the Spirit than in tracing out the practical implications of this doctrine. For instance, the Son and the Spirit are both "inner teachers," Calvin asserts, but their roles differ. The Holy Spirit loves to stay in the background, focusing all attention on the crucified and risen Lord. The Spirit never initiates a new work but delights to honor the finished work of Christ, revealing it to believers for their salvation and comfort. The Spirit works for Christ, and Christ works through the Spirit. In this reciprocal, mutually dependent divine work, believers are made doubly secure and are kept from such errors as mysticism or from imagining that the Spirit can be obtained without obtaining Christ: "We are partakers of the Holy Spirit in proportion to the intercourse which we make with Christ; for the Spirit will be found nowhere but in Christ, on whom he is said, on that account to have rested," Calvin argues. "But neither

---

52. Cf. Cheng, "Calvin on the Work of the Holy Spirit and Spiritual Gifts," 175–76; and H. Jackson Forstman, *Word and Spirit: Calvin's Doctrine of Biblical Authority* (Stanford, Calif.: Stanford University Press, 1962), 66–85.

53. This is clear from article 6 of the French Confession of Faith (1559), written by Calvin and his student Antoine de la Roche Chandieu. Philip Schaff, ed., *The Creeds of Christendom* (Grand Rapids: Baker, 1993), 3:356–82. Parts of this section and the next are condensed from my chapter on Calvin's piety in *Cambridge Companion to John Calvin*, ed. McKim, 125–52.

54. Calvin, *Institutes*, 3.1.2.

55. For a study on Calvin's sparse references to the Spirit's double procession, see Helleman, "John Calvin on the Procession of the Holy Spirit," 21–36.

Calvin on the Holy Spirit

can Christ be separated from his Spirit; for then he would be said to be dead, and to have lost all his power."[56]

If there is one doctrine that lies at the heart of Calvin's soteriological thought, it is union with Christ. "Calvin's doctrine of union with Christ is one of the most consistently influential features of his theology and ethics, if not the single most important teaching that animates the whole of his thought and his personal life," writes David Willis-Watkins.[57] Calvin's sermons, commentaries, and theological works are so permeated with reflection on union with Christ that it becomes his focus for Christian faith and practice.[58] In Calvin's own words: "That joining together of Head and members, that indwelling of Christ in our hearts—in short, that mystical union—are accorded by us the highest degree of importance, so that Christ, having been made ours, makes us sharers with him in the gifts with which he has been endowed."[59]

Calvin understands salvation to be built squarely upon the believer's union with Christ. Hence, this union must be our starting point in understanding what it means to be saved.[60] None of the subsequent elements of the order of salvation, such as justification, sanctification, and perseverance, are possible without the union with Christ that the Spirit effects through faith.[61] Calvin says, "We must understand that as long as Christ remains outside of us, and we are separated from him, all that he has suffered and done for the salvation of the human race remains useless and of no value for us."[62] Such union is a possibility only because Christ took on our human nature

---

56. Calvin, *Commentary*, on Eph. 3:17.

57. David Willis-Watkins, "The *Unio Mystica* and the Assurance of Faith According to Calvin," in *Calvin Erbe und Auftrag: Festschrift für Wilhelm Heinrich Neuser zum 65. Geburtstag*, ed. Willem van 't Spijker (Kampen: Kok, 1991), 78.

58. E.g., Charles Partee, "Calvin's Central Dogma Again," *Sixteenth Century Journal* 18, no. 2 (1987): 194. Cf. Otto Gründler, "John Calvin: Ingrafting in Christ," in *The Spirituality of Western Christendom*, ed. Rozanne Elder (Kalamazoo, Mich.: Cistercian, 1976), 172–87; Brian G. Armstrong, "The Nature and Structure of Calvin's Thought According to the *Institutes*: Another Look," in *John Calvin's Magnum Opus* (Potchefstroom, South Africa: Institute for Reformational Studies, 1986), 55–82; and Guenther Haas, *The Concept of Equity in Calvin's Ethics* (Waterloo, Ont.: Wilfrid Laurier University Press, 1997).

59. Calvin, *Institutes*, 3.11.9.

60. Howard G. Hageman, "Reformed Spirituality," in *Protestant Spiritual Traditions*, ed. Frank C. Senn (New York: Paulist Press, 1986), 61.

61. François Wendel, *Calvin: The Origins and Development of His Religious Thought*, trans. Philip Mairet (Grand Rapids: Baker, 1997), 238.

62. Calvin, *Institutes*, 3.1.1.

76   Theology Made Practical

and filled it with His virtue. Union with Christ in His humanity is historical, ethical, and personal, but it is important to note that there is no crass
mixture (*crassa mixtura*) of human substance between Christ and us. We
are not absorbed into Christ or united to Him in such a way that our human
personalities are annulled, even in the slightest degree. Nonetheless, as Calvin states, "not only does he cleave to us by an indivisible bond of fellowship,
but with a wonderful communion, day by day, he grows more and more into
one body with us, until he becomes completely one with us."[63]

This union with Christ takes place by the Holy Spirit and is a great mystery.[64] Only the Spirit, a divine person, can unite the God-man in heaven
with the believer on earth. The Spirit not only initiates this union but also,
at every step, empowers the communion (*communio*) with Christ that flows
from it. This involves participation (*participatio*) in all His benefits, which
are inseparable from union with Christ.[65] Just as the Spirit was key in uniting
heaven and earth in the incarnation, so in regeneration the same Spirit raises
the elect from earth to commune with Christ in the heavenlies and brings
Christ into the hearts and lives of the elect in this earthly realm.[66] While not
fully comprehensible, this communion with Christ is genuine and fills the
believer with wonder.[67] By the Spirit, Christ outside us (*extra nos*) becomes
Christ within us (*in nobis*).[68] As Calvin writes to the Italian Reformer Peter
Martyr: "We grow up together with Christ into one body, and he shares his
Spirit with us, through whose hidden operation he has become ours. Believers receive this communion with Christ at the same time as their calling. But
they grow from day to day more and more in this communion, in proportion to the life of Christ growing within them."[69]

---

63. Calvin, *Institutes*, 3.2.24.

64. Calvin, *Institutes*, 3.1.1. Dennis Tamburello points out that "at least seven instances
occur in the *Institutes* where Calvin uses the word *arcanus* or *incomprehensibilis* to describe
union with Christ" (2.12.7; 3.11.5; 4.17.1, 9, 31, 33; 4.19.35. *Union with Christ: John Calvin
and the Mysticism of St. Bernard* (Louisville: Westminster, 1994), 89, 144. Cf. William Borden
Evans, "Imputation and Impartation: The Problem of Union with Christ in Nineteenth-
Century American Reformed Theology" (PhD diss., Vanderbilt University, 1996), 6–68.

65. Van 't Spijker, "*Extra nos* and *in nobis* by Calvin in a Pneumatological Light," 39–62;
and Merwyn S. Johnson, "Calvin's Ethical Legacy," in *The Legacy of John Calvin*, ed. David
Foxgrover (Grand Rapids: Calvin Studies Society, 2000), 63–83.

66. Calvin, *Institutes*, 4.17.6; *Commentary*, on Acts 15:9.

67. Calvin, *Commentary*, on Eph. 5:32.

68. Van 't Spijker, "*Extra nos* and *in nobis* by Calvin in a Pneumatological Light," 44–53.

69. "Calvinus Vermilio" (#2266, 8 Aug 1555), *CO*, 15:723–24.

Calvin on the Holy Spirit

While Calvin never regards this union and communion with Christ as a participation in the essence of Christ's nature,[70] nevertheless it is so intimate that it can be described in terms of the one-flesh union in marriage: Christians are flesh of Christ's flesh and bone of His bone (Eph. 5:30). In fact, the spiritual union with Christ that the Holy Spirit forges in us is closer than any physical union. Calvin writes, "Let us know the unity that we have with our Lord Jesus Christ; to wit, that he wills to have a common life with us, and that what he has should be ours: nay, that he even wishes to dwell in us, not in imagination, but in effect; not in earthly fashion but spiritually; and that whatever may befall us, he so labors by the virtue of his Holy Spirit that we are united with him more closely than are the limbs with the body."[71] The true meaning of this union with Christ in both body and soul will be fully realized only when we rise from the dead on judgment day.[72]

So Christ and the Spirit work together for our salvation. Their work is distinct, though inseparable. Calvin can thus move easily from saying, "The Spirit dwelling in us" to "Christ dwelling in us."[73] In one sense, every action of the Spirit is the action of Christ. The Spirit bestows a saving nature on us through Christ, and Christ bestows on us a saving nature only through the Spirit.[74] Calvin hints of this in the title of his opening chapter in the third book of the *Institutes:* "The things spoken concerning Christ profit us by the secret working of the Spirit." Christ effects salvation through His Spirit, and the Holy Spirit makes that salvation real in the hearts of sinners.[75]

Calvin further develops this collaboration in salvation between Christ and the Spirit when he avers that the Spirit in His "whole fullness" is given by the Father to Christ in a special way, so that we, through the "Spirit of sanctification," might each be given the Spirit "according to the measure of Christ's gift."[76] The Spirit's work in us helps free us from worldliness and, by faith and hope, brings us to our eternal reward.[77] Calvin saw this work of the Spirit reflected in some of the titles that Holy Scripture gives to Him, such as

---

70. Calvin roundly defeats Osiander's doctrine of "essential righteousness" with Christ in *Institutes*, 3.11.5–12.

71. As quoted in Wendel, *Calvin: The Origins and Development of His Religious Thought*, 235.

72. Calvin, *Commentary*, on 1 Cor. 6:15.

73. Calvin, *Institutes*, 3.2.39.

74. Faber, "Saving Work of the Holy Spirit in Calvin," 3.

75. Calvin, *Institutes*, 3.1.1.

76. Calvin, *Institutes*, 3.1.2.

77. Calvin, *Institutes*, 3.1.2.

78 Theology Made Practical

the "spirit of adoption," "the guarantee and seal" of our inheritance, "water," "oil," and "anointing."[78]

The Spirit and Faith, Justification, and Sanctification

From God's perspective, on the one hand, the Spirit is the bond between Christ and His people. From our perspective, on the other hand, faith is the bond. There is no contradiction here at all, for one of the Spirit's primary tasks is to produce faith in the heart of a sinner. In Calvin's words, "Faith itself has no other source than the Spirit."[79] And when Calvin comes to a formal definition of faith, he gives the Holy Spirit a prominent role: "Now we shall possess a right definition of faith if we call it a firm and certain knowledge of God's benevolence toward us, founded upon the truth of the freely given promise in Christ, both revealed to our minds and sealed upon our hearts through the Holy Spirit."[80]

Human willpower and energy cannot contribute to this work, for faith is an entirely supernatural gift from the Spirit. It would be easier, Calvin suggests, to combine fire with water than to mix faith-righteousness and works-righteousness.[81] Calvin's definition of faith also underscores that the Spirit's saving work involves knowledge—not abstract, speculative, or external knowledge, but affective knowledge that reshapes will and act.

Spirit-worked faith joins the believer to Christ by means of the Word, enabling him to receive Christ Jesus the Lord as He is presented in the gospel and graciously offered by the Father.[82] Calvin prizes this faith, since it rises "from the flesh of Christ to his divinity" to penetrate "above all the heaven, even to those mysteries which the angels behold and adore."[83] The Holy Spirit uses this faith to bring the heavenly graces of Christ down into the human soul and to raise our souls up to heaven in return. Communion with Christ through faith is so real and profound that, even though Christ remains in heaven, He is so firmly grasped by faith and so fully possessed by

---

78. Calvin, *Institutes*, 3.1.3.
79. Calvin, *Institutes*, 3.1.4.
80. Calvin, *Institutes*, 3.2.7.
81. Calvin, *Institutes*, 3.11.13.
82. Calvin, *Institutes*, 3.2.30–32.
83. Calvin, *Commentary*, on John 12:45; 8:19.

us that He actually dwells in our hearts.[84] By faith we "come to possess the Heavenly Kingdom."[85]

Faith derives all its value from Jesus Christ. Without Christ, faith is of "no dignity or value," for it is "only instrumental."[86] But when focused on Christ, faith is of inestimable value, because by it we receive Christ and all His benefits, including the double grace of justification and sanctification, which together provide a twofold cleansing.[87] Justification offers imputed purity; sanctification, actual purity.[88]

Calvin presents an initial definition of justification as "the acceptance with which God receives us into his favor as righteous men."[89] He continues: "Since God justifies us by the intercession of Christ, he absolves us not by the confirmation of our own innocence but by the imputation of righteousness, so that we who are not righteous in ourselves may be reckoned as such in Christ."[90] Justification also includes the remission of sins together with the right to eternal life, about which the Spirit delights to assure the believer.

Justification by works is not possible for a sinner because of his sin. The believer, "excluded from the righteousness of works, grasps the righteousness of Christ through faith, and clothed in it, appears in God's sight not as a sinner but as a righteous man."[91] For Christ's sake, the believer is declared acquitted, "as if his innocence were confirmed."[92] Such truths lead Calvin to define justification more closely: "The sinner, received into communion with Christ, is reconciled to God by his grace, while, cleansed by Christ's blood, he obtains forgiveness of sins, and clothed with Christ's righteousness as if it were his own, he stands confident before the heavenly judgment seat."[93]

Deeply shaped by biblical and earlier Reformation reflections on justification, Calvin depicts justification as the central doctrine of the Christian

---

84. Calvin, *Commentary*, on Acts 15:9.
85. Calvin, *Institutes*, 3.2.1.
86. Calvin, *Institutes*, 3.11.7.
87. Calvin, *Institutes*, 3.11.1.
88. John Calvin, *Sermons on Galatians*, trans. Kathy Childress (Edinburgh: Banner of Truth Trust, 1997), 2:17–18.
89. Calvin, *Institutes*, 3.11.2.
90. Calvin, *Institutes*, 3.11.2.
91. Calvin, *Institutes*, 3.11.2.
92. Calvin, *Institutes*, 3.11.3.
93. Calvin, *Institutes*, 3.17.8.

80 Theology Made Practical

faith. In frequently quoted words, Calvin calls justification "the principal hinge by which religion is supported" and *the* soil from which the Christian life and piety develop.[94] Justification does two things in particular. With regard to God, it brings glory to God by satisfying the conditions for salvation. With regard to us, it offers the believer's conscience "peaceful rest and serene tranquility."[95] In the words of Romans 5:1: "Therefore being justified by faith, we have peace with God through our Lord Jesus Christ." The Spirit teaches believers that they need not worry about their status with God because they are justified by faith.

Of course justification never stands alone. As Richard Gaffin writes, it is "a component, with regeneration, of the principal 'twofold grace' that flows from the believer's underlying union with Christ. The 'hinge' of justification, if I may put it this way, is not a 'skyhook.' It is anchored firmly, without in any way diminishing its pivotal importance, in that union" with Christ.[96]

Sanctification is the pathway by which the believer, by means of the Spirit's gracious work, is increasingly conformed to Christ in heart, conduct, and devotion to God. It involves a continual remaking of the believer by the Holy Spirit as well as an increasing consecration of body and soul to God.[97] Calvin explains: "By contemplating the face of Jesus Christ in the mirror of the gospel, we may conform ourselves to him from glory to glory. Whereby the apostle means that in proportion as we draw nearer to Jesus Christ and know him more intimately, the grace and virtue of his Spirit will at the same time grow and be multiplied in us."[98]

In sanctification, the believer offers himself to God as a sacrifice. To be sure, this never comes without a great struggle, for it requires cleansing from the pollution of the flesh and the world.[99] Further, it entails repentance, mortification, daily conversion, and separation from pollution.[100] It is by the Spirit's grace, and only by that, the believer can persevere in sanctification. As Calvin says, the Holy Spirit did not begin the work of our salvation to leave it unfinished. The Spirit, Calvin states, is no "spasmodic visitor but a

---

94. Calvin, *Institutes*, 3.11.1; 3.15.7.

95. Calvin, *Institutes*, 3.13.1.

96. Richard B. Gaffin Jr., "Justification and Union with Christ," in *A Theological Guide to Calvin's Institutes*, 257.

97. Calvin, *Institutes*, 1.7.5; 3.1.2.

98. As quoted in Walters, *The Sovereign Spirit*, 106.

99. Calvin, *Commentary*, on John 17:17–19.

100. Calvin, *Commentary*, on 1 Cor. 1:2.

Calvin on the Holy Spirit

resident purifier of the inmost recesses of the soul."[101] The gift of the Spirit is not simply "for a single day, or for any short period," but He is like "a perennial fountain, which will never fail us."[102]

As the Spirit sanctifies us, He also moves the believer to work at his sanctification as well. Though all spiritual fruit in sanctification must ultimately be attributed to the Spirit, the believer is never passive in this work of sanctification. It is part of the paradox of grace that sanctification is both 100 percent God's work and 100 percent man's work. The Holy Spirit works in the believer even as the believer is empowered to act in godly ways by the Spirit. Walters concludes, "Calvin thus avoids the extremes of a spiritual absolutism on the one hand, and those of an equally invidious moralistic humanism on the other."[103]

Finally, we must note that for Calvin, justification and sanctification are inseparable. To try to separate one from the other is to attempt to tear Christ in pieces.[104] Or it is like trying to separate the sun's light from the heat the sun generates.[105] Gaffin summarizes Calvin's metaphor this way: "Christ, our righteousness, is the sun; justification, its light; sanctification, its heat. The sun is at once the sole source of both such that its light and heat are inseparable. At the same time, only light illumines and only heat warms, not the reverse. Both are always present, without the one becoming the other."[106] By the Spirit's influence, then, justification is never a dead-end street. Believers are justified by faith so that they might worship God in holiness of life.[107]

The Spirit and the Assurance and Application of Redemption

Calvin also teaches that the Holy Spirit witnesses to and assures the believer of his adoption.[108] Calvin writes, "The Spirit of God gives us such a testimony, that when he is our guide and teacher our spirit is made sure of the adoption

---

101. Walters, *The Sovereign Spirit*, 110.
102. Calvin, *Commentary* on John 4:13.
103. Walters, *The Sovereign Spirit*, 112.
104. Calvin, *Institutes*, 3.11.6.
105. Calvin, *Sermons on Galatians*, on Gal. 2:17–18.
106. Gaffin, "Justification and Union with Christ," 268.
107. Calvin, *Commentary*, on Rom. 6:2.
108. Much of this section is condensed from my more thorough treatment of Calvin's view of assurance in *The Quest for Full Assurance: The Legacy of Calvin and His Successors* (Edinburgh: Banner of Truth, 1999), 36–72.

82 Theology Made Practical

of God; for our mind of itself, without the preceding testimony of the Spirit, could not convey to us this assurance."[109] Calvin's repeated references to adoption embrace "the whole ethos of the Christian life," despite his lack of giving adoption its own specific section in the *Institutes.*[110] For Calvin, adoption is the apex of salvation as well as "a half-way point between justification and sanctification, inasmuch as in adoption there are both forensic and dynamic aspects."[111] In dynamic, experiential aspects, the Spirit persuades the believer to call out unashamedly, "Abba, Father."[112] The Holy Spirit assures us that our sins are forgiven, that the Father loves us with a love filled with goodness and benevolence, and that we have been elected in Christ for eternal life.[113] And he does all of this without detracting from the role of Christ. As the Spirit *of Christ*, he assures the believer by leading him to Christ and His benefits and by bringing those benefits to fruition in the believer.[114]

The unity of Christ and the Spirit has great implications for the doctrine of assurance. Some recent scholars have minimized Calvin's emphasis on the necessity of the Spirit's work in assuring a believer of God's promises. From their perspective, Calvin teaches that the *ground* of assurance is God's promises in Christ and in the Word of God, whereas the *cause* of assurance is the Spirit, who works it in the heart. Cornelis Graafland argues, however, that this distinction is far too simplistic, since the Spirit always works as the Spirit of Christ. Thus, the objective and subjective elements in assurance cannot be so easily separated. Objective salvation in Christ is inextricably linked to the subjective sealing by the Spirit. Graafland thus concludes: "Christ in and through his Spirit is the ground of our faith."[115] Moreover,

---

109. Calvin, *Commentary,* on Rom. 8:16. Cf. Calvin, *Institutes,* 3:2, 11, 34, 41; *Commentary,* on John 7:37–39; Acts 2:4; 3:8; 5:32; 13:48; 16:14; 23:11; Rom. 8:15–17; 1 Cor. 2:10–13; Gal. 3:2, 4:6; Eph. 1:13–14, 4:30; Calvin, *Tracts and Letters,* 3:253–54; and Parratt, "Witness of the Holy Spirit," 161–68.

110. Joel R. Beeke, *Heirs with Christ* (Grand Rapids: Reformation Heritage Books, 2008), 5–6. For a thorough study of Calvin on adoption, see Tim J. R. Trumper, "An Historical Study of the Doctrine of Adoption in the Calvinistic Tradition" (PhD diss., University of Edinburgh, 2001), 38–214. See also Griffith, "First Title of the Spirit," 135–53.

111. Walters, *The Sovereign Spirit,* 93.

112. Walters, *The Sovereign Spirit,* 95.

113. Calvin, *Commentary,* on Rom. 5:5; 8:33; 1 Cor. 2:12; *Institutes,* 3.1.3; 3.2.11.

114. Calvin, *Institutes,* 3.2.34.

115. Cornelis Graafland, "'Waarheid in het Binnenste': Geloofszekerheid bij Calvijn en de Nadere Reformatie," in *Een Vaste Burcht,* ed. K. Exalto (Kampen: Kok, 1989), 58–60. For more on the sealing of the Spirit, see Johannes DeBoer, *De Verzegeling met de Heilige Geest volgens de opvatting van de Nadere Reformatie* (Rotterdam: Brunder, 1968).

Calvin argues that a believer's objective reliance on God's promises as the primary ground for assurance must be subjectively sealed by the Holy Spirit. The reprobate may claim God's promises without experiencing the feeling (*sensus*), or consciousness, of those promises. The Spirit often works in the reprobate but in a far different manner than He works in the minds of the elect. The minds of the reprobate may be momentarily illumined, that it may seem they have the beginning of faith. But the truth is that they "never receive anything but a confused awareness of grace."[116]

By contrast, the elect are regenerated with an incorruptible seed.[117] They receive genuine heartwarming benefits that the reprobate will never taste. They receive the promises of God as truth in the inner man. They alone possess what can be called "the enlightening of the Spirit." They alone receive experiential, intuitive knowledge of God as He offers Himself to them in Christ.[118] Calvin says the elect alone come to "be ravished and wholly kindled to love God; [they] are borne up to heaven itself [and] admitted to the most hidden treasures of God."[119] "The Spirit, strictly speaking," Calvin further elaborates, "seals forgiveness of sins in the elect alone, so that they apply it by special faith to their own use."[120]

When Calvin distinguishes the elect from the reprobate, he speaks more about what the Spirit does *in us* than what Christ does *for us*, for here the line of demarcation is more clear. The terms he uses relate to inward experience, feeling, enlightenment, perception, even "violent emotion."[121] Well aware of the dangers of undue introspection, Calvin also recognizes that God's promises are only efficacious when they are brought by the Spirit within the scope, experience, and obedience of faith.[122]

Calvin is ever insistent that the Spirit's *chief method* of instilling assurance is to direct the believer to embrace the promises of God in Christ. Calvin rejects any attempt of the believer to find confidence in himself. Yet Calvin does not deny that a *subordinate means* to strengthen assurance is given by

---

116. Calvin, *Institutes*, 3.2.11.

117. Calvin, *Institutes*, 3.2.41.

118. Calvin, *Institutes*, 1:4, 1; 2:6, 4, 19.

119. Calvin, *Institutes*, 3.2.41.

120. Calvin, *Institutes*, 3.2.11.

121. "Too few scholars have been willing to recognize the intensely experiential nature of Calvin's doctrine of faith." M. Charles Bell, *Calvin and Scottish Theology: The Doctrine of Assurance* (Edinburgh: Handsel Press, 1985), 20.

122. Calvin, *Institutes*, 3.1.1; cf. Randall C. Zachman, *The Assurance of Faith: Conscience in the Theology of Martin Luther and John Calvin* (Minneapolis: Fortress, 1993), 198–203.

84 Theology Made Practical

the Spirit through good works and marks of grace that the Spirit enables the believer to do. Specifically, the Holy Spirit may assure the believer that his is not a temporary faith by revealing to him that he possesses "signs which are sure attestations" of faith,[123] such as "divine calling, illumination by Christ's spirit, communion with Christ, receiving Christ by faith, the embracing of Christ, perseverance of the faith, the avoidance of self-confidence, and [filial] fear."[124]

We can sum up Calvin's position by stating that in his view, all the members of the Trinity are involved in the believer's possession of assurance of faith. The election of the Father, the work of Christ, and the application of the Holy Spirit are complementary. When Calvin writes that "Christ is a thousand testimonies to me," he is saying that Christ is a primary source of assurance precisely because of the Spirit's application of Christ and His benefits to him as one elected by the Father. No one can be assured of Christ without the Spirit.[125] The Holy Spirit reveals to the believer through His Word that God is a well-disposed Father and also enables the believer to embrace Christ's promises by faith and with assurance.

The Spirit and Spiritual Gifts

A central theme in Calvin's understanding of the gifts of the Spirit is that they are given for the common good of the church.[126] When any gift deviates from this purpose, it loses its proper function. Moreover, Calvin refuses to limit the gifts of the Spirit to those specifically mentioned in texts like 1 Corinthians 12. In other words, he takes the mention of the various gifts of the Spirit in the New Testament to be exemplary of a wider range of gifts. In the *Institutes*, he thus mentions science, art, and sculpture as gifts of God.[127]

When it comes to specific gifts, Calvin argues that the gift of knowledge is "acquaintance with sacred things" or "ordinary information."[128] Wisdom,

---

123. Calvin, *Institutes*, 3.24.4.

124. Paul Helm, *Calvin and the Calvinists* (Edinburgh: Banner of Truth Trust, 1982), 28.

125. Calvin, *Institutes*, 3.2.35.

126. Stanley M. Burgess, *The Holy Spirit: Medieval Roman Catholic and Reformation Traditions* (Peabody, Mass.: Hendrickson, 1997), 166; for studies of Calvin and spiritual gifts not otherwise cited here, cf. Cheng, "Calvin on the Work of the Spirit and Spiritual Gifts," 195–204; P. F. Jensen, "Calvin, Charismatics and Miracles," *Evangelical Quarterly* 51 (1979): 131–44; and Paul Elbert, "Calvin and the Spiritual Gifts," *Journal of the Evangelical Theological Society* 22, no. 3 (September 1979): 235–56. Thanks to Derek Naves for assistance in this section.

127. Calvin, *Institutes*, 2.2.15; 1.11.8–16.

128. Calvin, *Commentary*, on 1 Cor. 12:8.

Calvin on the Holy Spirit

85

on the other hand, involves "revelations that are of a more secret and sublime order."[129] The gift of faith, mentioned in 1 Corinthians 12, does not represent saving faith but faith in the miracles performed in Christ's name. This was the faith possessed by Judas.[130] Calvin makes no comment about the gift of healing since, he says, "everyone knows what is meant"[131] by that. He does note, though, that miracles in conjunction with healing "manifest the goodness of God" and the destruction of Satan and his realm.[132] The gift of prophecy is Spirit-anointed preaching, not a supernatural understanding of the future.[133] The ability to discern between spirits has nothing to do with natural wisdom, Calvin avers. It was a special gift that God gave to the apostolic church so that believers could distinguish between true and false ministers.[134]

Calvin understands the tongues mentioned in Acts and 1 Corinthians to be the actual spoken languages of Israel's various neighboring nations. The ability to speak in those languages was not a skill acquired by study but was nothing less than a supernatural endowment. Similarly, the ability to interpret these languages was also divinely given. This gift edified the entire church, for it enabled those who heard the tongue to understand what was being said.[135] Through these gifts the gospel message was quickly disseminated throughout the entire Roman world.[136]

Calvin was also convinced that those gifts which were supernatural were no longer given in his day, for they had ceased at the passing of the apostles: "The gift of the tongues, and other such like things, are ceased long ago in the Church."[137] It is noteworthy that one reason Calvin ascribes to the disappearance of these gifts is sinful ambition and the wrong use of them. Though the gift of tongues was present in the early church, for example, God "took away that shortly after which he had given, and did not suffer the same to be corrupted with longer abuse."[138] The administration of those gifts has not been committed to the church today.[139]

---

129. Calvin, *Commentary*, on 1 Cor. 12:8.
130. Calvin, *Commentary*, on 1 Cor. 12:9.
131. Calvin, *Commentary*, on 1 Cor. 12:9.
132. Calvin, *Commentary*, on 1 Cor. 12:10.
133. Calvin, *Commentary*, on 1 Cor. 12:10.
134. Calvin, *Commentary*, on 1 Cor. 12:10.
135. Calvin, *Commentary*, on 1 Cor. 12:10.
136. Sweetman, "What Is the Meaning of These Gifts?," 120.
137. Calvin, *Commentary*, on Acts 10:44.
138. Calvin, *Commentary*, on Acts 10:46.
139. Calvin, *Institutes*, 4.19.18.

86   Theology Made Practical

In his commentary on Acts, Calvin summarizes his thought about the gifts of the Spirit:

> For although we do not receive [the Spirit], that we may speak in tongues, that we may be prophets, that we may cure the sick, that we may work miracles; yet it is given us for a better use, that we may believe with the heart unto righteousness, that our tongues may be framed unto true confession, (Rom. 10:10,) that we may pass from death to life, (John 5:24,) that we, which are poor and empty, may be made rich, that we may withstand Satan and the world stoutly.[140]

We should recognize such gifts, says Calvin, as the Spirit's work, acknowledging "that God has bestowed superlative gifts upon us for the purpose of perfecting what He has begun." Instead of filling us with pride, this should greatly humble us.[141]

The Spirit's Comprehensive Role

Calvin's Word-based understanding of the Holy Spirit's work is a central principle of his theology. Gwyn Walters puts it this way: "There are no major, and hardly any minor, aspects of theology which he can discuss without explicit reference to, and dependence upon, the Spirit of God. His doctrine of the Holy Spirit integrates his entire theology.... The Spirit is never relegated to the incidentals or periphery of faith."[142] Walters confirms Calvin's reputation of being the "theologian of the Holy Spirit," something that we have also seen in this essay. We must note that this essay sketches Calvin's theology in broad strokes and says nothing about other aspects of his pneumatology, such as the Spirit's role in relation to creation and the cosmos,[143]

---

140. Calvin, *Commentary*, on Acts 10:46.
141. Calvin, *Commentary*, on 1 Thess. 1:2.
142. Walters, *The Sovereign Spirit*, 233.
143. I. John Hesselink, "The Spirit of God the Creator in Calvin's Theology," in *Sola Gratia: Bron voor de Reformatie en uitdaging voor nu*, ed. A. van de Beek and W. M. van Laar (Zoetermeer, the Netherlands: Boekencentrum, 2004), 53–69; Bolt, "Spiritus Creator," 17–34; and Joseph A. Pipa Jr., "Creation and Providence," in *A Theological Guide to Calvin's Institutes*, 123–50.

the Christian life and ethics,[144] the church and the sacraments,[145] and preaching.[146]

Like other great theologians of the church who have enriched our understanding of the biblical teaching about the Spirit and His work, Calvin teaches us first and foremost that we need to be radically dependent upon the Holy Spirit for every temporal, spiritual, and eternal blessing. Without the Spirit, we cannot live spiritually. Without the Spirit, our religion is a sham, and we are consigned to the abyss of condemnation. Without the

---

144. John H. Leith, *John Calvin's Doctrine of the Christian Life* (Louisville: Westminster, 1989); I. John Hesselink, "Calvin, the Theologian of the Holy Spirit—the Holy Spirit and the Christian Life, in *Calvin in Asian Churches*, 113–27; Chung, "Calvin and the Holy Spirit," 40–55; Guenther H. Haas, "Calvin's Ethics," in *Cambridge Companion to John Calvin*, 93–105; David Clyde Jones, "The Law and the Spirit of Christ," in *A Theological Guide to Calvin's Institutes*, 301–19; William Edgar, "Ethics: The Christian Life and Good Works According to Calvin," in *A Theological Guide to Calvin's Institutes*, 320–46.

For Calvin on the Spirit's work in prayer, see Don Garlington, "Calvin's Doctrine of Prayer: An Examination of Book 3, Chapter 20 of the *Institutes of the Christian Religion*," *The Baptist Review of Theology* 1, no. 1 (Autumn 1991): 21–36; Robert Douglas Loggie, "Chief Exercise of Faith—An Exposition of Calvin's Doctrine of Prayer," *The Hartford Quarterly* 5 (Fall 1964): 65–81; Jae Sung Kim, "Prayer in Calvin's Soteriology," in *Calvinus Praeceptor Ecclesiae*, ed. Herman J. Selderhuis (Geneva: Droz, 2004), 265–74; Stephen Matteucci, "A Strong Tower for Weary People: Calvin's Teaching on Prayer," *The Founders Journal* 69 (Summer 2007): 19–24; David B. Calhoun, "Prayer: 'The Chief Exercise of Faith,'" in *A Theological Guide to Calvin's Institutes*, 347–67; and Joel R. Beeke, "The Communion of Men with God," in *John Calvin: A Heart for Devotion, Doctrine, and Doxology*, ed. Burk Parsons (Lake Mary, Fla.: Reformation Trust, 2008).

145. Hughes Oliphant Old, "Calvin's Theology of Worship," in *Give Praise to God: A Vision for Reforming Worship*, ed. Philip Graham Ryken et al. (Phillipsburg, N.J.: P&R, 2003), 412–35; Peter Ward, "Coming to Sermon: The Practice of Doctrine in the Preaching of John Calvin," *Scottish Journal of Theology* 58, no. 3 (2005): 319–32; I. John Hesselink, "The Role of the Holy Spirit in Calvin's Doctrine of the Sacraments," in *Essentialia et Hodierna: oblate P. C. Potgieter; Acta Theologica Supplementum*, ed. D. François Tolmie (Bloemfontein: Universiteit van die Oranje-Vrystaat, 2002), 66–88; Jill Raitt, "Three Inter-Related Principles in Calvin's Unique Doctrine of Infant Baptism," *Sixteenth Century Journal* 11, no. 1 (1980): 51–62; John W. Riggs, *Baptism in the Reformed Tradition* (Louisville: Westminster, 2002); Wallace, *Calvin's Doctrine of the Word and Sacrament*; Kilian McDonnell, *John Calvin, the Church, and the Eucharist* (Princeton: Princeton University Press, 1967); Brian A. Gerrish, *Grace and Gratitude: The Eucharistic Theology of John Calvin* (Minneapolis: Fortress, 1993); Thomas J. Davis, *The Clearest Promises of God: The Development of Calvin's Eucharistic Teaching* (New York: AMS, 1995); Keith Mathison, *Given for You: Reclaiming Calvin's Doctrine of the Lord's Supper* (Phillipsburg, N.J.: P&R, 2002); W. Robert Godfrey, "Calvin, Worship, and the Sacraments," in *A Theological Guide to Calvin's Institutes*, 368–89; Walters, *The Sovereign Spirit*, 146–75; Osterhaven, "John Calvin," 23–44.

146. Dawn DeVries, "Calvin's Preaching," in *Cambridge Companion to John Calvin*, ed. McKim, 106–24; and Brian G. Armstrong, "Role of the Holy Spirit in Calvin's Teaching on the Ministry," 99–116.

Spirit, there is no real ministry of the Word, no real church, and no real commemoration of the sacraments. How much we must thank God for the person and ministry of His precious, indispensable Spirit! And how much should we pray to live out the faith that the Spirit produces in us as we wait for greater measures of His sovereign outpouring in the life of our churches and in our lives!

—6—

Explicit and Implicit Appendixes to Calvin's View of Justification by Faith

David W. Hall

A search for the term "justification" in the database of Calvin's major writings shows that it is used over two hundred times in the *Institutes*—certainly indicating that this concept was of prevailing interest to Calvin.[1] This and other considerations have given rise to the claim that justification is the most important doctrine for the Protestant Reformation in general and for Calvin in particular. If that claim is sustained, then it would also stand to reason that other correlates such as Christian liberty and prayer, properly tied to justification, would consistently reflect both the meaning and the thrust of Calvin's denotation of justification.[2]

Calvin uses "justification" most frequently in the middle of the *Institutes* in book 3, chapters 11–12. Accordingly, once this doctrine is constructed in principle in those sections, other correlates are built on that foundation. Thus, if the faith rises or falls with justification by faith, certain other implied Christian teachings might be expected to give way (or be strengthened), depending on how this teaching is maintained. Similarly, if these correlates reflect Calvin's homology, a stronger understanding of his view of justification ensues. Moreover, because Calvin considers many of these auxiliary doctrines in depth in the second half of the *Institutes*, we see their importance. Indeed, most of the practical topics of Christian living are impacted by the meaning of justification.

---

1. John Calvin, *The Institutes of the Christian Religion*, trans. Henry Beveridge (Edinburgh: Calvin Translation Society, 1845–1846), accessed June 19, 2017, http://www.ccel.org/ccel/calvin/institutes.txt.

2. This chapter is a slightly revised version of a previously published essay that is used with permission. See David W. Hall, "Explicit and Implicit Appendixes to Calvin's View of Justification by Faith," in *Since We Are Justified by Faith: Justification in the Theologies of the Protestant Reformation*, ed. Michael Parsons, Studies in Christian History and Thought (Milton Keynes, Bucks: Paternoster, 2012), ch. 8.

90 Theology Made Practical

To better understand Calvin on this topic, in this chapter I discuss the following subjects:

1. Calvin's view of justification, including interactions with current theorists and the *Institutes*. As a vital and critical area, it begets overflows and correlates.

2. What Calvin explicitly calls the "proper appendix of justification"; namely, Christian liberty.

3. Other implicit areas in which Calvin draws on justification to make assertions for other loci: prayer, election, ecclesiology, civil government, and eschatology.

Summary of Justification from Calvin's *Institutes*

This much-debated area may not be as obscure or as difficult as some make it. A comprehensive reading of Calvin, whether the reader begins with Calvin's commentary on Romans or with the *Institutes*, demonstrates that his view on justification is clear and consistent. While creative theologians may always discover a stray thread in any theological wardrobe, Calvin's view can safely be categorized as consistent with the forensic view expressed in later Protestant and Puritan creeds and confessions.

In the *Institutes*, Calvin discussed justification following his treatise on the life of the Christian man. Along with cross-bearing and self-denial, this Christian life has an eschatological horizon that Christians may never forget. Calvin explained that the Christian is to understand and use the good gifts of God without becoming addicted to them.[3] Godly contentment should inspire the Christian to accept poverty or blessing, becoming enchanted with neither but always looking to his heavenly calling. With that backdrop, Calvin launches into his discussion of justification.

Justification is tied to regeneration as part of a "double grace" (*duplicem gratiam*).[4] The first of those graces is that the Christian is reconciled to God "through Christ's blamelessness," so that he sees that God is a gracious Father instead of a condemning judge.[5] Calvin's beginning definition of justification is this: the act of God by which He transforms us from criminals to children. The second grace is that "sanctified by Christ's spirit we may

---

3. Calvin, *Institutes*, 3.11.2.
4. Calvin, *Institutes*, 3.11.2.
5. Calvin, *Institutes*, 3.11.1.

Appendixes to Calvin's View of Justification by Faith   91

cultivate blamelessness and purity of life," or regeneration—which is used by Calvin here as a summary of the whole of the Christian life. In this context, Calvin calls this justification "the main hinge on which religion turns," asserting, "Unless you first of all grasp what your relationship to God is, and the nature of this judgment concerning you, you have neither a foundation on which to establish your salvation nor one on which to build piety toward God."[6] Thus, Calvin begins by contending that we must understand justification, for it is essential for both salvation and continuing piety.[7]

Calvin explained justification as being both "reckoned righteous in God's judgment" and as "accepted on account of his righteousness." Thus, God provides both the legal verdict and the moral atonement. As a result, the justified person is "reckoned in the condition not of a sinner but of a righteous man." God judicially alters the "condition" of a sinner and by the death of Christ "reckons" that sinner to be righteous. The justified sinner "grasps the righteousness of Christ through faith...is clothed in it, [and] appears in God's sight not as a sinner but as a righteous man." For Calvin, then, justification is "the acceptance with which God receives us into his favor as righteous men. And we say that it consists in the remission of sins and the imputation of Christ's righteousness."[8]

Calvin's initial definition is clear, unencumbered, and predictably orthodox. He proceeded to support his view of justification by citing only a few Scripture passages since "it would take too long to collect all the passages" that exhibit the meaning of justification. Furthermore, he viewed Paul's teaching on justification to be summarized by the term "acceptance," further emphasizing the judicial/forensic nature of justification. Calvin said, "Therefore, since God justifies us by the intercession of Christ, he absolves us not by

---

6. Calvin, *Institutes*, 3.11.1.

7. Among the recent discussions of Calvin on justification are the following: Mark A. Garcia, "Life in Christ: The Function of Union with Christ in the *Unio-Duplex Gratia* Structure of Calvin's Soteriology with Special Reference to the Relationship of Justification and Sanctification in Sixteenth-Century Context" (PhD diss., University of Edinburgh, 2004); Mark A. Garcia, *Life in Christ: Union with Christ and Twofold Grace in Calvin's Theology* (Milton Keynes: Paternoster, 2008); A. N. S. Lane, *Justification by Faith in Catholic–Protestant Dialogue* (New York: T&T Clark, 2002); J. Todd Billings, *Calvin, Participation, and the Gift: The Activity of Believers in Union with Christ*, Changing Paradigms in Historical and Systematic Theology (New York: Oxford University Press, 2008); Michael Horton, *Covenant and Salvation: Union with Christ* (Louisville: Westminster, 2007); and Dennis E. Tamburello, *Union with Christ: John Calvin and the Mysticism of St. Bernard* (Louisville: Westminster, 1996).

8. Calvin, *Institutes*, 3.11.2.

92 Theology Made Practical

the confirmation of our own innocence but by the imputation of righteousness, so that we who are not righteous in ourselves may be reckoned as such in Christ." Thus, Calvin equates justification with "acceptance," "imputation," "pardoning," "reckoning," and the divine commutation of justice.[9]

So careful was Calvin to focus on God's commutation of justice that he provided an extensive critique of Andreas Osiander's (1498–1552) view. Osiander, an early Lutheran theologian, taught contra Luther, "some strange monster" of essential righteousness, in which he advocated that Christ's essence was ontologically mingled with ours in justification. Calvin objected both to "infusion" of Christ's essence and "substantial" righteousness.[10] Calvin's point was this: God the judge justifies, and His act reckons our status according to what Christ is for us, not what Christ is in us. Osiander's problem was his "dividing" of Christ's natures; in contrast, Calvin emphasized that Christ's atoning work fully comprehended both natures and was performed as mediator. Instead of an ontological union, Calvin taught—and this guards us against the substantialism of Eastern Orthodoxy (to be discussed below)—that the union was a "mystical," or spiritual, one (note that this is much like the logic he employed later in his sacramentology).[11]

Calvin spied "more poison" in Osiander's view that "we are righteous together with God." It could hardly be clearer that Calvin held to a forensic view of justification, especially in light of this polemic against Osiander in his most important theological treatise. At one point Calvin affirmed that the essential meaning of justification was so clear as "reckoning" (an "expression taken from legal usage") that he wrote: "Anyone moderately versed in the Hebrew language, provided he has a sober brain, is not ignorant of the fact that the phrase arose from this [legal] source, and drew from it its tendency and implication."[12]

Bruce McCormack has drawn from Calvin's critique of Osiander and shows how this reflects Calvin's denotation of justification. Following Calvin's definition of justification,[13] McCormack recognizes Calvin's emphasis on justification as acquittal—certainly a legal concept, commenting that "'to justify' means nothing else than to acquit of guilt him who was accused as if

---

9. Calvin, *Institutes*, 3.11.3.
10. Calvin, *Institutes*, 3.11.5.
11. Calvin, *Institutes*, 3.11.10.
12. Calvin, *Institutes*, 3.11.11.
13. Calvin, *Institutes*, 3.11.2.

Appendixes to Calvin's View of Justification by Faith

his innocence were confirmed." The setting is a courtroom. The question is one of guilt or innocence. And the divine verdict is innocence. How can this be? Because the guilt for our sins was imputed to Christ, who then suffered the legal penalty that our guilt required. "This is our acquittal: the guilt that held us liable for punishment has been transferred to the head of the Son of God [Isa. 53:12]."[14]

McCormack observes further that the concept of acquittal presumes that "the righteousness on which it is based be complete." Accordingly, the acquitted person must truly be innocent of the charges, but "complete innocence is found in Christ alone. He alone was sinless. His obedience alone is perfect. But that, then, means that the ground of our justification must lie, at every moment of the Christian life, outside of ourselves.... Outside of us, Christ's righteousness is complete; in us, it is not. Therefore, if justification does indeed consist in acquittal, then the ground of our justification must be found to lie in the alien righteousness of Christ and in it alone."[15]

Moreover, McCormack confirms that

> the mechanism by means of which Christ's perfect righteousness is made to be ours is that of imputation. Imputation is a concept drawn from the realm of accounting (of bookkeeping). Guilt is not credited to the account of the sinner; Christ's righteousness is. The same mechanism is employed by Calvin to explain how our guilt is made to be Christ's—in other words, how he who knew no sin was made sin on our behalf.... That is, he who was about to cleanse the filth of those iniquities was covered with them by transferred imputation.... Our guilt was made his by imputation.... In any event, atonement and justification are twin doctrines for Calvin. Both are construed in strictly forensic terms.[16]

Finally, citing Calvin's critique of Osiander's view that the "essential righteousness" of Christ is taken to our nature, McCormack points out:

---

14. Bruce McCormack, "Union with Christ in Calvin's Theology: Grounds for a Divinization Theory?," in *Tributes to John Calvin: A Celebration of His Quincentenary*, ed. David W. Hall (Phillipsburg, N.J.: P&R, 2010), 517. See also Bruce McCormack, *Justification in Perspective: Historical Developments and Contemporary Challenges* (Grand Rapids: Baker, 2006); and Bruce McCormack, "What's at Stake in Current Debates over Justification: The Crisis of Protestantism in the West," in *Justification: What's at Stake in the Current Debates*, ed. Mark Husbands and Daniel J. Treier (Downers Grove, Ill.: InterVarsity, 2004).

15. McCormack, "Union with Christ in Calvin's Theology," 517.

16. McCormack, "Union with Christ in Calvin's Theology," 518.

94 Theology Made Practical

Against this conception, Calvin says that Osiander ought to have been "content with that righteousness which has been acquired for us by Christ's obedience and sacrificial death." The *acquired* righteousness of Christ: by this phrase Calvin clearly means to refer to the righteousness that accrues to Christ's sinless obedience in life and in death—in other words, to his *human* righteousness, that which is added to his divine righteousness.[17]

Cornelis Venema has recently observed that, for Calvin, any discussion of faith would be barren, deformed, and useless should it fail to include an elaboration of this twofold benefit.[18] Richard Gaffin similarly clarifies, notwithstanding, that Calvin did not teach that justification fails to lead to sanctification. Returning to the term "regeneration," Calvin believed that God always produces moral reform in the life of the truly justified: "He does not justify in part but liberally.... From this it follows that the doctrine of justification is perverted and utterly overthrown when doubt is thrust into men's minds, when the assurance of salvation is shaken and the free and fearless calling upon God suffers hindrance—nay, when peace and tranquility with spiritual joy are not established."[19] To be sure, as Gaffin notes, for Calvin,

> justification and sanctification are inseparable. As such, however, they are not confused but distinguished. Accenting inseparability, Calvin speaks not of two graces but of "two-fold grace" in the singular, although later in this section he does refer to regeneration as "the second of these gifts" or better, this "second grace," signaling some distinction. The nature of both this difference and inseparability, as well as the nature of the underlying union involved, Calvin will clarify as his discussion unfolds.[20]

Venema agrees that justification, the first benefit, is always accompanied by the second benefit, sanctification—although justification has a logical priority that the French Reformer could not ignore.[21] Such

---

17. McCormack, "Union with Christ in Calvin's Theology," 518–19.

18. Cornelis P. Venema, "Union with Christ, the 'Twofold Grace of God,' and the 'Order of Salvation' in Calvin's Theology," in *Calvin for Today*, ed. Joel R. Beeke (Grand Rapids: Reformation Heritage Books, 2010), 93.

19. Calvin, *Institutes*, 3.11.11.

20. Richard Gaffin, "Justification and Union with Christ," in *A Theological Guide to Calvin's Institutes*, 253–54.

21. Venema, "Union with Christ," 144–45.

Appendixes to Calvin's View of Justification by Faith 95

justification—juridical in nature—"consists in the remission of sins and the imputation of Christ's righteousness."[22] Calvin stood against the medieval confusion of justification with inherent righteousness. He saw justification as including divine acquittal as well as acceptance and reconciliation. Venema warns of the practical ills that flow from confusing justification with either sanctification or apotheosis: "Unless the difference between justification and sanctification is carefully maintained, the goodness and mercy of God will be seriously impugned and the assurance of faith will be threatened."[23]

Venema argues convincingly that Calvin expected his readers would easily conclude, by his sequence of topics, that justification was not by works but by faith alone—but as "simple pardon."[24] Furthermore, Calvin believed this precise ordering of topics would underscore the inseparability of justification and sanctification. In short, much of the discussion about Calvin on justification—especially if it leads to minimization of justification or an optimization of external factors—appears to be "much ado about nothing." Or, to put it another way: looking for Calvin to articulate or support a "new perspective" on justification is like expecting him to enunciate a new perspective on creation, the Trinity, or inspiration.

Gaffin puts things in focus when he summarizes:

> For Calvin sanctification as an ongoing, life-long process follows justification and in that sense justification is "prior" to sanctification and the believer's good works can be seen as the fruits and signs of having been justified. Only those already justified are being sanctified. But this is not the same thing as saying, what Calvin does *not* say, that justification is the source of sanctification or that justification causes sanctification. That source, that cause is Christ, in whom, Calvin is clear in this passage, at the moment they are united

---

22. Calvin, *Institutes*, 3.11.2.

23. Venema, "Union with Christ," 98. Venema's chapter also provides a helpful summary of the dialogue between Thomas Wenger and Marcus Johnson. Among other things, Venema makes it clear that the earlier discussion of sanctification before justification in Calvin should not discount how Calvin routinely treats sanctification as an effect of, fruit of, or following from justification (154). Moreover, in *Institutes* 3.3, Calvin explains the order of his loci, and in 3.11.1, when he speaks of justification as "the main hinge on which religion turns," while calling for a priority of comprehension given to it, Calvin states: "For unless you first of all grasp what your relationship to God is, and the nature of his judgment concerning you, you have neither a foundation on which to establish your salvation nor one on which to build piety toward God."

24. Venema, "Union with Christ," 106.

96 Theology Made Practical

to him by faith, sinners simultaneously receive a two-fold grace and so begin an ongoing process of being sanctified just as they are now also definitively justified.[25]

Gaffin further explains that Calvin called the idea that "imputation is non-forensic or somehow a nonjudicial transfer or communication" a "frivolous notion."[26]

Toward the conclusion of Calvin's discussion of justification, we begin to sense the practical test of doctrine in his writing.[27] Doctrine is founded, in Calvin's work, on proper exegesis and systematic consistency, and its practical effect confirms its right understanding. Thus, for Calvin, the erroneous constructs—whether Osiander's, the Romanist's, or the enthusiast's—of doctrine falsely conceived is further revealed in its practical bondage and hindrance.

This practical test leads us to the next sections of this essay. Calvin's doctrine always aimed at the needs of the soul and the glory of Christ: "In short, whoever wraps up two kinds of righteousness [i. e., Osiander's key flaw] in order that miserable souls may not repose wholly in God's mere mercy, crowns Christ in mockery with a wreath of thorns."[28]

With Calvin's view of justification established, let's move forward to see how he builds on what he has already constructed. Each appendage we consider will corroborate the meaning of justification as it has been explained above.

The Explicit Appendix: Christian Liberty

In his dispute with Osiander over the meaning of justification, Calvin labeled Osiander's view a "strange monster," thinking that it was tantamount to a revival of Manicheanism. Often those who separated essential parts, such as

---

25. Gaffin, "Justification and Union with Christ," 256. Gaffin also reports the substantial enlargement and placement of this topic in the second (and other) editions of Calvin's *Institutes*, showing the "roughly four-fold, expansion of the *Institutes* in the second, 1539 edition. Now and in subsequent editions (1543–45 and 1550–54) there is a separate chapter on justification (6 or 10, depending on the edition), positioned between chapters on repentance and the similarity and difference between the Old and New Testaments. This chapter, with its own title, "Concerning Justification by Faith and the Merits of Works," is approximately seven times the length of the treatment in 1536 and consists of eighty-seven numbered sections, without subtitling or other internal subdivisions." Further, Gaffin theorizes that Calvin's crystallization of this topic in his final edition was, in part, a response to the 1547 Council of Trent.

26. Gaffin, "Justification and Union with Christ," 263.

27. Calvin, *Institutes*, 3.11.11.

28. Calvin, *Institutes*, 3.11.12.

Appendixes to Calvin's View of Justification by Faith 97

practice from doctrine, were accused of Manicheanism. Calvin had a consistent view of justification, and he believed that justification had implications for Christian living.

In two different spheres—the civil sphere and the authoritarianism of Roman ecclesiology—Calvin was challenged to work out an enduring view of liberty. In book 3 of the *Institutes*, he took up the subject of Christian liberty, and his insights are helpful today. To begin, we must understand a key distinction from the conclusion of chapter 19 of that work.

Calvin spoke of two species of liberty: civil and spiritual.[29] He taught that human government is twofold: (1) spiritual government is internal, and it trains the conscience in matters of piety and worship; and (2) civil government refers to external matters. The church is to teach and handle the spiritual order, and the political rulers care for civil order. Calvin suggested that if we pay attention to this distinction, we will not "misapply to the political order the gospel teaching on spiritual freedom."[30] That division of labor would become an essential building block of stable societies; it would also supply ample protection for proper freedom.

With that in mind, it should be clear that church and state each had a valuable role to play in human life. They should not interfere with the proper jurisdiction of the other, however; God intended it to be that way.

As Calvin began his groundbreaking chapter on Christian liberty, he first sought to explain why this topic was so important. He argued that it was necessary for contemporaries to understand this, if only on an elementary level, lest they have their consciences burdened by the threat of endless rules and stifling captivity. Indeed, he asserted, this topic was a proper "appendage [Latin, *appendix*] to justification," meaning that if a person knew how he had been truly justified—that is, by God alone—he might also know that true liberty would result only as he followed God. Thus, from the outset, Calvin believed that liberty was a gift that should be used as God has designed it. It was a natural correlate of the right understanding of justification.

Pastor Calvin was sensitive to Protestants' tender consciences. He argued that if a pastor failed to explain this subject, his congregation would experience wavering and trepidation. The battle over justification, in other words, could be lost not only over what justification meant in theory but also over how it was practiced. Accordingly, if Christians who were justified did not

---

29. Calvin, *Institutes*, 3.9.15.
30. Calvin, *Institutes*, 3.19.15.

98 Theology Made Practical

understand this "thing of prime necessity," they would "hesitate and recoil" in many things, hardly being able to undertake anything without crippling doubts. Calvin also taught that for those with a good understanding of justification who "seriously fear" God, this topic yielded "incomparable benefit."[31]

So vital was this doctrine for Calvin that he concluded: "Unless this freedom be comprehended, neither Christ nor gospel truth, nor inner peace of soul, can be rightly known."[32] Thus, he advised that this "so necessary a part of doctrine" not be suppressed. For Calvin, the doctrine of justification—with a correct understanding of the role of law—leads to a Christocentric and ethical liberation.

Being regenerated by God, believers are to "voluntarily obey" His will, not out of a servile fear.[33] Instead of being in terror, the believer should know the love of God, and liberty flows from that. This understanding of justification also meant the end of various perfectionistic schemes. Calvin's followers were to be perfect in Christ, not in themselves. That also implied the end of legalism. As such, believers were permitted either to use things as helpful or not, as long as they did not seek to overturn the moral law. Accordingly, there were many things in life that Calvin classified as "indifferent." To fail to make that distinction would, he thought, mean "no end of superstition."[34] As long as believers used created things properly, they had liberty to enjoy them. The goal of this liberty was to "give peace to trembling consciences."[35]

Calvin also offered a hierarchy of norms to help people make decisions. Matters of Christian liberty must be "subordinated to love"; by that, he meant that sometimes we must voluntarily restrict ourselves so that we do not cause others to stumble. Thus, liberty is not absolute in Calvin's scheme. It is a good gift from God, but it must be kept in perspective. Moreover, while the law of liberty must be subject to the law of charity, the norm of love is not the final test either, for the law of love must "abide under purity of faith."[36]

Calvin had seen oppression of liberties and he based his view of liberties on God's Word and in a fashion that avoided misuses of it. Christian liberty was the proper appendage of justification. Calvin knew, however, that

---

31. Calvin, *Institutes*, 3.19.1.
32. Calvin, *Institutes*, 3.19.1.
33. Calvin, *Institutes*, 3.19.4.
34. Calvin, *Institutes*, 3.19.7.
35. Calvin, *Institutes*, 3.19.9.
36. Calvin, *Institutes*, 3.19.13.

Appendixes to Calvin's View of Justification by Faith   99

sanctification was always intertwined with justification. Christian practice, if not formed by God's Word, could virtually nullify the doctrine of justification. The final chapters of books 3 and 4 in the *Institutes* treat those matters.

Implicit Appendixes

The logic in the final section of this essay is as follows: If we understand justification (J) as Calvin did, it leads necessarily to the doctrine of Christian liberty (L). For those who have an understanding of both justification and Christian liberty (J + L), certain other implications (I) follow. In each case below, the simple "J + L → I" logic shows the internal consistency of Calvin's thought. The implications of justification also serve to liberate each of these individual loci from spiritual bondage—a significant consequence.

Prayer

The way a person understands justification affects the way he or she prays. In his study of Calvin's soteriology and prayer, Jae Sung Kim has noted the difference that theoretical formulations make for the practice of prayer. He notes, "One of the distinctive contributions of John Calvin to reformed theology is the firm establishment of the doctrine of application of redemption." In an important essay, Kim seeks to "expose a distinct aspect of Calvin's soteriology, which emphasizes that justification by faith should be complemented by prayer in the Holy Spirit."[37] Kim writes that the focus of Calvin's idea on the application of redemption "starts with recognizing faith as the primary gift and secret work of the Holy Spirit to unite us with Christ.... The chief role of the Holy Spirit in the application of redemption is to unite us with Christ."[38] Moreover, Kim sees both prayer and faith as God's gifts, noting that

> these two subjects are closely related in Calvin's biblical soteriology, especially in his numerous polemical arguments against the Roman Catholics and some radical Lutheran extremes. One of Calvin's controversial arguments on Reformed soteriology shows us a new understanding of justification by faith. The imputation of Christ's righteousness is not only alien but has been compared with the

---

37. Jae Sung Kim, "Prayer in Calvin's Soteriology," in *Tributes to John Calvin: A Celebration of His Quincentenary*, ed. David W. Hall (Phillipsburg, N.J.: P&R, 2010), 343–55.

38. Kim, "Prayer in Calvin's Soteriology," 343–55.

100 Theology Made Practical

doctrine of infusion and self-attained righteousness of the Council of Trent. In this sense, Calvin's doctrine of prayer is also very different from the Roman Catholics.[39]

Kim's important observation is borne out from a perusal of some of Calvin's "rules for prayer." In his third rule for prayer, Calvin taught that any person who "stands before God to pray, in his humility giving glory completely to God, abandon[s] all thought of his own glory, cast[s] off all notion of his self-worth, in fine, put[s] away all self-assurance."[40] In this we can see both the difference between the prevailing Roman view of prayer, as well as how similar the terminology ("humility," "abandon all thought of his own glory," "put away self-assurance") is to that of Calvin's explanation of forensic justification. Moreover, Calvin adds that confidence is derived in prayer "solely from God's mercy."[41] Is Calvin not calling for *sola misericordae ora* in the same way that he calls for *sola gratia* and *sola fides* concerning justification? It is difficult to imagine a logical disjunction. It is not in our "own righteousness" that we have the enjoyment of a "pure conscience before the Lord" in prayer.[42] On the contrary, faith necessarily joins the "acknowledgement of our misery, destitution, and uncleanness"—the same starting point for forensic justification. Calvin also denied that observing fixed hours for prayer could ever pay "our debt to God,"[43] drawing clearly and consistently on forensic terminology.

Calvin argued that appealing to the intercession of saints assaulted the dignity of Christ's work. To hold such would imply that "Christ were insufficient or too severe."[44] It is a dishonoring of Christ that "strips him of the title of sole Mediator" to pray to others; moreover this "obscures the glory of his birth and makes void the cross."[45] Thus Kim observes that the doctrine of prayer links two important subjects in the final edition of the *Institutes*, Christian liberty and predestination.[46]

Prayer is almost, but not quite (except as a part of sanctification) elevated to the *ordo salutis* in Calvin's work. Kim summarizes:

---

39. Kim, "Prayer in Calvin's Soteriology," 343–55.
40. Calvin, *Institutes*, 3.20.8.
41. Calvin, *Institutes*, 3.20.9.
42. Calvin, *Institutes*, 3.20.10.
43. Calvin, *Institutes*, 3.20.50.
44. Calvin, *Institutes*, 3.20.21.
45. Calvin, *Institutes*, 3.20.21.
46. Kim, "Prayer in Calvin's Soteriology," 344.

Appendixes to Calvin's View of Justification by Faith

In order to escape from Roman Catholic's [sic] error, Calvin attacks the practice of penance, especially the three steps of the Scholastics: contrition of heart, confession of mouth, and satisfaction of works. For Calvin, God simply requires repentance and faith. Our sanctification is the object of regeneration and our efforts strive to overcome bad habits. The first step in the Christian life is self-denial, which is the departure from self to thorough obedience to God. Then, bearing the cross leads us to mature trust in God's will.[47]

Thus, justification as a critical part of soteriology has bearing on prayer. It is no coincidence that Romanists and Calvinists view prayer differently. The same would be true for proponents of any of the other differing views of justification. Calvin put it this way: "God finds nothing in man to arouse him to do good to him but that he comes first to man in his free generosity. For what can a dead man do to attain life?"[48] Calvin applies this scriptural logic further, drawing on Hosea 2:19: "If a covenant of this sort, which is clearly the first union of us with God, depends upon God's mercy, no basis is left for our righteousness.... If justification is the beginning of love, what righteousness of works will preceded it?"[49] The logic of justification, which was applied to prayer, was subsequently applied to election.

Election

The way a person understands justification affects the way he or she views God's sovereignty in divine election. On review, Calvin's defense of divine election may surprise some people by its unanticipated gentleness and pastoral tone. He opined that the only possible way to understand this is for "reverent minds" to accept what God has written. He argued practically that one of the benefits for the believer who understands election is the resulting comfort: "We shall never be clearly persuaded, as we ought to be, that our salvation flows from the wellspring of God's free mercy until we come to know his eternal election, which illumines God's grace by this contrast: that he does not indiscriminately adopt all into the hope of salvation but gives to some what he denies to others."[50] Moreover, he reiterated that "our salvation comes about solely from God's mere generosity"; the opposing view of

---

47. Kim, "Prayer in Calvin's Soteriology," 354.
48. Calvin, *Institutes*, 3.14.5.
49. Calvin, *Institutes*, 3.14.6.
50. Calvin, *Institutes*, 3.21.1.

102   Theology Made Practical

salvation fails to tear up pride by its roots. Nothing, said Calvin, has more potential to make us humble than to realize that our standing with Christ is undeserved. Furthermore, this teaching, along with forensic justification, "is our only ground for firmness and confidence" and alone will free us from all fear."[51]

Calvin explicitly linked election and justification in a key section that draws upon numerous Scripture texts. In one section, he stated again that "freely given mercy," not "regard to human worth" (the dynamic of justification), is the engine for this loving election that dares to adopt any into God's family. Also in this context Calvin wrote of "justification" as "another sign of [the] manifestation" of election.[52] In the next chapter, Calvin asserted that "we were adopted in Christ into the eternal inheritance because in ourselves we were not capable of such great excellence."[53]

Church Government

The bulk of book 4, following Calvin's elaboration of justification, discusses various matters of church government. One might think that in these areas, the shadow of justification does not extend. On the contrary! The conceptions of church power and the ethos of ecclesiology are affected by the subjects and manner of God's justification. A different view of justification would lead to a different ecclesiology.

Calvin's sixth chapter in his original 1536 edition of the *Institutes* addressed three topics: Christian liberty, ecclesiastical power, and political administration. The longest section in his sixth chapter is on ecclesiology proper. Calvin viewed this in his day as an extension of Christian freedom, for the tyranny of church masters who invaded the conscience threatened Christian liberty.[54] It is noteworthy that Calvin viewed church government as important for spiritual liberty—thus, the need to devote so much writing to that subject during the Reformation era. Justification, thus, even overflowed into church order, with proper ecclesiology being infused with theology. It is not too much to assert that Calvin viewed himself as setting forth an ecclesiology of liberty as opposed to the prevailing tyranny of "innumerable," "limitless," and "entangling" church governance that "traps to catch

---

51. Calvin, *Institutes*, 3.21.1.
52. Calvin, *Institutes*, 3.21.7.
53. Calvin, *Institutes*, 3.22.1.
54. Calvin, *Institutes* (1536), 184.

Appendixes to Calvin's View of Justification by Faith   103

and ensnare souls."[55] If this language sounds similar to Calvin's comments on justification, there is a good explanation for this found in homology.

His divine-right ecclesiology would later be extended by his disciples, but on the level of principle his advocacy of *sola Scriptura* in this topic is as clear as in other theological loci. With Scripture acknowledged as his authority even for ecclesiology, Calvin asserted that "if faith depends on God's word alone, if it looks to it and reposes in it alone, what place is now left for the word of men?"[56] That reliance on an alien source is similar to his view on justification as the grant of an alien righteousness. Legislative power, thought Calvin, or the authority to "frame new laws," was denied to the apostles; only ministerial power—the right to echo and assert what God had already declared—was given to the church.[57] God, the sole ruler over souls, was the sole ruler over the church of all souls.

Civil Government

The way a person understands justification affects the way he or she constructs the role of the civil magistrate. While it may seem "alien to the spiritual doctrine of faith," Calvin found it necessary to tie political matters to faith. Indeed, for Calvin, the whole plan of God's salvation implied numerous ethical correlates and a correct formulation in government matters yields "greater zeal for piety" that may flourish in us "to attest our gratefulness."[58] For Calvin, political matters flow from a proper appropriation of other doctrines and also produced something as practical as thankfulness.

Moreover, Calvin's calling magistrates "the vicars of God" uses terms that remind a careful reader of the substitutionist vocabulary found similarly in Calvin's soteriological formulations.[59] For Calvin, the concept that the civil government works for both the saved and the unsaved implies two other important factors: (1) justification, under that formulation, is an internal-forensic work, not a moralistic one; and (2) Calvin's view permits the nonjustified to have equal protection, which states influenced by Calvin's instruction have tended to provide.

---

55. Calvin, *Institutes* (1536), 185.
56. Calvin, *Institutes* (1536), 189.
57. Calvin, *Institutes* (1536), 189.
58. Calvin, *Institutes*, 4.20.1.
59. Calvin, *Institutes*, 4.20.6.

104   Theology Made Practical

Eschatology

The way a person understands justification affects his or her expectations of a future hope. It is well known that Calvin proffered an underdeveloped eschatology, at least in his *Institutes*. Some people claim that he is a modern-day postmillennialist based on remarks in his commentary on Daniel and other Old Testament prophetic books. Seldom, however, is Calvin viewed as having a premillennial bent, probably because he so frequently lambasted the "chiliasts." I am happy to leave to other scholars the exact determination of his view but will make some remarks here.[60] My only insight into Calvin's eschatology and its affinity to his view on justification is to point out one trenchant and pastoral comment he made near the outset of this discussion. Calvin castigated Christians for being tied to earthly things and suggested that we would do better spending more time on our "heavenly life." Then he showed the pastoral advantages for raw doctrine: "Accordingly, he alone has fully profited in this gospel who has accustomed himself to continual meditation upon the blessed resurrection."[61]

In his commentary on Romans 8:30, Calvin had no qualms about tying justification to glorification. At one point, Calvin defined justification as spanning "the unremitted continuance of God's favor, from the time of our calling to the hour of our death," and asserted that since "Paul uses this word [justification] throughout the Epistle for *gratuitous imputation of righteousness* [emphasis added], there is no necessity for us to deviate from this meaning."[62]

Calvin, of course, did not create this logic of justification. He merely followed the apostle Paul in Romans 5:1, who wrote "*Therefore* being justified by faith" [emphasis added] and then listed several blessings, including peace, access, standing, and perseverance.

Observations and Conclusion

For Calvin, those who rightly understood justification would "turn aside from the contemplation of [their] own works and look solely upon God's mercy and Christ's perfection."[63] Accordingly, Calvin observed a certain

---

60. See Heinrich Quistorp, *Calvin's Doctrine of Last Things* (Eugene, Ore.: Wipf and Stock, 2009). Also, see Jim Llewellyn Codling, *Calvin: Ethics, Eschatology, and Education* (Newcastle: Cambridge Scholars Publishing, 2010); or Hank Bowen, "Calvin's Eschatological World and Life View," *Reformed Herald* 65, no. 8/9 (2009): 20–24.

61. Calvin, *Institutes*, 3.25.1.

62. Calvin, *Commentary*, on Rom. 8:30.

63. Calvin, *Institutes*, 3.11.16.

Appendixes to Calvin's View of Justification by Faith 105

"order of justification" consistent with his earlier definitions. This orderly design begins with God's "freely given goodness" to sinners, finding no good in the human subject. Then God "touches" sinners with this goodness, causing them to turn away from any sense of moral virtue. Sinners seek salvation wholly in God's mercy by faith and acknowledge that they have been reconciled to God. A sinner is justified because of Christ's mediatorial activity, and, once regenerated, "he ponders the everlasting righteousness laid up for him not in good works to which he inclines but in the sole righteousness of Christ."[64] Such apprehension leads properly to Christian liberty as an appendage and to many other aspects of true piety.

Without such justification and its appendixes, Calvin saw only a "strange monster," or salvation by works. Assurance of salvation is also assailed: "For when we rise up toward God [with works], that assurance of ours vanishes in a flash and dies."[65] In summary, for Calvin "this whole discussion will be foolish and weak unless every man admit his guilt before the Heavenly Judge, and concerned about his own acquittal, willingly cast himself down and confess his nothingness."[66] Such is the safeguard afforded by a correct understanding of justification.

Calvin's view of justification is tied even to humility, or the thought that we have nothing if we are left to ourselves. In fact, the "gateway to salvation," according to Calvin, does not lie open for us "unless we have laid aside all pride and taken upon ourselves perfect humility; secondly, that…this humility is an unfeigned submission of our heart."[67]

Two correlates of free justification are that (1) God's glory is undiminished; and (2) our consciences have rest and serenity. Drawing on the *Institutes* 3.13.3, Cornelis Venema has recently called attention to how assurance itself is tied, in Calvin's thinking, to a right view of justification.[68] Calvin expected that the believer's inability to discern the difference between justification and sanctification would dramatically reduce his assurance of faith. Moreover, Venema is helpful to note how sanctification, rightly following justification, liberates the believer from being tempted to present God (mercenary-like) with an overdue bill. For when sanctification is within the matrix of free

---

64. Calvin, *Institutes*, 3.11.16.
65. Calvin, *Institutes*, 3.12.2.
66. Calvin, *Institutes*, 3.12.1.
67. Calvin, *Institutes*, 3.12.6.
68. Venema, "Union with Christ," 111.

106 Theology Made Practical

justification, "it represents the free, Spirit-authored life of a forgiven sinner in the presence of his gracious heavenly Father."[69] The logic is that if sanctification is not buttressed upon God's prior pardon/acquittal, it invariably "becomes tainted with the infections of 'anxiety' before God ('Have I been sufficiently obedient?'), 'pride' ('Surely my good works contribute something to my acceptance with God.'), and a 'mercenary' spirit ('No doubt, my obedience will prove valuable since God will 'repay' me in kind.')."[70]

For Calvin, the divine righteousness that brings justification is not sufficiently presented unless God "alone be esteemed righteous, and communicate the free gift of righteousness to the undeserving."[71] Moreover, "God's glory is somewhat diminished if man glories in himself." Thus, Calvin's view of justification is strongly forensic—not ontological—and it results in the fruit of godliness. Justification and its appendixes, rightly understood, can permit no human glorying, and "man cannot without sacrilege claim for himself even a crumb of righteousness."[72] Calvin advised seeking peace of soul "solely in the anguish of Christ our Redeemer."[73] Most clearly he wrote, "Faith is something merely passive, bringing nothing of ours to the recovering of God's favor but receiving from Christ that which we lack."[74]

Calvin's doctrine of justification is clear from his writings. Thankfully, he confirmed his forensic view[75] repeatedly as he discussed explicit and implicit appendixes to justification—all of which form spokes that are connected to the hub on which our religion rises or falls. Moreover, his doctrine of justification overflows with numerous practical effects.

---

69. Venema, "Union with Christ," 113.

70. Venema, "Union with Christ," 113.

71. Calvin, *Institutes*, 3.13.1.

72. Calvin, *Institutes*, 3.13.2.

73. Calvin, *Institutes*, 3.13.4.

74. Calvin, *Institutes*, 3.13.5.

75. Calvin saw a distinction between how Paul uses the term "justification" ("the gratuitous imputation of righteousness before the tribunal of God") and what James means by it ("the manifestation of righteousness by the conduct, and that before men"). Calvin, *Commentary*, James 2:21.

PART 3:
Calvin's Pastoral and Political Theology

Calvin's Experiential Preaching

Joel R. Beeke

John Calvin embraced a high view of preaching. He called the preaching office "the most excellent of all things," commended by God that it might be held in the highest esteem. "There is nothing more notable or glorious in the church than the ministry of the gospel," he concluded.[1] In commenting on Isaiah 55:11, he said, "The Word goeth out of the mouth of God in such a manner that it likewise goeth out of the mouth of men; for God does not speak openly from heaven but employs men as his instruments."[2]

Calvin viewed preaching as God's normal means of salvation and benediction. He said that the Holy Spirit is the "internal minister" who uses the "external minister" in preaching the Word. The external minister "holds forth the vocal word and it is received by the ears," but the internal minister "truly communicates the thing proclaimed [which] is Christ."[3] Thus, God Himself speaks through the mouth of His servants by His Spirit. "Wherever the gospel is preached, it is as if God himself came into the midst of us," Calvin wrote.[4] Preaching is the instrument and the authority that the Spirit uses in His saving work of illuminating, converting, and sealing sinners. "There is…an inward efficacy of the Holy Spirit when he sheds forth his power upon hearers, that they may embrace a discourse [sermon] by faith."[5]

Calvin taught that the preached Word and the inner testimony of the Spirit should be distinguished but cannot be separated. Word and Spirit are joined together organically; without the Spirit, the preached Word only adds to the condemnation of unbelievers. On the other hand, Calvin admonished

---

1. Calvin, *Institutes*, 4.3.3.
2. Calvin, *Commentary*, on Isa. 55:11.
3. Calvin, *Tracts and Letters*, 1:173.
4. Calvin, *Commentary*, on Matt. 24:14.
5. Calvin, *Commentary*, on Ezek. 1:3.

110　　　　　　　　　　　Theology Made Practical

the radicals who accented the Spirit at the expense of the Word. Calvin said that only the spirit of Satan separates itself from the Word.[6]

This stress on preaching moved Calvin to be active on several fronts in Geneva. First, he showed his convictions through his example. Calvin preached from the New Testament on Sunday mornings, the Psalms on Sunday afternoons, and the Old Testament at 6:00 a.m. on one or two weekdays. Following this schedule during his last stay in Geneva from 1541 to 1564, Calvin preached nearly four thousand sermons, more than 170 sermons a year. On his deathbed, he spoke of his preaching as more significant than his writings.[7]

Second, Calvin often preached to his congregation about their responsibility to hear the Word of God aright. He taught his members in what spirit they should come to the sermon, what to listen for in preaching, and what was expected of those who hear. For Calvin, since all true preaching is biblical preaching and ministers are to preach only what God commands by opening His Word, people were to test sermons by this criterion. Unscriptural sermons were to be rejected; scriptural sermons were to be accepted and obeyed. Calvin's goal was that the people would grasp the importance of preaching, learn to desire preaching as a supreme blessing, and participate as actively in the sermon as the preacher himself. Their basic attitude should be one of "willingness to obey God completely and with no reserve," Calvin said.[8]

Calvin was motivated to stress profitable hearing of the Word because he believed that few people listen well. The following statement is a typical assessment of Calvin: "If the same sermon is preached, say, to a hundred people, twenty receive it with the ready obedience of faith, while the rest hold it valueless, or laugh, or hiss, or loathe it."[9] At least forty similar comments occur in Calvin's sermons (especially on Deuteronomy), commentaries (e.g., on Ps. 119:101; Acts 11:23), and the *Institutes* (especially 3.21 to 3.24). If profitable hearing was a problem in Calvin's day, how much more so today, when ministers have to compete for their congregation's attention with all the mass media that bombard them on a daily basis? Third, the Genevan system Calvin established emphasized preaching. The Genevan *Ordinances* stipulated that

---

6. Willem Balke, "Het Pietisme in Oostfriesland," *Theologia Reformata* 21 (1978): 320–27.

7. William Bouwsma, *John Calvin: A Sixteenth-Century Portrait* (New York: Oxford University Press, 1988), 29.

8. Leroy Nixon, *John Calvin: Expository Preacher* (Grand Rapids: Eerdmans, 1950), 65.

9. Calvin, *Institutes*, 3.24.12.

Calvin's Experiential Preaching

on Sundays sermons be preached in each of the three churches at daybreak and again at 9:00 a.m. After the children were catechized at noon, a third sermon was preached in each church at 3:00 p.m. Weekday sermons were also scheduled in the churches on Mondays, Wednesdays, and Fridays at varying hours so that they could be heard one after the other. That way people could take in three sermons in one day, if they so desired. By the time Calvin died, at least one sermon was preached in every church every day of the week.

Calvin's gifts and high view of preaching both theologically and in practice motivates us to study his sermons. In this chapter, I want to first briefly define experiential preaching, then step back to look in broad overview at how Calvin preached before focusing more narrowly on the question of how he preached experientially and how such preaching interfaced with corollary doctrines such as assurance of faith, election, and self-examination.

Experiential Preaching Defined

Experiential, or experimental, preaching addresses the vital matter of how Christians experience the truth of Christian doctrine in their lives. The term *experimental* comes from the Latin *experimentum*, meaning "trial." It is derived from the verb *experior*, meaning "to try, prove, or put to the test." That same verb can also mean "to find or know by experience," thus leading to the word *experientia*, meaning knowledge gained by experiment. Calvin used *experiential* and *experimental* interchangeably, since both words in biblical preaching indicate the need for measuring experienced knowledge against the touchstone of Scripture.

Experimental preaching stresses the need to know the great truths of the Word of God by experience. A working definition of experimental preaching is this: Experimental preaching seeks to explain in terms of biblical truth how spiritual matters ought to go, how they do go, and what is the goal of the Christian life. It aims to apply divine truth to the whole range of the believer's personal experience as well as to his relationships with family, the church, and the world around him.

Experimental preaching is discriminatory preaching. It clearly defines the difference between a Christian and a non-Christian, opening the kingdom of heaven to one and shutting it to the other. Discriminatory preaching offers the forgiveness of sins and eternal life to all who embrace Christ as Savior and Lord by true faith, but it also proclaims the wrath of God and His eternal condemnation upon those who are unbelieving, unrepentant, and

112 Theology Made Practical

unconverted. Such preaching teaches that unless our religion is experiential, we will perish—not because experience itself saves, but because the Christ who saves sinners must be experienced personally as the foundation upon which the house of our eternal hope is built (Matt. 7:22–27; 1 Cor. 1:30; 2:2).

Experimental preaching is applicatory. It applies the text to every aspect of a listener's life, promoting a religion that is truly a power and not mere form (2 Tim. 3:5). Robert Burns defined such religion as "Christianity brought home to men's business and bosoms" and said the principle on which it rests is "that Christianity should not only be known, and understood, and believed, but also felt, and enjoyed, and practically applied."[10]

Experiential preaching, then, teaches that the Christian faith must be experienced, tasted, and lived through the saving power of the Holy Spirit. It stresses the knowledge of scriptural truth, "which [is] able to make [us] wise unto salvation through faith which is in Christ Jesus" (2 Tim. 3:15). Specifically, such preaching teaches that Christ, who is the living Word (John 1:1) and the very embodiment of the truth, must be experientially known and embraced. It proclaims the need for sinners to experience who God is in His Son. As John 17:3 says, "And this is life eternal, that they might know thee the only true God, and Jesus Christ, whom thou hast sent." The word "know" in this text, as well as in other biblical usages, does not indicate a casual acquaintance but a deep, abiding relationship. For example, Genesis 4:1 uses the word "know" to suggest marital intimacy: "And Adam knew Eve his wife; and she conceived, and bare Cain." Experiential preaching stresses the intimate, personal knowledge of God in Christ.

Such knowledge is never divorced from Scripture. According to Isaiah 8:20, all our beliefs, including our experiences, must be tested against Holy Scripture. "If I can't find my experiences back in the Bible, they are not from the Lord but from the devil," Martin Luther once said. That is really what the word "experimental" intends to convey. Just as scientific experiment tests a hypothesis against a body of evidence, so experimental preaching involves examining Christian experience in the light of the teaching of the Word of God.

---

10. Robert Burns, introduction to the *Works of Thomas Halyburton* (London: Thomas Tegg, 1835), xiv–xv.

Calvin's Preaching

Calvin preached serially from various Bible books, striving to show clearly the meaning of a passage and how it should impact the lives of his hearers. Much like a homily in style, his sermons have no divisions or points other than what the text dictates. As Paul Fuhrman writes, "They are properly homilies as in the ancient church: expositions of Bible passages [in] the light of grammar and history, [providing] application to the hearers' life situations."[11]

Calvin was a careful exegete, an able expositor, and a faithful applier of the Word. His goals in preaching were to glorify God, to cause believers to grow in the grace and knowledge of Christ Jesus, and to unite sinners with Christ, so "that men be reconciled to God by the free remission of sins."[12] This aim of saving sinners blended seamlessly with his emphasis on scriptural doctrines. He wrote that ministers are "keepers of the truth of God; that is to say, of His precious image, of that which concerneth the majesty of the doctrine of our salvation, and the life of the world."[13] Calvin frequently admonished ministers to keep this treasure safe by handling the Word of God carefully, always striving for pure, biblical teaching. That did not exclude bringing contemporary events to bear on people's lives, however. As current events related to the passage being expounded, Calvin felt free to apply his sermon to those events in practical, experiential, and moralistic ways.[14]

The image of the preacher as a teacher moved Calvin to emphasize the importance of careful sermon preparation. How he accomplished that himself with his frequency of preaching and heavy workload remains a mystery, but he obviously studied the text to be expounded with great care and read widely what others had said about it. He preached extemporaneously, relying heavily on his remarkable memory. He often declared that the power of God could best be exhibited in extemporaneous delivery.

That is why there are no extant manuscripts of Calvin's sermons. As far as we know, he never wrote out any sermons. The only reason that we have more than two thousand of Calvin's sermons is that Denis Raguenier wrote

---

11. Paul T. Fuhrmann, "Calvin, Expositor of Scripture," *Interpretation* 6, no. 2 (April 1952): 191.

12. Calvin, *Commentary*, on John 20:23.

13. John Calvin, *The Mystery of Godliness* (Grand Rapids: Eerdmans, 1950), 122.

14. A. Mitchell Hunter, "Calvin as a Preacher," *Expository Times* 30, no. 12 (September 1919): 563.

114   Theology Made Practical

them down in shorthand from 1549 until his death in 1560.[15] Apparently, Calvin never intended for them to be published.

The average length of texts covered in each of Calvin's sermons was four or five verses in the Old Testament and two or three verses in the New Testament. His sermons were fairly short for his day (perhaps due in part to his asthmatic condition), probably averaging thirty-five to forty minutes. He is reported to have spoken "deliberately, often with long pauses to allow people to think," though others say that he must have spoken rapidly to complete his sermon on time.[16]

Calvin's style of preaching was plain and clear. In a sermon titled "Pure Preaching of the Word," Calvin wrote, "We must shun all unprofitable babbling, and stay ourselves upon plain teaching, which is forcible."[17] Rhetoric for its own sake or vain babbling must be shunned, though true eloquence, when subjected to the simplicity of the gospel, is to be coveted. When Joachim Westphal charged Calvin with "babbling" in his sermons, Calvin replied that he stuck to the main point of the text and practiced "cautious brevity."[18]

Calvin's sermons abound with application throughout. In some cases, application consumes more time than exposition. Short, pungent applications, sprinkled throughout his sermons, constantly urge, exhort, and invite sinners to act in obedience to God's Word. "We have not come to the preaching merely to hear what we do not know, but to be incited to do our duty," Calvin said to his flock.[19]

T. H. L. Parker suggests that Calvin's sermons follow a certain pattern:

1. Prayer

2. Recapitulation of previous sermon

3a. Exegesis and exposition of the first point

3b. Application of the first point and exhortation to obedience of duty

4a. Exegesis and exposition of the second point

---

15. John H. Gerstner, "Calvin's Two-Voice Theory of Preaching," *Reformed Review* 13, no. 2 (1959): 22.

16. Philip Vollmer, *John Calvin: Theologian, Preacher, Educator, Statesman* (Richmond, Va.: Presbyterian Committee of Publication, 1909), 124; George Johnson, "Calvinism and Preaching," *Evangelical Quarterly* 4, no. 3 (July 1932): 249.

17. Calvin, *Mystery of Godliness*, 55.

18. As quoted in John C. Bowman, "Calvin as a Preacher," *Reformed Church Review* 56 (1909): 251–52, cited in Gerstner, "Calvin's Two-Voice Theory of Preaching," 18.

19. *CR*, 79:783, as quoted in Gerstner, "Calvin's Two-Voice Theory of Preaching," 20.

4b. Application of the second point and exhortation to obedience of duty

5. Closing prayer, which contains a brief, implicit summary of the sermon.[20]

John Gerstner points out that, though this was the structural order that Calvin often did follow and probably intended to follow, he frequently departed from it because "he was so eager to get at the application that he often introduced it in the midst of the exposition. In other words, application was the dominant element in Calvin's preaching, to which all else was subordinated."[21]

Calvin's Stress on Piety in Preaching

Calvin understood true religion as fellowship between God and man. Calvin called the part of the fellowship that moves from God to man "revelation"; he called the part of the fellowship that moves from man to God, which involves man's obedient response, "piety." Such piety functions through God's grace by faith and involves such devout acts as childlike trust, humble adoration, godly fear, and undying love. Calvin's applications in preaching often aimed for exciting these kinds of graces.

For Calvin, the goal of the preacher is to promote such piety, even as the preacher himself must remain acutely aware that the listener cannot produce this piety himself. He is only a recipient of such piety by the grace of the Holy Spirit and is not the author of it. Nevertheless, the Spirit accompanies the Word with this divine gift of pious grace.

Calvin's piety, like his theology, is inseparable from the knowledge of God. The true knowledge of God results in pious activity that stretches its goal beyond personal salvation to embrace the glory of God. Where God's glory is not served, piety cannot exist. This compels discipline, obedience, and love in every sphere of the believer's life. For Calvin, the law gives love its mandate and content to act, to obey God out of discipline, and so to live to His glory. Indeed, love is the fulfilling of the law. Thus, for Calvin, true piety was both a vertical (Godward) and horizontal (manward) relationship of love and law.

---

20. T. H. L. Parker, *The Oracles of God: An Introduction to the Preaching of John Calvin* (London: Lutterworth, 1947), 70–71.

21. Gerstner, "Calvin's Two-Voice Theory of Preaching," 22.

116 Theology Made Practical

Grace and law, therefore, are both prominent in Calvin's theology and preaching. Keeping the law is especially important because of its supreme purpose to lead us to consecrate our entire lives to God. Lionel Greve writes, "Grace has priority in such a way that Calvin's piety may be considered as a quality of life and response to God's grace that transcended law but at the same time included it." He concludes, "Calvin's piety may be termed 'transcendent piety.' It transcends the creature because it is founded in grace but yet includes the creature as he is the subject of faithfulness. He is the subject in such a way that his piety is never primarily for his welfare…. The general movement of Calvin's piety is always Godward. The benefits of God's goodness are merely byproducts of the main purpose—glorifying God."[22]

Calvin's combined emphases on God's glory and the believer's Spirit-worked piety led him to a theology of experience. Experience was a theological and spiritual necessity for him. That is quite understandable, given his emphasis on the Spirit's work in the life of the believer—an emphasis that earned him the title "theologian of the Holy Spirit." So we ought not be surprised that his pneumatological, experiential emphasis of piety also spilled over into his sermons. The question is not whether Calvin was an experiential preacher—that is obvious from his sermons, commentaries, and even in his *Institutes*. The question is, What role does experience (*experientia*) play in his theology and preaching?

Calvin and Experience

Calvin valued experience as long as it was rooted in Scripture and sprang out of the living reality of faith. He repeatedly defined the experience of believers as beyond verbal expression. For example, he wrote, "Such, then, is a conviction that requires no reasons, such a knowledge with which the best reason agrees—in which the mind truly reposes, more securely and constantly than in any reasons: such finally, a feeling that can be born only of heavenly revelation. I speak of nothing other than what each believer experiences within himself—though my words fall far beneath a just explanation of the matter."[23] Calvin went on to say that believers' recognition of God "consists more in living experience than in vain and high-flown speculations." But

---

22. Lionel Greve, "Freedom and Discipline in the Theology of John Calvin, William Perkins, and John Wesley: An Examination of the Origin and Nature of Pietism" (PhD diss., Hartford Seminary Foundation, 1976), 149.

23. Calvin, *Institutes*, 1.7.5.

Calvin's Experiential Preaching

then he hastened to add: "Indeed, with experience as our teacher, we find God just as he declares himself in his Word."[24]

False experience fabricates a god that does not square with the Scripture, but true experience always flows out of the truths of Scripture and underscores them. Holy Scripture is consistent with sacred, Spirit-worked experience, since Calvin understood that the Bible is not a book of abstract or scholastic doctrines but a book of doctrines that is rooted in real, experiential, daily living. Thus, experience plays an important role in Calvin's exegesis. Willem Balke writes, "Experience can serve as a hermeneutical key in the explanation of the Scriptures. The Bible places us in the center of the struggle of faith, *coram Deo*, and therefore Calvin can recommend himself as exegete as he does in the introduction to the Commentary on the Psalms (1557) since he has experienced what the Bible testifies."[25]

Calvin viewed his multifaceted experiences as a Reformer as an important qualification for exegeting and preaching God's Word. Though he related his experiential qualification particularly to the Psalms—since the Psalms pertain best to the suffering people of God and are, as he called them, "an anatomy of all parts of the soul"[26]—all his sermons and commentaries reveal that he believed no book of Scripture could be reduced to mere doctrine.

Though Calvin ascribed a large place to experience in his exegesis and preaching, he understood that experience has significant limitations. When divorced from the Word, experience is altogether unreliable and always incomplete. Calvin concluded that concentrating on the depths of the human heart, which always remain a focal point for the mystic, is not the way to God. Rather, he agreed with Luther that the only way to God is by Word-centered faith. The believer does not learn to know God's will from "*nuda experientia* [bare experience]," Calvin said, but only through the testimony of Scripture.[27]

If Scripture is not the foundation of our experience of faith, Calvin said, we will be left only with vague feelings that have no anchor. True faith, however, anchors itself in the Word. We ought not measure the presence of God

---

24. Calvin, *Institutes*, 1.10.2.

25. Willem Balke, "The Word of God and *Experientia* according to Calvin," in *Calvinus Ecclesiae Doctor*, ed. W. H. Neuser (Kampen: Kok, 1978), 22. Much of what I write in this and the following subheading is a summary and fine-tuning of Balke's helpful effort to grapple with Calvin's understanding of experience in the life of the believer.

26. Calvin, *Commentary*, preface to Psalms, 1:xxxvii.

27. *CO*, 31:424.

118   Theology Made Practical

in our lives by our experience, for that would soon bring us to despair. "If we should measure out the help of God according to our feelings," Calvin wrote, "our faith would soon waver and we would have no courage or hope."[28]

Thus, Calvin is careful not to be an experientialist—that is, one who frequently calls attention to his own experiences in a rather mystical manner. He well understands that experience is to be defined by the testimony of the written Word.

Calvin avoided both experientialism and dry scholasticism. He did not see the Bible as a collection of doctrines but rather viewed biblical doctrines as "embedded in the life and faith of the church and of the individual, in the natural habitat of the verification of faith in Christian and ecclesiastical existence."[29]

Experientia Fide or *Sensus Fide*

The experience or sense of faith (*experientia fide* or *sensus fide*), according to Calvin, is also inseparable from the ministry of the Holy Spirit. The Spirit renews the very core of man. That work involves illumination and sealing; the Spirit's illumination of the mind and His efficacious work in the heart coalesce. The Spirit's sealing work certifies the authority of the Word and the reality of the Spirit's saving work. It promotes confidence in God's promises of mercy and experience of them. This doctrine, Calvin said, is "not of the tongue, but of life. It is not apprehended by the understanding and memory alone, as other disciplines are, but it is received only when it possesses the whole soul, and finds a seat and resting place in the inmost affection of the heart."[30]

Such *experientia fide* is thus not a part of the believer's ability, but it is the creative effect of the Spirit, who uses the Word. It contains both objective and subjective truth. The Spirit testifies both in the Word of God and in the heart of the believer, and the believer hears and experiences its reality. Through the Spirit's objective and subjective testimony, the believer is persuaded experientially of the absolute truth of God and of His Word. Being made willing by the powerful operations of the Spirit, the heart, will, and emotions all respond in faith and obedience to the triune God. Since the Spirit is the Spirit of the Son, whose great task it is to lead the believer to

---

28. *CO*, 31:103.
29. Balke, "Word of God and *Experientia* according to Calvin," 22.
30. Calvin, *Institutes*, 3.6.4.

Calvin's Experiential Preaching

Christ and through Him to the Father, the center of faith's experience is, as John called it, having "fellowship...with the Father, and with his Son" (1 John 1:3). True experience always leads, then, to true communion and to *praxis pietatis*.

This is not to say that true experience is always that easily dissected and understood. The experience of faith contains numerous paradoxes. For example, a paradox exists in the life of faith when we are called to believe that God is still with us when we feel that He has deserted us. Or, how can we believe that God is favorably inclined to us when He strips us at times of all consciousness of that favor and seems to providentially postpone fulfilling His merciful promises?[31]

The believer can experience such apparent contradictions on a daily basis, Calvin said. He can feel forsaken of God, even when he knows deep within that he is not (Isa. 49:14–16). These conflicting experiences transpire within one heart and seem, like hope and fear, to cancel each other out. If fear gets the upper hand, Calvin wrote, we ought to simply throw ourselves wholly on the promises of God.[32] Those promises will give us courage to go on in spite of temptations to doubt. Moreover, it is especially when we acknowledge God as present by faith, though we cannot see or feel His goodness and power, that we truly honor His lordship and His Word.[33] To believe in God when experience seems to annul His promises takes great faith, but it is precisely this experience of faith that enables believers to remain undisturbed when their entire world seems to be shaken.[34]

Experience and Assurance of Faith

Calvin's doctrine of assurance reaffirmed the basic tenets of Martin Luther and Ulrich Zwingli and disclosed emphases of his own. Like Luther and Zwingli, Calvin said that faith is never merely assent (*assensus*) but involves both knowledge (*cognitio*) and trust (*fiducia*). Faith rests firmly upon God's Word; faith always says amen to the Scriptures.[35] Hence, assurance must be

---

31. *CO*, 31, 344.
32. *CO*, 31, 548.
33. *CO*, 31, 525.
34. *CO*, 31, 703; 32:194.
35. Calvin, *Commentary*, on John 3:33; Ps. 43:3. Cf. K. Exalto, *De Zekerheid des Geloofs bij Calvijn* (Apeldoorn: Willem de Zwijgerstichting, 1978), 24. Edward Dowey mistakenly dichotomizes the Scriptures and assurance when he asserts that the center of Calvin's doctrine of faith is assurance rather than the authority of the Scriptures. For Calvin, the separation of

120   Theology Made Practical

sought *in* the Word and flows *out of* the Word.[36] Assurance is as inseparable from the Word as sunbeams are from the sun.

Faith and assurance are also inseparable from *Christ and the promise of Christ*, for the totality of the written Word is the living Word, Jesus Christ, in whom all God's promises are "yea and amen."[37] Calvin made much of the promises of God as the ground of assurance, for these promises are based on the nature of God, who cannot lie. The promises are fulfilled by Christ; therefore Calvin directed sinners to Christ and to the promises as if they were synonyms.[38] Since faith takes its character from the promise on which it rests, faith takes on the infallible stamp of God's own Word. Consequently, faith possesses assurance in its own nature. Assurance, certainty, trust: such is the essence of faith.

More specifically, Calvin argued that faith involves something more than objectively believing the promises of God; it involves personal, subjective assurance. In believing God's promises to sinners, the true believer recognizes and celebrates that God is gracious and benevolent to him in particular. Faith is an assured knowledge "of God's benevolence toward *us*... revealed to *our* minds...sealed upon *our* hearts."[39] Calvin wrote, "Here, indeed, is the hinge on which faith turns: that we do not regard the promises of mercy that God offers as true only outside ourselves, but not at all in us; rather that we make them ours by inwardly embracing them."[40]

Thus, as Robert Kendall notes, Calvin repeatedly described faith as "certainty (*certitudino*), a firm conviction (*solido persuasio*), assurance (*securitas*), firm assurance (*solida securitas*), and full assurance (*plena securitas*)."[41] While faith consists of knowledge, it is also marked by heartfelt assurance that is "a sure and secure possession of those things which God has promised us."[42]

---

the Word of God from assurance is unthinkable. *The Knowledge of God in Calvin's Theology* (New York: Columbia University Press, 1965), 182.

36. Calvin, *Commentary*, on Matt. 8:13; John 4:22.

37. Calvin, *Commentary*, on Gen. 15:6; Luke 2:21.

38. Calvin, *Institutes*, 3.2.32; *Commentary*, on Rom. 4:3, 18; Heb. 11:7, 11.

39. Calvin, *Institutes*, 3.2.7 (emphasis added).

40. Calvin, *Institutes*, 3.2.16; cf. 3.2.42.

41. Robert T. Kendall, *Calvin and English Calvinism to 1649* (New York: Oxford University Press, 1979), 19; cf. Calvin, *Institutes*, 3.2.6, 3.2.16, 3.2.22.

42. Calvin, *Institutes*, 3.2.41; 3.2.14.

Calvin's Experiential Preaching

Calvin also emphasized throughout his commentaries that assurance is integral to faith.[43] In expounding 2 Corinthians 13:5, Calvin even stated that those who doubt their union to Christ are reprobates: "[Paul] declares, that all are *reprobates*, who doubt whether they profess Christ and are a part of His body. Let us, therefore, reckon *that* alone to be right faith, which leads us to repose in safety in the favour of God, with no wavering opinion, but with a firm and steadfast assurance."[44]

Throughout his lofty doctrine of faith, however, Calvin repeated these themes: unbelief dies hard; assurance is often contested by doubt; severe temptations, wrestlings, and strife are normative; Satan and the flesh assault faith; trust in God is hedged with fear.[45] Calvin freely acknowledged that faith is not retained without a severe struggle against unbelief, nor is it left untainted by doubt and anxiety. He wrote: "Unbelief is, in all men, always mixed with faith.... For unbelief is so deeply rooted in our hearts, and we are so inclined to it, that not without hard struggle is each one able to persuade himself of what all confess with the mouth, namely, that God is faithful. Especially when it comes to reality itself, every man's wavering uncovers hidden weakness."[46]

In expounding John 20:3, Calvin seemed to contradict his assertion that true believers know themselves to be such when he testified that the disciples had faith without awareness of it as they approached the empty tomb: "There being so little faith, or rather almost no faith, both in the disciples and in the women, it is astonishing that they had so great zeal; and, indeed, it is not possible that religious feelings led them to seek Christ. *Some seed of faith, therefore, remained in their hearts, but quenched for a time, so that they were not aware of having what they had.* Thus the Spirit of God often works in the elect in a secret manner."[47]

This prompts us to ask how Calvin can say that faith is characterized by full assurance, yet still allow for the kind of faith that lacks assurance. The two statements appear antithetical. Assurance is free from doubt, yet not free. It does not hesitate, yet can hesitate. It contains security, but may be beset with anxiety. The faithful have assurance, yet waver and tremble.

---

43. Calvin, *Commentary*, on Acts 2:29; 1 Cor. 2:12.
44. Calvin, *Commentary*, on 2 Cor. 13:5.
45. Calvin, *Institutes*, 3.2.7; *Commentary*, on Matt. 8:25; Luke 2:40.
46. Calvin, *Institutes*, 3.2.4, 3.2.15.
47. Calvin, *Commentary*, on John 20:3; Cf. Calvin, *Institutes*, 3.2.12 (emphasis added).

122 Theology Made Practical

Calvin used at least four principles to address this complex issue. Each helps make sense of his apparent contradictions.

First, consider Calvin's need to distinguish between *the definition of faith* and *the reality of the believer's experience*. After explaining faith in the *Institutes* as embracing "great assurance," Calvin wrote:

> Still, someone will say: "Believers *experience* something far different: In recognizing the grace of God toward themselves they are not only tried by disquiet, which often comes upon them, but they are repeatedly shaken by gravest terrors. For so violent are the temptations that trouble their minds as not to seem quite compatible with that certainty of faith." Accordingly, we shall have to solve this difficulty if we wish the above-stated doctrine to stand. Surely, while we teach that faith *ought* to be certain and assured, we cannot imagine any certainty that is not tinged with doubt, or any assurance that is not assailed.[48]

In short, Calvin distinguished between the *ought to* of faith and the *is* of faith in daily life. His definition of faith serves as a recommendation about how believers ought "habitually and properly to think of faith."[49] Faith should always aim at full assurance, even if it cannot reach perfect assurance in experience. In principle, faith gains the victory (1 John 5:4); in practice, it recognizes that it has not yet fully apprehended (Phil. 3:12–13).

Nevertheless, the practice of faith validates faith that trusts in the Word. Calvin was not as interested in experiences as he was in validating Word-grounded faith. Experience confirms faith, Calvin said. Faith "requires full and fixed certainty, such as men are wont to have from things experienced and proved."[50]

Thus, bare experience is not Calvin's goal, but experience grounded in the Word, flowing out of the fulfillment of the Word. Experimental knowledge of the Word is essential.[51] For Calvin, two kinds of knowledge are needed: knowledge by faith (*scientia fidei*) that is received from the Word, "though it is not yet fully revealed," and the knowledge of experience

---

48. Calvin, *Institutes*, 3.2.17 (emphasis added).
49. Paul Helm, *Calvin and the Calvinists* (Edinburgh: Banner of Truth Trust, 1982), 26.
50. Calvin, *Institutes*, 3.2.15.
51. Calvin, *Institutes*, 1.7.5.

Calvin's Experiential Preaching

(*scientia experentiae*) "springing from the fulfilling of the Word."[52] The Word of God is primary to the former and to the latter, for experience teaches us to know God as He declares Himself to be in His Word.[53] Experience not consonant with Scripture is never an experience of true faith. In short, though the believer's experience of true faith is far weaker than he desires, there is an essential unity in the Word between faith's perception (the *ought-to* dimension of faith) and experience (the *is* dimension of faith).

The second principle that helps us understand Calvin's tension in assurance of faith is *flesh versus spirit*. Calvin wrote:

> It is necessary to return to that division of flesh and spirit which we have mentioned elsewhere. It most clearly reveals itself at this point. Therefore the godly heart feels in itself a division because it is partly imbued with sweetness from its recognition of the divine goodness, partly grieves in bitterness from an awareness of its calamity; partly rests upon the promise of the gospel, partly trembles at the evidence of its own iniquity; partly rejoices at the expectation of life, partly shudders at death. This variation arises from imperfection of faith, since in the course of the present life it never goes so well with us that we are wholly cured of the disease of unbelief and entirely filled and possessed by faith. Hence arise those conflicts, when unbelief, which reposes in the remains of the flesh, rises up to attack the faith that has been inwardly conceived.[54]

Like Luther, Calvin set the *ought to/is* dichotomy against the backdrop of spirit/flesh warfare.[55] Christians experience this spirit/flesh tension acutely because it is instigated by the Holy Spirit.[56] The paradoxes that permeate experiential faith (e.g., Romans 7:14–25 in the classical Reformed interpretation) find resolution in this tension: "So then with the mind [spirit] I myself serve the law of God; but with the flesh the law of sin" (v. 25).

---

52. Balke, "The Word of God and *Experientia* according to Calvin," in *Calvinus Ecclesiae Doctor*, 25. Cf. Charles Partee, "Calvin and Experience," *Scottish Journal of Theology* 26 (1973): 169–81; Balke, "Word of God and *Experientia* according to Calvin," 23–24.

53. Calvin, *Institutes*, 1.10.2.

54. Calvin, *Institutes*, 3.2.18.

55. Cf. C. A. Hall, *With the Spirit's Sword: The Drama of Spiritual Warfare in the Theology of John Calvin* (Richmond, Va.: John Knox Press, 1970).

56. Cf. Victor A. Shepherd, *The Nature and Function of Saving Faith in the Theology of John Calvin* (Macon, Ga.: Mercer University Press, 1983), 24–28.

124 Theology Made Practical

Calvin set the sure consolation of the spirit side by side with the imperfection of the flesh, for these are what the believer finds within himself. Since the final victory of the spirit over the flesh will be fulfilled only in Christ, the Christian will perpetually struggle in this life. His spirit fills him "with delight in recognizing the divine goodness" even as his flesh activates his natural proneness to unbelief.[57] He is beset with "daily struggles of conscience" as long as the vestiges of the flesh remain.[58] The believer's "present state is far short of the glory of God's children," Calvin wrote. "Physically, we are dust and shadow, and death is always before our eyes. We are exposed to a thousand miseries…so that we always find a hell within us."[59] While still in the flesh, the believer may even be tempted to doubt the whole gospel.

Even as the believer is tormented with fleshly doubts, his spirit trusts God's mercy by invoking Him in prayer and by resting upon Him through the sacraments. By these means, faith gains the upper hand over unbelief. "Faith ultimately triumphs over those difficulties which besiege and… imperil it. [Faith is like] a palm tree [that] strives against every burden and raises itself upward."[60]

In short, Calvin taught that from *the spirit* of the believer rise hope, joy, and assurance; from *the flesh*, fear, doubt, and disillusionment. Though spirit and flesh operate simultaneously, imperfection and doubt are integral only to the flesh, not to faith; the works of the flesh often *attend* faith but do not *mix* with it. The believer may lose spiritual battles along the pathway of life, but he will not lose the ultimate war against the flesh.

Third, despite the tensions between definition and experience, spirit and flesh, Calvin maintained that faith and assurance are not so mixed with unbelief that the believer is left with probability rather than certainty.[61] The smallest germ of faith contains assurance in its essence, even when the believer is not always able to grasp this assurance due to weakness. The Christian may be tossed about with doubt and perplexity, but the seed of faith, implanted by the Spirit, cannot perish. Precisely because it is the Spirit's seed, faith retains assurance. This assurance increases and decreases in

---

57. Calvin, *Institutes*, 3.2.18, 3.2.20.
58. Calvin, *Commentary*, on John 13:9.
59. Calvin, *Commentary*, on 1 John 3:2.
60. Calvin, *Institutes*, 3.2.17.
61. Cf. Cornelis Graafland, *De Zekerheid van het geloof: Een onderzoek naar de geloofbeschouwing van enige vertegenwoordigers van reformatie en nadere reformatie* (Wageningen: H. Veenman & Zonen, 1961), 31n.

Calvin's Experiential Preaching

proportion to the rise and decline of faith's exercises, but the seed of faith can never be destroyed. Calvin said: "The root of faith can never be torn from the godly breast, but clings so fast to the inmost parts that, however faith seems to be shaken or to bend this way or that, its light is never so extinguished or snuffed out that it does not at least lurk as it were beneath the ashes."[62]

Calvin thus explained "weak assurance in terms of weak faith without thereby weakening the link between faith and assurance."[63] Assurance is normative but varies in degree and constancy in the believer's consciousness of it. So, in responding to weak assurance, a pastor should not deny the organic tie between faith and assurance but should urge the pursuit of stronger faith through the use of the means of grace in dependence upon the Spirit.

Experience, the Trinity, and Election

Through a fourth sweeping principle—namely, a *Trinitarian framework* for the doctrine of faith and assurance, Calvin spurred the doubt-prone believer onward. As surely as the election of the Father must prevail over the works of Satan, the righteousness of the Son over the sinfulness of the believer, and the assuring witness of the Spirit over the soul's infirmities—so certainly assured faith shall and must conquer unbelief.

Calvin's arrangement of book 3 of the *Institutes* reveals the movement of the grace of faith from God to man and man to God. The grace of faith is from the Father, in the Son, and through the Spirit, by which, in turn, the believer is brought into fellowship with the Son by the Spirit and consequently is reconciled to and walks in fellowship with the Father.

For Calvin, a complex set of factors establishes assurance, not the least of which is the Father's election and preservation in Christ. Hence he writes that "predestination duly considered does not shake faith, but rather affords the best confirmation of it,"[64] especially when viewed in the context of calling: "The firmness of our election is joined to our calling [and] is another means of establishing our assurance. For all whom [Christ] receives, the Father is said to have entrusted and committed to Him to keep to eternal life."[65]

---

62. Calvin, *Institutes*, 3.2.21.
63. A. N. S. Lane, "The Quest for the Historical Calvin," *Evangelical Quarterly* 55 (1983): 103.
64. Calvin, *Institutes*, 3.24.9.
65. Calvin, *Institutes*, 3.24.6.

126 Theology Made Practical

Decretal election is a sure foundation for preservation and assurance; it is not coldly causal. Gordon Keddie writes: "Election is never seen, in Calvin, in a purely deterministic light, in which God...is viewed as 'a frightening idol' of 'mechanistic deterministic causality' and Christian experience is reduced to either cowering passivity or frantic activism, while waiting some 'revelation' of God's hidden decree for one's self. For Calvin, as indeed in Scripture, election does not threaten, but rather undergirds, the certainty of salvation."[66]

Such a foundation is possible only in a Christ-centered context; hence Calvin's constant emphasis on Christ as the mirror of election "wherein we must, and without self-deception may, contemplate our own election."[67] Election turns the believer's eyes from the hopelessness of his inability to meet any conditions of salvation to focus on the hope of Jesus Christ as God's pledge of undeserved love and mercy.[68]

Through union with Christ, "the assurance of salvation becomes real and effective as the assurance of election."[69] Christ becomes ours in fulfillment of God's determination to redeem and resurrect us. Consequently, we ought not to think of Christ as "standing afar off, and not dwelling in us."[70] Since Christ is for us, to contemplate Him truly is to see Him forming in us what He desires to give us, Himself above all. God has made Himself "little in Christ," Calvin stated, so that we might comprehend and flee to Christ alone who can pacify our consciences.[71] Faith must begin, rest, and end in Christ. "True faith is so contained in Christ, that it neither knows, nor desires to know, anything beyond Him," Calvin said.[72] Therefore, "we ought not to separate Christ from ourselves or ourselves from Him."[73]

---

66. Gordon J. Keddie, "'Unfallible Certenty of the Pardon of Sinne and Life Everlasting': The Doctrine of Assurance in the Theology of William Perkins," *Evangelical Quarterly* 48 (1976): 231; cf. G. C. Berkouwer, *Divine Election*, trans. Hugo Bekker (Grand Rapids: Eerdmans, 1960), 10–12.

67. Calvin, *Institutes*, 3.24.5; cf. John Calvin, *Sermons on the Epistle to the Ephesians* (repr., Edinburgh: Banner of Truth Trust, 1973), 47; John Calvin, *Sermons from Job* (Grand Rapids: Eerdmans, 1952), 41–42; and *CO*, 8:318–21; 9:757.

68. Calvin, *Institutes*, 3.24.6; and William H. Chalker, "Calvin and Some Seventeenth Century English Calvinists" (PhD diss., Duke University, 1961), 66.

69. Wilhelm Niesel, *The Theology of Calvin*, trans. Harold Knight (Grand Rapids: Baker, 1980), 196. Cf. Calvin, *Institutes*, 3.1.1; and Shepherd, *Nature and Function of Saving Faith*, 51.

70. Calvin, *Institutes*, 3.2.24.

71. Calvin, *Commentary*, on 1 Peter 1:20.

72. Calvin, *Commentary*, on Eph. 4:13.

73. Calvin, *Institutes*, 3.2.24.

Calvin's Experiential Preaching

In this Christological manner, Calvin reduced the distance between God's objective decree of election from the believer's subjective lack of assurance that he is elect. For Calvin, election answers rather than raises the question of assurance. In Christ, the believer sees his election; in the gospel, he hears of his election.

The question remains, however: How do the elect enjoy communion with Christ, and how does that produce assurance? Calvin's answer is pneumatological: the Holy Spirit applies Christ and His benefits to the hearts and lives of guilty, elect sinners, through which they are assured by saving faith that Christ belongs to them and they to Him. The Holy Spirit especially confirms within them the reliability of God's promises in Christ. Thus, personal assurance is never divorced from the election of the Father, the redemption of the Son, the application of the Spirit, and the instrumental means of saving faith.

The Holy Spirit has an enormous role in the application of redemption, Calvin said. As personal comforter and seal, the Holy Spirit assures the believer of his gracious adoption: "The Spirit of God gives us such a testimony, that when he is our guide and teacher our spirit is made sure of the adoption of God; for our mind of itself, without the preceding testimony of the Spirit, could not convey to us this assurance."[74] The Holy Spirit's work underlies all assurance of salvation without detracting from the role of Christ, for the Spirit is the Spirit *of Christ* who assures the believer by leading him to Christ and His benefits, and by working out those benefits within him.[75]

Experience and Self-Examination

Nevertheless, Calvin was acutely aware that a person may think that the Father has entrusted him to Christ when such is not the case. It is one thing to underscore Christ's task in the Trinitarian, salvific economy as the recipient and guardian of the elect; the center, author, and foundation of election; the guarantee, promise, and mirror of the believer's election and salvation. But it is quite another to know how to inquire about whether a person has been joined to Christ by a true faith. Many appear to be Christ's who are estranged from Him. Said Calvin: "It daily happens that those who seemed

---

74. Calvin, *Commentary*, on Rom. 8:16. Cf. *Commentary*; on John 7:37–39; Acts 2:4; 3:8; 5:32; 13:48; 16:14; 23:11; Rom. 8:15–17; 1 Cor. 2:10–13; 2 Cor. 1:21–22; Gal. 3:2, 4:6; Eph. 1:13–14, 4:30; *Institutes*, 3.2.11, 34, 41; commentary on); Calvin, *Tracts and Letters*, 3:253–54; and Parratt, "Witness of the Holy Spirit," 161–68.

75. Calvin, *Institutes*, 3.2.34.

128   Theology Made Practical

to be Christ's fall away from him again.... Such persons never cleaved to Christ with the heartfelt trust in which certainty of salvation has, I say, been established for us."[76]

Calvin never preached to console his flock into false assurance of salvation.[77] Many scholars minimize Calvin's emphasis on the need for a subjective, experiential realization of faith and election by referring to Calvin's practice of approaching his congregation as saved hearers. They misunderstand. Though Calvin practiced what he called "a judgment of charity" (i.e., addressing as saved those church members who maintain a commendable, external lifestyle), he also frequently asserted that only a minority receive the preached Word with saving faith. He said: "For though all, without exception, to whom God's Word is preached, are taught, yet scarce one in ten so much as tastes it; yea, scarce one in a hundred profits to the extent of being enabled, thereby, to proceed in a right course to the end."[78]

For Calvin, much that resembles faith lacks a saving character. He thus speaks of faith that is unformed, implicit, temporary, illusionary, false, a shadow-type, transitory, and under a cloak of hypocrisy.[79] Self-deception is a real possibility, Calvin said. Because the reprobate often feel something much like the faith of the elect,[80] self-examination is essential. He wrote: "Let us learn to examine ourselves, and to search whether those interior marks by which God distinguishes his children from strangers belong to us, viz., the living root of piety and faith."[81] Happily, the truly saved are delivered from self-deception through proper examination directed by the Holy Spirit. Calvin said: "In the meantime, the faithful are taught to examine themselves

---

76. Calvin, *Institutes*, 3.24.7.

77. Cf. Cornelis Graafland, "'Waarheid in het Binnenste': Geloofszekerheid bij Calvijn en de Nadere Reformatie," in *Een Vaste Burcht*, ed. K. Exalto (Kampen: Kok, 1989), 65–67.

78. Calvin, *Commentary*, on Ps. 119:101.

79. Calvin, *Institutes*, 3.2.3, 5, 10–11. For Calvin on temporary faith, see David Foxgrover, "'Temporary Faith' and the Certainty of Salvation," *Calvin Theological Journal* 15 (1980): 220–32; A. N. S. Lane, "Calvin's Doctrine of Assurance," *Vox Evangelica* 11 (1979): 45–46; Exalto, *De Zekerheid des Geloofs bij Calvijn*, 15–20, 27–30.

80. Calvin, *Institutes*, 3.2.11.

81. Calvin, *Commentary*, on Ezek. 13:9. David Foxgrover shows that Calvin relates the need for self-examination to a great variety of topics: knowledge of God and ourselves, judgment, repentance, confession, affliction, the Lord's Supper, providence, duty, and the kingdom of God. "John Calvin's Understanding of Conscience" (PhD diss., Claremont Graduate School, 1978), 312–13. Cf. J. P. Pelkonen, "The Teaching of John Calvin on the Nature and Function of the Conscience," *Lutheran Quarterly* 21 (1969): 24–88.

Calvin's Experiential Preaching 129

with solicitude and humility, lest carnal security insinuate itself, instead of the assurance of faith."[82]

Even in self-examination, Calvin emphasized Christ. He said we must examine ourselves to see if we are placing our trust in *Christ alone*, for this is the fruit of biblical experience. Anthony Lane says that for Calvin, self-examination is not as much "Am I *trusting* in Christ?" as it is "Am I trusting in *Christ?*"[83] Self-examination must always direct us to Christ and His promise. It must never be done apart from the help of the Holy Spirit, who alone can shed light upon Christ's saving work in the believer's soul. Apart from Christ, the Word, and the Spirit, Calvin said, "if you contemplate yourself, that is sure damnation."[84]

Conclusion

Calvin was an experiential theologian and preacher who strove to balance how spiritual matters should go in the Christian life, how they do go, and what their end goal is. He hedged himself in from excesses by confining himself to the limits of Scripture and by always tying the Spirit's experiential work to Scripture. At the same time, he used experiential preaching as a way to minister to the needs of believers and as a discriminatory tool for unbelievers. Above all, all his experiential emphases strove to lead the believer to end in glorifying the Trinity through Jesus Christ.

---

82. Calvin, *Institutes*, 3.2.7.
83. Lane, "Calvin's Doctrine of Assurance," 47.
84. Calvin, *Institutes*, 3.2.24.

—8—
"A Sacrifice Well Pleasing to God":
John Calvin and the Missionary Endeavor
of the Church

Michael A. G. Haykin

Often it has been maintained that the sixteenth-century Reformers had a poorly developed missiology and that overseas missions to non-Christians was something to which they gave little thought.[1] Yes, this argument runs, they rediscovered the apostolic gospel, but they had no vision to spread it to the uttermost parts of the earth.[2] Possibly the first author to question early Protestantism's failure to apply itself to missionary work was the Roman Catholic theologian and controversialist Robert Bellarmine (1542–1621). Bellarmine argued that one of the marks of a true church was its continuity with the missionary passion of the apostles. In his mind, Roman Catholicism's missionary activity was indisputable, and this supplied a strong support for its claim to stand in solidarity with the apostles. As Bellarmine maintained:

> In this one century the Catholics have converted many thousands of heathens in the new world. Every year a certain number of Jews are converted and baptized at Rome by Catholics who adhere in loyalty to the Bishop of Rome.... The Lutherans compare themselves to the apostles and the evangelists; yet though they have among them a very large number of Jews, and in Poland and Hungary have the Turks as their near neighbors, they have hardly converted so much as a handful.[3]

---

1. Earlier versions of this essay first appeared in the online journal *Reformation 21*, 13 (September 2006) and in Michael A. G. Haykin and C. Jeffrey Robinson Sr., *To the Ends of the Earth: Calvin's Vision and Legacy* (Wheaton, Ill.: Crossway, 2014). Used with permission.

2. See Kenneth J. Stewart, "Calvinism and Missions: The Contested Relationship Revisited," *Themelios* 34, no.1 (April 2009), especially the third section, http://themelios .thegospelcoalition.org/article/calvinism-and-missions-the-contested-relationship-revisited.

3. Robert Bellarmine, *Controversiae*, book 4, as quoted in Stephen Neill, *A History of Christian Missions* (Harmondsworth, Middlesex, U.K.: Penguin, 1964), 221.

132 Theology Made Practical

Such a characterization fails to account for the complexity of this issue. First, in the earliest years of the Reformation, none of the major Protestant bodies possessed significant naval and maritime resources to take the gospel outside the bounds of Europe. The Iberian Catholic kingdoms of Spain and Portugal, on the other hand, the acknowledged leaders among missionary-sending regions at the time, had plenty of these resources. It is noteworthy that other European Roman Catholic nations like Poland and Hungary also lacked sea-going capabilities and evidenced no more cross-cultural missionary concern than did Lutheran Saxony or Reformed Zurich. It is thus plainly wrong to make the simplistic assertion that Roman Catholic nations were committed to overseas missions whereas no Protestant power was so committed.[4]

Second, it is vital to recognize that, as Scott Hendrix has shown, the Reformation was the attempt to "make European culture more Christian than it had been. It was, if you will, an attempt to reroot faith, to rechristianize Europe."[5] In the eyes of the Reformers, this program involved two accompanying convictions. First, they considered what passed for Christianity in late medieval Europe as sub-Christian at best, pagan at worst. As Calvin put it in his *Reply to Sadoleto* in 1539: "The light of divine truth had been extinguished, the Word of God buried, the virtue of Christ left in profound oblivion, and the pastoral office subverted. Meanwhile, impiety so stalked abroad that almost no doctrine of religion was pure from admixture, no ceremony free from error, no part, however minute, of divine worship untarnished by superstition."[6] The Reformers, then, viewed their task as a missionary endeavor; they were planting true Christian churches.[7]

In what follows, a brief examination of the missiology of John Calvin clearly shows the error of the perspective that the Reformation was by and large a nonmissionary movement.[8] John Calvin's theology of missions is developed by looking first at the theme of the victorious advance of

---

4. Stewart, "Calvinism and Missions."

5. Scott Hendrix, "Rerooting the Faith: The Reformation as Re-Christianization," *Church History* 69 (2000): 561.

6. John Calvin and Jacopo Sadoleto, *A Reformation Debate*, ed. John C. Olin (Grand Rapids: Baker, 1976), 74–75.

7. Hendrix, "Rerooting the Faith," 558–68.

8. David B. Calhoun, "John Calvin: Missionary Hero or Missionary Failure," *Presbyterion: Covenant Seminary Review* 5, no.1 (Spring 1979): 17. Cf. Joel R. Beeke, "John Calvin: Teacher and Practitioner of Evangelism," in *Puritan Reformed Spirituality* (Darlington, England: Evangelical Press, 2006), chap. 3.

John Calvin and the Missionary Endeavor of the Church   133

Christ's kingdom that looms so large in his writings. Statements from Calvin regarding the means and motivations for extending this kingdom are then examined to further show his concern for the spread of the gospel to the ends of the earth. Finally, there is a brief look at the way Calvin's Geneva functioned as a missionary center.

The Victorious Advance of Christ's Kingdom

A frequent theme in Calvin's writings and sermons is the victorious advance of Christ's kingdom in the world. God the Father, Calvin said in his prefatory address to Francis I in his theological masterpiece, the *Institutes of the Christian Religion*, has appointed Christ to "rule from sea to sea, and from the rivers even to the ends of the earth." The reason for the Spirit's descent at Pentecost, Calvin noted further in a sermon on Acts 2, was in order for the gospel to "reach all the ends and extremities of the world." In a sermon on 1 Timothy 2:5–6, one of a series of sermons on 1 Timothy 2, Calvin underlined again the universality of the Christian faith: Jesus came not simply to save a few but "to extend his grace over all the world."[9]

In that same sermon series, Calvin thus declared that "God wants his grace to be known to all the world, and he has commanded that his gospel be preached to all creatures; we must (as much as we are able) seek the salvation of those who today are strangers to the faith, who seem to be completely deprived of God's goodness."[10] It was this global perspective on the significance of the gospel that also gave Calvin's theology a genuine dynamism and forward movement. It has been rightly said that if it had not been for the so-called Calvinist wing of the Reformation, many of the great gains of that era would have died on the vine.[11]

Means for the Extension of Christ's Kingdom

Calvin was quite certain that the extension of Christ's kingdom is first God's work. Commenting on Matthew 24:30, he asserted that it is not "by human

---

9. The three Calvin quotes in this paragraph are quoted in Calhoun, "John Calvin: Missionary Hero or Missionary Failure," 17.

10. For this quote from Calvin's sermon 13 on 1 Timothy 2:8, I am indebted to Elsie McKee, "Calvin and Praying for 'All People Who Dwell on Earth,'" *Interpretation* 63 (2009): 134.

11. Jean-Marc Berthoud, "John Calvin and the Spread of the Gospel in France," in *Fulfilling the Great Commission* ([London]: Westminster Conference, 1992), 44–46.

134   Theology Made Practical

means but by heavenly power…that the Lord will gather His Church."[12] Or consider his comments on the phrase "a door having also been opened to me" in 2 Corinthians 2:12:

> [The meaning of this metaphor is] that an opportunity of further-ing the gospel had presented itself. Just as an open door makes an entrance possible, so the Lord's servants make progress when opportunity is given them. The door is shut when there is no hope of success. Thus when the door is shut we have to go a different way rather than wear ourselves out in vain efforts to get through it but, when an opportunity for edification presents itself, we should realize that a door has been opened for us by the hand of God in order that we may introduce Christ into that place and we should not refuse to accept the generous invitation that God thus gives us.[13]

For Calvin, the metaphor of an open door spoke volumes about the way in which the advance of the church is utterly dependent on the mercy of a sovereign God. This does not mean that Christians are to be passive in their efforts to reach the lost and can sit back and wait for God to do it all. In his comments on Isaiah 12:5, Calvin dealt with this common misinterpretation of God's divine sovereignty: "[Isaiah] shows that it is our duty to proclaim the goodness of God to every nation. While we exhort and encourage oth-ers, we must not at the same time sit down in indolence, but it is proper that we set an example before others; for nothing can be more absurd than to see lazy and slothful men who are exciting other men to praise God."[14]

As David Calhoun rightly observes: "The power to save [souls] rests with God but He displays and unfolds His salvation in our preaching of the gospel."[15] While missions and evangelism are indeed God's work, God delights to use His people as His instruments.

The first major way in which God uses His people for the conversion of others is through prayer—our prayers for the conversion of unbelievers.[16] In Calvin's words, God "bids us to pray for the salvation of unbelievers,"[17] and Scripture passages like 1 Timothy 2:4 encourage us not to "cease to pray

---

12. As quoted in Calhoun, "John Calvin: Missionary Hero or Missionary Failure," 18.

13. Calvin, *Commentary*, on 2 Cor. 2:12.

14. Calvin, *Commentary*, on Isa. 12:5.

15. Calhoun, "John Calvin: Missionary Hero or Missionary Failure," 18.

16. In this regard, see the masterful essay by McKee, "Calvin and Praying," 130–40.

17. As quoted in McKee, "Calvin and Praying," 133.

John Calvin and the Missionary Endeavor of the Church

for all people in general."[18] We see this conviction at work in Calvin's own prayers, a good number of which have been recorded for us at the end of his sermons. Each of his sermons on Deuteronomy, for instance, ends with a prayer that runs something like this: "May it please [God] to grant this [saving] grace, not only to us, but also to all peoples and nations of the earth."[19] In fact, in the liturgy that Calvin drew up for his church in Geneva is this prayer:

> We pray you now, O most gracious God and merciful Father, for all people everywhere. As it is your will to be acknowledged as the Saviour of the whole world, through the redemption wrought by your Son Jesus Christ, grant that those who are still estranged from the knowledge of him, being in the darkness and captivity of error and ignorance, may be brought by the illumination of your Holy Spirit and the preaching of your gospel to the right way of salvation, which is to know you, the only true God, and Jesus Christ whom you have sent.[20]

Moreover, Calvin admonished believers not to be discouraged if they do not see fruit immediately issuing as a result of their prayers. As he stated in his comments on Genesis 17:23:

> So, at this day, God seems to enjoin a thing impossible to be done, when he requires his gospel to be preached everywhere in the whole world, for the purpose of restoring it from death to life. For we see how great is the obstinacy of nearly all men, and what numerous and powerful methods of resistance Satan employs; so that, in short, all the ways of access to these principles are obstructed. Yet it behooves individuals to do their duty, and not to yield to impediments; and, finally, our endeavors and our labors shall by no means fail of that success, which is not yet apparent.[21]

Then, believers must actively employ their strength to bring God's salvation to others. In his sermon on Deuteronomy 33:18–19, Calvin thus argued that it is not enough to be involved in God's service. Christians need to draw

---

18. As quoted in McKee, "Calvin and Praying," 138.

19. Calhoun, "John Calvin: Missionary Hero or Missionary Failure," 19n23; McKee, "Calvin and Praying," 139–40.

20. As quoted in McKee, "Calvin and Praying," 139.

21. Calvin, *Commentary*, on Gen. 17:23.

Theology Made Practical

others to serve and adore God.[22] Specifically, how does God use the strength of Christians? Calvin's answer is by their words and deeds. Given Calvin's high appreciation for the Word of God, one would naturally expect that this would be seen as a major means of witness. Thus, Calvin stated that whenever the Old Testament prophets foretold "the renewal of the Church or its extension over the whole globe," they always assigned "the first place to the Word."[23] Acting on this conviction, Calvin encouraged the translation and printing of the Scriptures in the work of reformation in Geneva. This also explains his devotion to regular expository preaching and his penning of commentaries on all the books of the New Testament (except for 2 and 3 John and Revelation) and on a number of Old Testament books. Preaching is also central here, as Calvin noted: "God wants his grace to be known in all the world, and he has commanded that his gospel be preached to all people."[24]

Witness, though, is borne not only by the Word but also by our deeds. Calvin established an academy in Geneva to train men to be missionaries especially for his native land, France. A significant number of these men did indeed go back as missionaries, and some died as martyrs. Five such missionaries, for example—Martial Alba, Pierre Ecrivain, Charles Favre, Pierre Navihères, and Bernard Seguin—came from Lausanne to Geneva in the spring of 1552, where they got to know Calvin as they prepared to go back to France as missionaries in the region of Lyons. As they were on the road to Lyons, they met a man who asked if he could travel with them. They had no suspicions of the man. He seemed hospitable, and on arrival at Lyons, he urged them to come and stay with him. They did so, and he subsequently betrayed them into the hands of the authorities in April 1552. As soon as Calvin heard of their arrest, he began a letter-writing campaign, seeking to bring pressure on the French king Henri II through a number of German Protestant allies. By the spring of 1553, however, it became obvious that he would not be able to obtain their release. Calvin wrote to the five who were facing death and were martyred on May 15, 1553. The students never saw this letter, for they were burned on May 16:

> Since it pleases [God] to employ you to the death in maintaining his quarrel [with the world], he will strengthen your hands in the

---

22. John Calvin, Sermon 196 on Deuteronomy 33:18–19, in *CO*, 29:175. English translation here by the author.

23. As quoted in Calhoun, "John Calvin: Missionary Hero or Missionary Failure," 22.

24. As quoted in McKee, "Calvin and Praying," 134.

John Calvin and the Missionary Endeavor of the Church 137

fight, and will not suffer a single drop of your blood to be spent in vain. And though the fruit may not all at once appear, yet in time it shall spring up more abundantly than we can express. But as he hath vouchsafed you this privilege, that your bonds have been renowned, and that the noise of them has been everywhere spread abroad, it must needs be, in despite of Satan, that your death should resound far more powerfully, so that the name of our Lord be magnified thereby. For my part, I have no doubt, if it please this kind Father to take you unto himself, that he has preserved you hitherto, in order that your long-continued imprisonment might serve as a preparation for the better awakening of those whom he has determined to edify by your end. For let enemies do their utmost, they never shall be able to bury out of sight that light which God has made to shine in you, in order to be contemplated from afar.[25]

In this instance Calvin saw the act of martyrdom as a powerful witness for the gospel, though it was a witness without words.

Calvin was also convinced that all Christians must be prepared to witness, by both word and deed, about God's grace and mercy in Christ to all whom they can. It is noteworthy that when it comes to spreading the gospel, he made no distinction between the responsibility of pastors and other Christians. All believers must be involved.[26]

It should also be noted that Calvin and the Genevan pastors helped further the work of Reformation evangelism in Europe through print media. By the time of Calvin's death, his interest in Christian publishing resulted in about thirty-four printing houses in Geneva, which printed Bibles and Christian literature in a variety of European languages. During the 1550s, Geneva was a busy center for publishing Bible editions and translations. There was, for example, Robert Estienne's Greek New Testament of 1551, which divided the text into verses for the first time; a new edition of the Vulgate; an Italian translation and Spanish translation in 1555 and 1556 respectively; and at least twenty-two editions of the French Bible. And in 1560 a complete English translation of the Bible was printed sometime between April 10 and May 30. This was the Geneva Bible, the bedrock of early English Puritanism.

---

25. John Calvin to Martial Alba, Pierre Ecrivain, Charles Favre, Pierre Navihères, and Bernard Seguin (letter 318), in *Letters of John Calvin*, ed. Jules Bonnet, trans. Mr. Constable (1858; repr., New York: Lenox Hill, 1972), 2:406.

26. Calhoun, "John Calvin: Missionary Hero or Missionary Failure," 22.

138 Theology Made Practical

There is one means that Calvin expected God to use to spread the gospel that we today in the West probably do not expect—that is, evangelism through Christian rulers and magistrates. For example, Calvin viewed Elizabeth I's (r. 1558–1603) coming to the throne as a hopeful sign for the advance of the gospel in England. Over the years he also corresponded extensively with a number of French noblewomen, especially Jeanne d'Albret (1528–1572), queen of Navarre. This French noblewoman played a significant role in the French Reformation, and Calvin recognized his need of her support and that of the other nobility if new territories were to be opened up to the spread of the evangelical faith.

Motivations for Extending Christ's Kingdom

What was to motivate the believer to bear witness to the faith? First and foremost was the glory of God. As Calvin stated in his sermon on Deuteronomy 33:18–19: "When we know God to be our Father, should we not desire that he be known as such by all? And if we do not have this passion, that all creatures do him homage, is it not a sign that his glory means little to us?"[27]

In other words, if we are truly passionate about God's glory, our passion will result in witness. The Christian life, in all its apostolic fullness, is marked by self-denial, the recognition that the Christian does not belong to himself or herself but belongs totally to God and is to live for God's glory. In Calvin's words:

> Even though the law of the Lord provides the finest and best-disposed method of ordering a man's life, it seemed good to the Heavenly Teacher to shape his people by an even more explicit plan to that rule which he had set forth in the law. Here [in Romans 12], then, is the beginning of this plan: the duty of believers is "to present their bodies to God as a living sacrifice, holy and acceptable to him."... We are consecrated and dedicated to God in order that we may hereafter think, speak, meditate, and do nothing except to his glory.[28]

Moreover, bearing witness to the faith is pleasing to God. Consider in this regard Calvin's letter to a Christian landowner on the island of Jersey written around the year 1553:

---

27. Calvin, sermon 196 on Deuteronomy 33:18–19, in *CO*, 29:175.
28. Calvin, *Institutes*, 3.7.1.

John Calvin and the Missionary Endeavor of the Church 139

We praise God for having inclined your heart to try if it will be possible to erect, by your means, a small church on the place where you reside. And indeed, according as the agents of the Devil strive by every act of violence to abolish the true religion, extinguish the doctrine of salvation, and exterminate the name of Jesus Christ, it is very just that we should labor on our side to further the progress of the gospel, that, by these means, God may be served in purity, and the poor wandering sheep may be put under the protection of the sovereign Pastor to whom everyone should be subject. And you know that it is a sacrifice well pleasing to God, to advance the spread of the Gospel by which we are enlightened in the way of salvation, to dedicate our life to the honor of him who has ransomed us at so costly a price in order to bear rule in the midst of us.[29]

So we are to evangelize because we have been commanded to do so by Christ.[30] Compassion for people's lost condition should also drive Christians to witness. "If we have any humanity in us," Calvin declared in a sermon on Deuteronomy 33, "seeing men going to perdition,... ought we not be moved by pity, to rescue the poor souls from hell, and teach them the way of salvation?"[31] A Christian who is not involved in witness is really a contradiction in terms. As Calvin remarks in his commentary on Isaiah 2:3: "The godly will be filled with such an ardent desire to spread the doctrines of religion, that everyone not satisfied with his own calling and his personal knowledge will desire to draw others along with him. And indeed nothing could be more inconsistent with the nature of faith than that deadness which would lead a man to disregard his brethren, and to keep the light of knowledge choked up within his own breast."[32]

Geneva as a Missionary Center

Geneva was not a large city. During Calvin's lifetime it reached a peak of slightly more than twenty-one thousand by 1560, of whom a goodly number were religious refugees.[33] Nevertheless, it became *the* missionary center of

---

29. John Calvin to a Seigneur of Jersey, 1553 (letter 339), in *Letters of John Calvin*, 2:453.
30. Calhoun, "John Calvin: Missionary Hero or Missionary Failure," 20.
31. Calvin, Sermon 196 on Deuteronomy 33:18–19, in *CO*, 29:175.
32. Calvin, *Commentary*, on Isa. 2:3.
33. Alister E. McGrath, *A Life of John Calvin: A Study in the Shaping of Western Culture* (Cambridge, Mass.: Blackwell, 1990), 121.

140 Theology Made Practical

Europe in this period of the Reformation. Calvin sought to harness the energies and gifts of many of the religious refugees so as to make Geneva central to the expansion of Reformation thought and piety throughout Europe. This meant training and preparing many of these refugees to go back to their native lands as evangelists and reformers.

Understandably Calvin was vitally concerned about the evangelization of his native land, France, and his French countrymen. It has been estimated that by 1562 some 2,150 congregations had been established in France with around two million members, many of them converted through the witness of men trained in Geneva.[34] That two million comprised 50 percent of the upper and middle classes and a full 10 percent of the entire population. The growth is enormous when one reckons that at the time of Calvin's conversion, in the early 1530s, there were probably no more than a couple thousand evangelicals in France.

But Calvin was concerned not only for reformation in France but also for reformation of the church in places like Scotland and England, Spain, Poland, Hungary, and the Netherlands. He even encouraged a mission to Brazil in 1555, which turned out to be a failure.[35] It is noteworthy that when the church in Geneva heard of this Brazilian opportunity, contemporary chronicler and participant in the mission to Brazil Jean de Léry recorded that "upon...hearing this news, the church of Geneva at once gave thanks to God for the extension of the reign of Jesus Christ in a country so distant and likewise so foreign and among a nation entirely without the knowledge of the true God."[36]

Little wonder that in light of all these missionary projects, Calvin wrote: "When I consider how very important this corner [Geneva] is for the propagation of the kingdom of Christ, I have good reason to be anxious that it should be carefully watched over."[37]

---

34. W. Stanford Reid, "Calvin's Geneva: A Missionary Centre," *The Reformed Theological Review* 42, no. 3 (September–December, 1983): 69.

35. See the story of this important mission in G. Baez-Camargo, "The Earliest Protestant Missionary Venture in Latin America," *Church History* 21 (1952): 135–45; Amy Glassner Gordon, "The First Protestant Missionary Effort: Why Did It Fail?," *International Bulletin of Missionary Research* 8, no. 1 (January 1984): 12–18; and Stewart, "Calvinism and Missions."

36. Jean de Léry, *Journal de Bord de Jean de Léry en la Terre de Brésil 1557, présenté et commenté par M.R. Mayeux* (Paris, 1957) as quoted in R. Pierce Beaver, "The Genevan Mission to Brazil," in *The Heritage of John Calvin,* ed. John Bratt (Grand Rapids: Eerdmans, 1973), 61.

37. Calvin, *Tracts and Letters,* 5:227.

A Concluding Word

There have been assertions in modern times that the Christian tradition which came down from Calvin is essentially uncomfortable with missionary zeal and is inherently antimissionary. Some of those making these assertions are knowledgeable historians who are rightly esteemed in their respective schools. Possibly they are confusing biblical Calvinism with the hyper-Cavinism that has frequently developed on the fringes of the Reformed tradition. Every movement has its fringe element that no more represents the center than chalk resembles cheese.

—9—

Calvin on Principles of Government

David W. Hall

Compared to his writing on other subjects, John Calvin offers far less commentary on political matters in the *Institutes of the Christian Religion*, his magnum opus. But seldom have so few words had such political impact. While many theologians who followed Calvin would scarcely brave a comment on matters of state in a systematic theology text, he addressed political topics without trepidation. The resulting forty pages of discussion on the civil government in the final chapter of the *Institutes* blazed a trail for others. Thankfully, many treatises have already addressed this key area of human culture.[1]

The concluding chapter of the *Institutes* is also, in some ways, the culmination of a tradition. It followed decades of Renaissance thought and perched atop centuries of medieval and scholastic theological reflection on political principles. Calvin was not alone in addressing these matters; it was not uncharacteristic for leading theologians of the period to expound on matters of state. The subsequent expansion and replication of Calvin's thought by his

---

1. Among the scholars who have explicated Calvin's political thought and impact are Harro Hopfl, *The Christian Polity of John Calvin* (Cambridge: Cambridge University Press, 1982); Quentin Skinner, *The Foundations of Modern Political Thought: The Age of Reformation*, vol. 2 (Cambridge: Cambridge University Press, 1978); Abraham Kuyper, *Lectures on Calvinism* (1898; repr., Grand Rapids: Eerdmans, 1953); Robert Kingdon, *Calvin and Calvinism: Sources of Democracy* (Lexington, Mass.: D. C. Heath, 1970); Ralph C. Hancock, *Calvin and the Foundations of Modern Politics* (Ithaca, N.Y.: Cornell University Press, 1989); John Witte Jr., *The Reformation of Rights: Law, Religion and Human Rights in Early Modern Calvinism* (Cambridge: Cambridge University Press, 2007); John T. McNeill, "Calvin and Civil Government," in *Readings in Calvin's Theology*, ed. Donald McKim (Grand Rapids: Baker, 1984); Herbert D. Foster, *Collected Papers of Herbert D. Foster* (privately printed, 1929); John T. McNeill, "John Calvin on Civil Government," in *Calvinism and the Political Order*, ed. George L. Hunt (Philadelphia: Westminster, 1965); Douglas Kelly, *The Emergence of Liberty in the Modern World* (Phillipsburg, N.J.: Presbyterian and Reformed, 1992); Franklin Charles Palm, *Calvinism and the Religious Wars* (New York: Henry Hold, 1932); Karl Holl, *The Cultural Significance of the Reformation* (Cleveland: Meridian, 1959); and Keith L. Griffin, *Revolution and Religion: American Revolutionary War and the Reformed Clergy* (New York: Paragon House, 1994).

144 Theology Made Practical

followers, however, virtually created a new trajectory of political discourse. It is no exaggeration to observe that before Calvin, certain political principles were viewed as radical, while after him, they became widely accepted. This is true in all realms of government—both in church and in state.

Any proper analysis of Calvin's political thought should begin with his discussion in the *Institutes*, but an accurate understanding of Calvin will also take into account his other writings and, importantly, the manner in which his disciples codified his teachings into a school of political thought. This chapter begins with Calvin's theology of civil government and concludes by showing how those same principles were yoked to Reformed ecclesiology. As such, Calvin's theory of governance is seen as unified.

Calvin's *Institutes*: Blueprint for Civil Government

Calvin's political thought in the *Institutes of the Christian Religion* is still credited with immense political impact, even by the Reformer's critics. Asserting that the state was not merely a necessary evil for Calvin, Karl Holl recognized that Calvinism, even more than Lutheranism, provided a theological basis to oppose unjust governments.[2] Everywhere Calvinism spread, so did its impulse to limit government.[3] Dutch Calvinist prime minister Abraham Kuyper (1837–1920) summarized the essence of Calvin's theocentric emphasis:

> It is therefore a political faith which may be summarily expressed in these three theses: 1. God only, and never any creature, is possessed of sovereign rights, in the destiny of nations, because God alone created them, maintains them by his Almighty power, and rules them by his ordinances. 2. Sin has, in the realm of politics, broken down the direct government of God, and therefore the exercise of authority, for the purpose of government, has subsequently been invested in men, as a mechanical remedy. And 3. In whatever form this authority may reveal itself, man never possesses power over his fellow man in any other way than by the authority which descends upon him from the majesty of God.[4]

---

2. Holl, *Cultural Significance of the Reformation*, 65–66.

3. Hancock, *Calvin and the Foundations of Modern Politics*, 1. The author asserts that the Protestant Reformation was "an essentially modern movement that in some way laid the foundations for our modern openness."

4. Kuyper, *Lectures on Calvinism*, 85.

Calvin on Principles of Government

Calvinism, Kuyper continued, "protests against State omni-competence, against the horrible conception that no right exists above and beyond existing laws, and against the pride of absolutism, which recognizes no constitutional rights." Calvinism "built a dam across the absolutistic stream, not by appealing to popular force, nor to the hallucination of human greatness, but by deducing those rights and liberties of social life from the same source from which the high authority of government flows, even the absolute sovereignty of God."[5]

Such thoughts are indeed contained in Calvin's *Institutes of the Christian Religion*, which underwent considerable evolution between editions. The original 1536 edition composed in Basel[6] combined the chapter on civil government with Calvin's treatment of Christian liberty and ecclesiastical power. In the 1559 edition, Calvin explained that civil government was the second part of a twofold government, properly chartered to "establish civil justice and outward morality."[7]

Calvin's major sections addressed these topics:

1. the magistrate,[8] who is "the protector and guardian of the laws,"[9]
2. the laws, which provide objectivity for governors,[10]
3. the people,[11] an early statement of the contract theory later rightly associated with Ponet, Beza, the *Vindiciae*, Buchanan, and Althusius.

Calvin believed that civil government provided an example of how God had compassionately provided for humankind; the sphere of human government, thus, was a gracious token for human culture much like the law itself. The task of the civil ruler was to ensure "that a public manifestation of religion may exist among Christians, and that humanity be maintained among men." If no civil government existed or if depraved people perceived that they could go scot-free, they surely would opt for sin, and society would deteriorate into chaos.[12] On one occasion, Calvin likened such anarchy to

---

5. Kuyper, *Lectures on Calvinism*, 85.
6. Skinner, *Foundations of Modern Political Thought*, 192. Skinner suggests that by 1559 Calvin had begun to change his views, permitting at least a discussion of the propriety of active resistance.
7. Calvin, *Institutes*, 4.20.1.
8. Calvin, *Institutes*, 4.20.3–13.
9. Calvin, *Institutes*, 4.20.3.
10. Calvin, *Institutes*, 4.20.14–21.
11. Calvin, *Institutes*, 4.20.22–32.
12. Calvin, *Institutes*, 4.20.2.

146 Theology Made Practical

living "pell-mell, like rats in straw." He argued that God does not bid persons to "lay aside their authority and retire to private life, but submit to Christ the power with which they have been invested, that he alone may tower over all."[13] Calvin believed that "powers are from God, not as pestilence, and famine, and wars, and other visitations for sin, are said to be from him; but because he has appointed them for the legitimate and just government of the world. For though tyrannies and unjust exercise of power, as they are full of disorder, are not an ordained government; yet the right of government is ordained by God for the well-being of mankind."[14]

In marked contrast to the Anabaptists of his day, Calvin recognized service in a political office as entirely appropriate, even going as far as to speak of civil service as the most sacred and honorable of human callings. Calvin referred to civil rulers favorably as "vicars of God,"[15] "the highest gift of [God's] beneficence to preserve the safety of men,"[16] and as "ordained protectors and vindicators of public innocence, modesty, decency, and tranquility [whose] sole endeavor should be to provide for the common safety and peace of all."[17] Thus, Calvinism did not inspire an inherently negative view of civil government. Elsewhere Calvin stated that the appointed goal of the civil government was "to cherish and protect the outward worship of God, to defend sound doctrine of piety and the position of the church, to adjust our life to the society of men, to form our social behavior to civil righteousness, to reconcile us with one another, and to promote general peace and tranquility."[18] By early 1553, he had summoned the magistrates of Geneva to be "the vindicators, not the destroyers, of sacred laws."[19] The use of the sword was the necessary corollary to human depravity. Civil magistrates were to be honored as superiors in keeping with the fifth commandment to honor those placed in authority. Even evil rulers kept God's law to some degree, and disobedience was justified only in response to actions contrary to God's law. The task of civil government, according to Calvin's commentary on Romans, was as follows:

---

13. Calvin, *Institutes*, 4.20.5. The "pell-mell" quote is from the French, as translated in the Battles edition, 1490n15.

14. Calvin, *Commentary*, on Rom. 13:2.

15. Calvin, *Institutes*, 4.20.6.

16. Calvin, *Institutes*, 4.20.25.

17. Calvin, *Institutes*, 4.20.9.

18. Calvin, *Institutes*, 4.20.2

19. Beza, *Life of John Calvin*, in *Tracts and Letters*, 1:c.

Calvin on Principles of Government

Magistrates may hence learn what their vocation is, for they are not to rule for their own interest, but for the public good; nor are they endued with unbridled power, but what is restricted to the well-being of their subjects; in short, they are responsible to God and to men in the exercise of their power. For as they are deputed by God and do his business, they must give an account to him: and then the ministration which God has committed to them has a regard to the subjects, they are therefore debtors to them.[20]

Calvin believed that both politics and providence were operative; indeed, he suggested that the kingdom of God was already present, although not completely realized: "For spiritual government, indeed, is already initiating in us upon earth certain beginnings of the Heavenly Kingdom, and in this mortal and fleeting life affords a certain forecast of an immortal and incorruptible blessedness."[21] He advised, "Let no man be disturbed that I now commit to civil government the duty of rightly establishing religion."[22] Few would be greatly disturbed by such a statement, since it was the common notion of Calvin's time for government to uphold religion. Calvin acknowledged this: "All have confessed that no government can be happily established unless piety is the first concern."[23] He also stated that the civil magistrate should care for both tables of the law.[24] Later conflicts between church and state, however, would beg for reevaluations of this maxim. Furthermore, he included a limitation for his theory— that is, no administration was permitted to tailor the worship of God to their own imaginations nor prohibit the practice of true religion.[25]

Lest we brand Calvin a theocrat, however, his comments on John 18:36, in which Jesus states that His servants did not strive for enforcement of an earthly kingdom, may reassure. His view of the separation of jurisdictions (which is not identical to the Lutheran two-kingdom view), enunciated in the mid-sixteenth century, is still helpful. Discussing the conditions under which it is appropriate to defend "the kingdom of Christ by arms," Calvin wrote:

---

20. Calvin, *Commentary*, on Rom. 13:4.
21. Calvin, *Institutes*, 4.20.2.
22. Calvin, *Institutes*, 4.20.3.
23. Calvin, *Institutes*, 4.20.9.
24. Calvin, *Institutes*, 4.20.9.
25. Calvin, *Institutes*, 4.20.3.

148   Theology Made Practical

> Though godly kings defend the kingdom of Christ by the sword, still it is done in a different manner from that in which worldly kingdoms are wont to be defended; for the kingdom of Christ, being spiritual must be founded on the doctrine and power of the Spirit. In the same manner, too, its edification is promoted; for neither the laws and edicts of men, nor the punishments inflicted by them, enter into the consciences.... It results, however, from the depravity of the world that the kingdom of Christ is strengthened more by the blood of the martyrs than by the aid of arms.[26]

For Calvin, serving in civil government could be "the most sacred and by far the most honorable of all callings in the whole life of mortal men."[27] He wrote that if civil rulers properly understood their callings—that is, "that they are occupied not with profane affairs or those alien to a servant of God, but with a most holy office, since they are serving as God's deputies"—they would serve with more equity.[28] Echoing Aristotle's morphology of the state and its tendency toward deterioration from monarchy to tyranny and from democracy to anarchy, Calvin advocated "a system compounded of aristocracy and democracy." He also saw a legitimate place for checks and balances, realizing the need for "censors and masters to restrain [the monarch's] willfulness."[29]

The civil magistrate did not act on his own, but "carries out the very judgments of God" in bearing the sword to punish lawbreakers.[30] Calvin cited King David as condoning the destruction of the wicked in the land as an example of the right to wage war. But, far from legitimating vengeance, violence, or undue cruelty, the magistrate was to avoid both exorbitant severity and "superstitious affectation of clemency." Alluding to a proverb from Seneca, Calvin concurred, "It is indeed bad to live under a prince with whom nothing is permitted; but much worse under one by whom everything is allowed."[31] He argued: "Now if [rulers'] true righteousness is to pursue the guilty and the impious with drawn sword, should they sheathe their sword and keep their hands clean of blood, while abandoned men wickedly range about with slaughter and massacre, they will become guilty of the greatest

---

26. Calvin, *Commentary*, on John 18:36.
27. Calvin, *Institutes*, 4.20.4.
28. Calvin, *Institutes*, 4.20.6.
29. Calvin, *Institutes*, 4.20.8.
30. Calvin, *Institutes*, 4.20.10.
31. Calvin, *Institutes*, 4.20.10.

Calvin on Principles of Government

impiety, far indeed from winning praise for their goodness and righteousness thereby!"[32]

In a phrase that would become incendiary, Calvin noted that not only kings but also "people must sometimes take up arms to execute public vengeance."[33] The same basis for waging war was used both to justify revolution and to put down sedition. If the magistrates were to punish private evildoers, then they could certainly punish mobs and protect the country from an external foe. Regardless of class, the noble governor was to protect the people equally from robbers or invaders. If he did not, he would be considered a robber and worthy of censure. Calvin's logic rested in the idea that the governor has the right to wage war, as he saw it, on "both natural equity and the nature of the office."[34] If additional grounds were needed to refute pacifism, Calvin would argue that governors could still defend their subjects, an exclusively New Testament basis was not necessary, and that Christ did not compel soldiers to resign.[35]

That Calvin gave attention to a far-ranging set of civic concerns is evidenced by his discussion of the magistrate's right to tax in the *Institutes*. He recommended prudent limits, arguing that taxes should support only public necessity, for "to impose them upon the common folk without cause is tyrannical extortion."[36] Obedience was a Christian duty in this area; princes, however, were not to indulge in "waste and expensive luxury," lest they earn God's displeasure. Calvin alluded to excessive taxation in a later comment: "Others drain the common people of their money, and afterward lavish it on insane largesse."[37]

Another major topic of discussion for Calvin is the use of the Old Testament judicial law, which he called "the silent magistrate." In a proper republic, laws were "the stoutest sinews of the commonwealth."[38] Not as theocratic as some might expect, Calvin affirmed that just as the Old Testament ceremonial laws (laws regulating ritual and diet, not viewed as permanent like the moral law) had been "abrogated while piety remained safe and unharmed, so too, when these judicial laws were taken away, the perpetual duties and

---

32. Calvin, *Institutes*, 4.20.10.
33. Calvin, *Institutes*, 4.20.11.
34. Calvin, *Institutes*, 4.20.11.
35. Calvin, *Institutes*, 4.20.12.
36. Calvin, *Institutes*, 4.20.13.
37. Calvin, *Institutes*, 4.20.24.
38. Calvin, *Institutes*, 4.20.14.

150   Theology Made Practical

precepts of love could still remain."[39] He admitted that different nations were free to make laws as they saw best, but with this qualification: "Yet these must be in conformity to that perpetual rule of love, so that they indeed vary in form but have the same purpose."[40] And while some of his day thought that a commonwealth could be "duly framed" only if it included a theonomic approach, Calvin called that idea "perilous," "seditious," "false and foolish."[41]

Calvin taught that even if all the specifics and particulars of the Mosaic judicial law were not binding, the moral principle within each command continued. The moral law,[42] which Calvin viewed as nothing other than a "testimony of natural law" and conscience, was never abrogated, contrary to the ceremonial and judicial codes: "Consequently, the entire scheme of this equity of which we are now speaking has been prescribed in it. Hence, this equity alone must be the goal and rule and limit of all laws. Whatever laws shall be framed to that rule, directed to that goal, bound by that limit, there is no reason why we should disapprove of them, howsoever they may differ from the Jewish law or among themselves."[43] Notwithstanding, Calvin did not teach that the Mosaic law was to be in force everywhere. Since Calvin is seldom accused of laxness, his comments must be taken seriously. So taken, they do not call for disavowal of the equitable principles of the Old Testament judicial law but merely for the adaptation of nonessential and nonmoral aspects. It was, as Calvin realized, possible to maintain the

---

39. Calvin, *Institutes*, 4.20.14. See Calvin's definition of this tripartite taxonomy in this section.

40. Calvin, *Institutes*, 4.20.15.

41. Calvin, *Institutes*, 4.20.14.

42. R. Scott Clark has recognized the formal identity between Calvin and Thomas Aquinas on natural law. But believing that original sin corrupted moral and intellectual capabilities, Calvin constricted the sweep of natural law. Like Thomas, notes Clark, Calvin was "influenced by the classics, but unlike [Thomas] Aquinas, he defined natural law very precisely by identifying it with the decalogue or moral law." "Calvin on the *Lex Naturalis*," *Stulos Theological Journal* 6, nos.1–2 (May–November 1998): 3. Further attempting to correct the claims of Calvin scholar John T. McNeill, Clark notes that Abelard, Luther, and others equated natural law with the Ten Commandments (9, 11) rather than appealing to strict moral neutrality. Calvin, according to Clark, identified the Decalogue with natural law, as was "the general custom in Protestantism" in the early seventeenth century. Clark concludes: "For Calvin and for his successors...it was a given that God had entered into a probationary, federal-covenantal relationship with Adam, and that the *lex moralis*...is the same law which he codified at Sinai and which Calvin called the *lex naturalis*. It was part of the warp and woof of 16th and 17th-century Reformed theology to think of these things synonymously as components of the creational order" (20).

43. Calvin, *Institutes*, 4.20.16.

Calvin on Principles of Government

applicability of God's law while not necessarily advocating all the cultural specifics of the original Hebrew code. Some of his political descendants would adhere to this notion more than others.

Derivative of the proper understanding of laws and the magistracy was Calvin's acknowledgment that Christians could certainly avail themselves of public courts.[44] Access to legal process was not evil in itself, and the right to sue was a logical corollary of Calvin's refutation of pacifism, this time applied to the personal right to defend property legally. But Calvin warned against greed, revenge, and an excessive reliance on litigation.[45] Typical of his ethic, he recommended moderation, sometimes taking an economic loss, and to summarize: "Love will give every man the best counsel."[46]

In his third section, Calvin enumerated the duties of the Christian citizen, beginning with a call to honor the office as established by God as the first duty. Moreover, subjects should prove their obedience by paying taxes, obeying proclamations, and serving to protect the nation. Furthermore, Calvin warned Christians not to intrude excessively into the authority of the magistrate as long as he honored the office.[47]

Calvin's discussion of governmental largesse led him to acknowledge the common reaction to call oppressive governors "tyrants."[48] Still, he warned that the mere existence of some overtaxation or misappropriation was not the same as divine warrant to overthrow the tyrant. There was still a scriptural priority on submitting to governors who "have their sole authority from him."[49] Moreover, Calvin devoted several sections, relying heavily upon narratives in Daniel and Jeremiah, to discussing how God's providence presumptively called for submission to civil rulers.[50]

Despite such clarion calls to submit to the civil ruler, in some cases the lesser magistrates were justified in overturning a wicked ruler. That, however, was not to be carried out merely by private individuals. Calvin's argument, which was drawn upon by his disciples, was that rulers (whether in home, church, or civil spheres) also had obligations. The abuse of such obligations could negate their authority and relegate them to tyrant status.

---

44. Calvin, *Institutes*, 4.20.17.
45. Calvin, *Institutes*, 4.20.18–21.
46. Calvin, *Institutes*, 4.20.21.
47. Calvin, *Institutes*, 4.20.23.
48. Calvin, *Institutes*, 4.20.24.
49. Calvin, *Institutes*, 4.20.25.
50. Calvin, *Institutes*, 4.20.26–29.

152   Theology Made Practical

Calvin acknowledged that, at times, divine providence was satisfied in the overthrowing of wicked rulers, but he still preferred to allow the Lord to correct unbridled despotism.[51] Calvin urged believers to consider that through prayer God might change the hearts of rulers.[52] Concerning revolution, he advocated a peaceful, incremental revolution via the intermediate magistrates:

> For if there are now any magistrates of the people, appointed to restrain the willfulness of kings, (as in ancient times the ephors…), I am so far from forbidding them to withstand, in accordance with their duty, the fierce licentiousness of kings, that, if they wink at kings who violently fall upon and assault the lowly common folk, I declare that their dissimulation involves nefarious perfidy, because they dishonestly betray the freedom of the people, of which they know that they have been appointed protectors by God's ordinance.[53]

The obvious exception to any of these rules, however, was that people were not merely free but were also obligated to resist the magistrate who compelled ungodly activity. Calvin taught that there were exceptions to the above considerations but also that obedience to God was primary: "Obedience [to a ruler] is never to lead us away from obedience to Him," a good example of qualified absolutism.[54] He reasoned: "How absurd would it be that in satisfying men you should incur the displeasure of him for whose sake you obey men themselves!" Still, this argument is balanced with Calvin's conclusion that we should "comfort ourselves with the thought that we are rendering that obedience which the Lord requires when we suffer anything rather than turn aside from piety."[55]

The other aspect of Calvin's argument that resistance is appropriate under certain conditions is his argument from relative authorities. He maintained

---

51. Calvin, *Institutes*, 4.20.30.

52. Calvin, *Institutes*, 4.20.29.

53. Calvin, *Institutes*, 4.20.31.

54. "Qualified absolutism" is the term I use in David W. Hall, *Savior or Servant: Putting Government in Its Place* (Oak Ridge, Tenn.: Kuyper Institute, 1996). See also Ralph Keen, "The Limits of Power and Obedience in the Later Calvin," *Calvin Theological Journal* 27, no. 2 (November 1992): 252–77, for a good harmonization between the earlier and later statements by Calvin on the propriety of resistance. Although Calvin is sometimes accused of shifting toward a more republican posture, as if influenced by Beza, Keen summarizes: "It is simply necessary to recognize that the position is not pro-monarchical in itself (that is, as a political doctrine) but pro-monarchical in the theological sense of being an endorsement of the divine presence in governments" (259).

55. All quotes from this paragraph are from Calvin, *Institutes*, 4.20.32.

Calvin on Principles of Government

that a lower authority (an elder, a father, or a magistrate) could not contradict the rule or norms of a higher authority. Calvin expressed it this way: "As if God had made over his right to mortal men, giving them the rule over mankind! Or as if earthly power were diminished when it is subjected to its Author."[56] A blend of necessary factors, then, determined if revolution was in order. The following factors were necessary: a tyrant who exceeded his divinely charted boundaries; a tyrant who, in so doing, contradicted some other divine mandate; and lower magistrates to bring constitutional correction.

Calvin's Political Theology in Other Works on the Old and New Testaments

Geneva's premier Reformer, though, was more than the sum of precise theology. He was also an able commentator and communicator. Driven by the need to record biblical insights for posterity, Calvin composed commentaries on most biblical books. His commentaries contained practical discussions as well as doctrinal treatises, expounding on subjects ranging from human relationships to work ethic concerns. Several parts of Calvin's commentaries develop certain significant themes more broadly than either his sermons or the *Institutes* permitted. Representative samples, concentrating on several key texts, along with other illuminating glosses, are provided below in order to present a fuller view of Calvin's thought.

In his comments on Genesis 49, Calvin noted: "In order to make the distinction between a legitimate government and tyranny, I acknowledge that counselors were joined with the king, who should administer public affairs in a just and orderly manner."[57] Calvin also expressed his approval of classical republican traditions: "In as much as God had given them the use of the franchise, the best way to preserve their liberty for ever was by maintaining a condition of rough equality, lest a few persons of immense wealth should oppress the general body. Since, therefore, the rich, if they had been permitted constantly to increase their wealth, would have tyrannized over the rest, God put a restraint on immoderate power by means of this law."[58]

Calvin's resistance theory is further exhibited in his commentary on the rebellion of the Hebrew midwives.[59] He characterized any obedience to

---

56. Calvin, *Institutes*, 4.20.32.
57. Cited in Hopfl, *Christian Polity of John Calvin*, 162.
58. Calvin, *Commentary*, on Deut. 25:1.
59. James Smylie notes that King James VI did not approve of the Geneva Bible's note on Exodus 1, seeing all too clearly that the Marian exiles in Geneva felt quite free to recommend

154 Theology Made Practical

the murderous command of Pharaoh as preposterously unwise, a detestable effrontery, and ill-conceived in its attempt to "gratify the transitory kings of earth" while taking "no account of God."[60] Most clear in that context, Calvin wrote that God did not delegate His rights to princes, "as if every earthly power, which exalts itself against heaven, ought not rather most justly to be made to give way."

Exodus 18

Calvin's commentary on Exodus 18 displays his appreciation for the robust Hebrew contributions to republicanism.[61] In between Nimrod[62] and Moses, the notion of a republic vanished or seemed unknown. Calvin realized that all that the Israelites had known for four centuries was the monarchical rule by pharaohs. Thus, the republican-type plan suggested by Jethro appears as an innovation that did not originate in the mind of man, thought Calvin.

Rather than commending either a democracy or a monarchy, Jethro advised Moses and the people to select a plurality of prudent representative leaders (Ex. 18:21).[63] Moses instituted a graduated series of administrations with greater and lesser magistrates, and that long before the golden age of Greco-Roman governance, the Enlightenment, or other modern revolutions. The early federal scheme adopted in Exodus 18 seemed to Calvin and his followers (as it had to Aquinas and Machiavelli) to be republicanism. Commenting on the parallel in Deuteronomy 1:14–16, Calvin spied popular suffrage ("elected by the votes of the people...the most desirable kind of liberty...which allows of election, so that no one should rule except he be

---

resistance. See James H. Smylie, "America's Political Covenants, the Bible, and Calvinists," *Journal of Presbyterian History* 75, no. 3 (Fall 1997): 156, 163. The marginal note on Exodus 1:19 of the 1560 Geneva Bible reads: "Their disobedience her[e]in was lawful, but their dissembling evil."

60. Calvin, *Commentary*, on Ex. 1:17.

61. See Daniel Elazar, *Covenant and Polity in Biblical Israel* (New Brunswick, N.J.: Transaction Publishers, 1998), 1:437–47 for a full treatment of the progressive and enduring features of the early Israeli republic.

62. Even prior to Algernon Sidney, Lambert Daneau called Nimrod the first true monarch.

63. For examples of early American exposition on the character needed for office holders, complete with a discussion similar to Calvin's on this Exodus passage, see *Election Day Sermons*, ed. David W. Hall (Oak Ridge, Tenn: Kuyper Institute, 1996), 143–68. T. H. Breen provides one of the most thorough studies of American expectations for civil rulers in *The Character of the Good Ruler: A Study of Puritan Political Ideas in New England, 1630–1730* (New York: W. W. Norton, 1970). See also David Hall, *Twenty Messages to Consider before Voting* (Powder Springs, Ga.: Covenant Foundation: 2016) for exemplars of election sermons.

Calvin on Principles of Government

approved by us").[64] Thus, Calvin viewed the Hebrew republic as an early instance of rule by the consent of the governed.

Later, Calvinist Johannes Althusius (1563–1638) agreed, seeing an early form of republican-federal government in Exodus 18. Certainly it would be a stretch to claim that Calvin was *the* pioneer of a modern democratic ethos; his writings and sermons on these passages from the Pentateuch, however, illustrated God's inestimable gift to the Jewish commonwealth, specifically the freedom to elect judges and magistrates. Most of the disciples of Calvin and Beza provided ample commentary on numerous Old Testament passages that, in their opinion, provided general (if not specific) guidance for the shaping of particular governments. These various Old Testament precedents, thought most Reformers, were transferable to the politics of their own settings. Many of these same precedents were drawn upon later by Protestants in many governments. The seeds sown by Calvin blossomed amid the Western political discourse.

1 Samuel 8

Calvin's sermon on 1 Samuel 8, one of the most widely expounded political passages in Scripture, provides more insight into his political matrix. His 1561 exposition discusses the dangers of monarchy, the need for proper limitation of government, and the place of divine sovereignty over human governments. It is an example of Calvinism at its best, carefully balancing individual liberty and proper government.

Calvin began his sermon on 1 Samuel 8 by asserting that the people of Israel were not required to elect a king.[65] Warning against hierarchical "plundering and robbery," Calvin reasoned that the Lord does not give kings the right to use their power to subject the people to tyranny. Indeed, when the liberty to resist tyranny seems to be taken away by princes who have taken over, one can justly ask this question: since kings and princes are bound by covenant to the people,… if they break faith and usurp tyrannical power by which they allow themselves everything they want: is it not possible for the people to consider together taking measures in order to remedy the evil?

---

64. Calvin, *Commentary*, on Deut. 1:15.

65. Quotations are from the translation of Calvin's sermon on 1 Samuel 8 by Douglas Kelly, in *Calvin Studies Colloquium*, ed. Charles Raynal and John Leith (Davidson, N.C.: Davidson College Presbyterian Church, 1982).

156 Theology Made Practical

Calvin preached that "there are limits prescribed by God to their power, within which they ought to be satisfied: namely, to work for the common good and to govern and direct the people in truest fairness and justice; not to be puffed up with their own importance, but to remember that they also are subjects of God." Leaders were always to keep in mind the purpose (that is, the glory of God) for which they had been providentially appointed.

Calvin noted Samuel warning citizens about "the royal domination they will have to bear, and that their necks will have to be patiently submitted to his yoke." Calvin inferred something very significant from this: that intervening magistrates, not citizens themselves, should seek to correct abuses and tyranny. His doctrine was that "there are legitimate remedies against such tyranny, such as when there are other magistrates and official institutions to whom the care of the republic is committed, who will be able to restrict the prince to his proper authority so that if the prince attempts wrong action, they may hold him down." He observed that if the intervening magistrates did not free the people from tyranny, perhaps the people were being disciplined by God's providence.

Even though Calvin was more permissive of monarchy than most of his successors, his calls to submit to the governor were not without limit. God established magistrates properly "for the use of the people and the benefit of the republic." Accordingly, royal powers were circumscribed "not to undertake war rashly, nor ambitiously to increase their wealth; nor are they to govern their subjects on the basis of personal opinion or lust for whatever they want." Kings had authority only insofar as they met the conditions of God's covenant. Accordingly, he proclaimed from the pulpit of St. Peter's, "Subjects are under the authority of kings; but at the same time, kings must care about the public welfare so they can discharge the duties prescribed to them by God with good counsel and mature deliberation."

Anticipating the later teaching of Beza and Knox, Calvin taught in this sermon that lawful obedience to a ruler "does not mean that it is ever legitimate for princes to abuse them willfully.... This authority is therefore not placed in the hands of kings to be used indiscriminately and absolutely." In an early statement of limitations on political power, he said that private property was not "placed under the power and will of kings." Kings, too, were to obey the laws, lest they convince themselves that they may do anything they wish. Rather, rulers should employ "all their ingenuity for the welfare of their subjects," considering themselves bound by God's law. Calvin had the foresight to explain that magistrates were instituted to be "ministers and servants of God and the people."

This Genevan beacon, whose sermonic ideas later reached the shores of America, enumerated the ways kings abuse their power from the Samuel narrative, and he distinguished a tyrant from a legitimate prince: "A tyrant rules only by his own will and lust, whereas legitimate magistrates rule by counsel and by reason so as to determine how to bring about the greatest public welfare and benefit." Calvin decried the oppressive custom of government servants "taking part in the plundering to enrich themselves off the poor."

In this sermon, Calvin forewarned about the price associated with hierarchical government and warned that if political consequences resulted from poor political choices, perhaps that was an instance of God's judging a nation. Calvin did not call for rebellion, as Knox later did. However, similar sermons, along with reactions to the depravity witnessed in the St. Bartholomew's Day Massacre, demanded that Calvinistic political theory progress to the next level and more directly address the propriety of resistance to oppressive government.

Daniel 6

Although some theologians claim to see discrepancies between Calvin's early thought in the *Institutes* and his later commentaries and sermons on the matter of resistance, a review of his commentary on Daniel 6:21–23 reveals no radical discontinuity. Admittedly, certain events, such as the 1572 St. Bartholomew's Day Massacre,[66] forced development and clarification within the Calvinistic political tradition, but Calvin's own view about the legitimacy of reforming bad government need not be considered internally inconsistent.

Calvin expected his commentary on the Old Testament book of Daniel to become a handbook for princes. His belief that "the throne of [God's] sceptre is nothing else but the doctrine of the gospel" shows that God's conquest was not to be one of physical coercion. Meanwhile, not only were governors limited but they were also expected to be virtuous, avoiding pride, bridling their lusts, and supporting piety. Whenever rulers and governors did not "willingly submit to the yoke of Christ," societal turbulence ensued. Calvin's commentary also decried corrupt judges who gratified their own appetites.[67]

---

66. For more on this historically significant event, see chapter 4 in David W. Hall, *The Genevan Reformation and the American Founding* (Lanham, Md.: Lexington Books, 2003).

67. Calvin, *Commentary*, introduction to Daniel, lxiv–lxxv.

158 Theology Made Practical

Except for a few comments (for example, on Daniel 6:22), Calvin consistently discouraged rebellion except in extraordinary circumstances. Calvin, like Lutheran leaders, taught similarly that princes "who are not free agents though being under the tyranny of others, if they permit themselves to be overcome contrary to their conscience, lay aside all their authority and are drawn aside in all directions by the will of their subjects."[68] Calvin's frequent disparagement of ungodly kings in his sermons on Job and Deuteronomy in 1554 to 1555 and in his lectures on Daniel in 1561 indicate that he was not, in principle, a monarchist, as he indicated in the *Institutes*: "Men's vices and inadequacies make it safer and better that the many hold sway. In this way may rulers help each other, teach and admonish one another, and if one asserts himself unfairly, they may act in concert to censure, repressing his willfulness."[69]

Calvin's commentary on Daniel 6 virtually enshrines all the major principles contained in the *Institutes*, demonstrating great consistency.[70] Calvin displayed his suspicion of aggregate power in that commentary: "In the palaces of kings we often see men of brutal dispositions holding high rank, and we need not go back to history for this." Of the low and contemptible character of some rulers, he wrote, "But now kings think of nothing else than preferring their own panders, buffoons, and flatterers; while they praise none but men of low character."

Calvin also alluded to the necessity for fixed laws and universal norms, warning that "many are necessarily injured, and no private interest is stable unless the law be without variation; besides, when there is a liberty of changing laws, license succeeds in place of justice. For those who possess the supreme power, if corrupted by gifts, promulgate first one edict and then another. Thus justice cannot flourish where change in the laws allows of so much license." Of the need for resistance against a totalitarian power that wrongly attempts to command the conscience, Calvin noted that "Daniel could not obey the edict [making public prayer a crime] without committing an atrocious insult against God and declining from piety."

Calvin most clearly articulated his doctrine of contingent submission to the governor in his gloss on Daniel 6:22. Daniel, he wrote, "was not so bound to the king of the Persians when [the king] claimed for himself as

---

68. Cited in *On God and Political Duty* (Indianapolis: Bobbs-Merrill, 1956), 100–101.
69. Calvin, *Institutes*, 4.20.8.
70. Calvin, *Commentary*, on Dan. 6.

a god what ought not to be offered to him." Earthly regimes were "constituted by God, only on the condition that he deprives himself of nothing, but shines forth alone, and all magistrates must be set in regular order and every authority in existence must be subject to his glory." Daniel did not err when he disobeyed an illegitimate request from the king. As to duty, Calvin commented on this verse: "For earthly princes lay aside their power when they rise up against God, and are unworthy to be reckoned among the number of mankind. We ought, rather, utterly defy them than to obey them."

Calvin's doctrine of contingency—that is, that governors should be supported contingent upon their ruling as divinely instituted—was also manifest in his explanation of Acts 4:19–20. He stated that, regardless of their title, we should obey officials only "upon this condition, if they lead us not away from obeying God."[71] Commenting a chapter later, he summarized: "Therefore, we must obey rulers so far that the commandment not be broken." His balance is displayed in a related comment: "If a magistrate do his duty as he ought, a man shall in vain say that he is contrary to God.... We must obey God's ministers and officers if we will obey him." But if rulers lead away from obedience to God, they are dishonorable and "darken his glory." Using a parallel analogy, should a father order something unlawful in the home, he forfeits honor and "is nothing else but a man." Similarly, "If a king or ruler or magistrate becomes so lofty that he diminishes the honor and authority of God, he is but a man.... For he who goes beyond his bounds in his office must be despoiled of his honor, lest, under a color or visor, he deceive."[72]

Commenting on Jesus's teaching to render to Caesar what is Caesar's and to God what is God's, Calvin stated that obedience to a poor magistrate did not "prevent us from having within us a conscience free in the sight of God," and concluded, "Those who destroy political order are rebellious against God, and therefore, that obedience to princes and magistrates is always joined to the worship and fear of God; but that on the other hand, if princes claim any part of the authority of God, we ought not to obey them any farther than can be done without offending God."[73]

Even in view of the later New Testament teaching to fear God and honor the king (1 Peter 2:17), certain priorities must not be forgotten. Calvin commented, "The fear of God ought to precede, that kings may obtain their

---

71. Calvin, *Commentary*, on Acts 4:19–20.
72. Calvin, *Commentary*, on Acts 5:29.
73. Calvin, *Commentary*, on Mark 12:17.

160 Theology Made Practical

authority. For if any one begins his reverence of an earthly prince by rejecting that of God, he will act preposterously, since this is a complete perversion
of the order of nature." Calvin noted that "earthly princes lay aside all their
power when they rise up against God, and are unworthy of being reckoned
in the number of mankind." Rather than fulfilling unjust laws, although care
in determining this was commended as well, the Geneva Reformer advised
the following: "We ought rather utterly to defy than to obey them whenever
they are so restive and wish to spoil God of his rights, and, as it were, to seize
upon his throne and draw him down from heaven."[74]

Romans 13

Calvin's discussion of Romans 13 begins by explaining that all civil power
originates with the sovereign God—not with man, as later secular schemes
suggested. He then discussed the role of civil government and the duty of the
Christian to submit to that government except in extreme circumstances.
The civil government was given, wrote Calvin, to prevent the damage of
human sinfulness. Although it was restraining, it was a gracious institution
for society. Calvin, it should be remembered, believed that any government
was better than no government at all: "Further, some kind of government,
however deformed and corrupt it may be, is still better and more beneficial
than anarchy."[75]

In sum, however, he concluded: "Now this passage confirms what I have
already said, that we ought to obey kings and governors, whoever they may
be, not because we are constrained, but because it is a service acceptable
to God; for he will have them not only to be feared, but also honored by a
voluntary respect."[76] In addition, he called for magistrates to protect religion
and public decency—"endeavor to promote religion and to regulate morals
by wholesome discipline."[77]

Calvin called for ethical and religious considerations to be included
in good government, argued for republicanism on an authoritative basis,
pleaded with believers to exemplify virtue and be submissive as a norm, and
paved the way for later political developments by stating that the governor

---

74. Calvin, *Commentary*, on Dan. 6:22.
75. Calvin, *Commentary*, on 1 Peter 2:14. He also commented on Romans: "There can
then be no tyranny which does not in some respects assist in consolidating the society of men."
Calvin, *Commentary*, on Rom. 13:3.
76. Calvin, *Commentary*, on Rom. 13:7.
77. See Calvin, *Commentary*, on 1 Tim. 2:2.

Calvin on Principles of Government

161

could be resisted under certain conditions. His disciples later augmented and expanded the conditions under which such revolution was acceptable.

Calvin's Homology: In Civil and in Ecclesiastical Governance

We should not incorrectly estimate Calvin's political contributions.[78] Some scholars persistently see a disconnect between Calvin and his disciples or between Calvin's principles of government for the state compared to those for the church. With a little more care to detail, however, one will likely find an organic connection between Calvin's governmental principles in both areas.[79] Moreover, the homology between disciplines reinforces the unwavering championing of certain ideas and structures.

The structural dynamics between Calvin's political principles and his ecclesiology show that, to him, corporate governments as revealed from God have organic similarities. When we compare multiple loci, a homology presents itself clearly.

In terms of two spheres of government, one may even pose the question in this fashion: Did Calvin first form ecclesiological principles that would later have application to the civil sphere? Or did Calvin import and revise principles from the civil sector and then tailor them to the church?

The latter seems improbable logically, as well as historically. Calvin did not give as much attention to civil governing principles until later in his life. Thus, it is a distinct possibility that Calvin was a churchman par excellence first, and over time some of his sturdy principles in church government were adapted to secular contexts. Such would seem to fit both the logic and the historical considerations.

It is also possible, however, that Calvin developed both equally—though one loci was more pressingly urgent than the other in 1541—and both flow from the same core principles. Such is what Harro Hopfl cites as "homology," or the sameness of principles between disciplines. Hopfl identifies the following signatures of political Calvinism:

- Calvin detested rulers who acted as if their will made right (*sic volo sic iubeo*).

---

78. For my study of this, see *Calvin in the Public Square: Liberal Democracies, Rights, and Civil Liberties* (Phillipsburg, N.J.: P&R, 2009).

79. For a fuller treatment of this see my chapter "Calvin's Principles of Government: Homology in Church and State," in *Tributes to John Calvin* (Phillipsburg, N.J.: P&R, 2010).

162   Theology Made Practical

- Because no single individual possessed "power and breadth of vision enough to govern" unilaterally, a council was needed.
- Even in a monarchy, a council was required.
- Tyranny was exhibited in a ruler's unwillingness to tolerate restraint or live within the law. Any ruler should be *sub Deo et sub lege* (under God and under law).[80]

These limitations on rulers in either sphere shaped the resulting political practices approved by Calvinists. Hopfl's summary is helpful:

> There is an unmistakable preference for an aristocratic form with popular admixtures of sorts, and for small territorial units. Monarchy is explicitly rejected for ecclesiastical polity on scriptural grounds; in civil polity no such outright rejection was possible because of the earlier *parti pris* in favor of the divine authorization of all forms of government and Calvin's almost inflexible opposition to political resistance. Nonetheless, the animus against monarchs is clear enough, and civil monarchy remains a discrepant and disturbing element in an otherwise carefully synchronized arrangement of mutual constraints.[81]

As Doumergue noted, Calvin was the "founder of stable and powerful democracies, a defender not of 'egalitarianism,' but of 'equality before the law.'"[82]

In another set of texts, Calvin railed against tyrannical prelates as much as civil tyrants. Calvin opposed tyranny in both church and state government. Calvin taught similarly that princes "who are not free agents through being under the tyranny of others, if they permit themselves to be overcome contrary to their conscience, lay aside all their authority and are drawn aside in all directions by the will of their subjects."[83]

In his work on Daniel, Calvin noted that rulers were to "avoid depraved counsels, since they are besieged on every side by perfidious men, whose only object is to gain by their false representations."[84] The temptation of

---

80. Hopfl, *Christian Polity of John Calvin*, 112, 162, 164, 165, 166.
81. Hopfl, *Christian Polity of John Calvin*, 171. In this and other sections, Hopfl notes "a very clear but imperfect homology" between church government and civil polity in Calvin.
82. As quoted in Hancock, *Calvin and the Foundation of Modern Politics*, 66.
83. Calvin, *On God and Political Duty*, 100–101.
84. Calvin, *Commentary*, on Dan. 6:14–15.

Calvin on Principles of Government

rulers to succumb to their own depravity necessitated strong constraints, for the examples of political self-indulgence were not rare in the world but recurred perennially. Calvin also diagnosed envy in magistrates, which enticed them to break the law, and "they trample upon justice without modesty and without humanity."[85]

Commenting on Micah 5:5, Calvin suggested that rulers should be elected, interpreting the Hebrew word for "shepherds" as synonymous with "rulers." He asserted:

> In this especially consists the best condition of the people, when they can choose, by common consent, their own shepherds; for when any one by force usurps the supreme power, it is tyranny. And when men become kings by hereditary right, it seems not consistent with liberty. "We shall then set up for ourselves princes," says the Prophet: that is, the Lord will not only give breathing time to his Church, and will also cause that she may set up a fixed and well-ordered government, and that by the common consent of all.[86]

Calvin advocates this election by common suffrage in his commentary on Acts: "It is tyrannous if any one man appoint or make ministers at his pleasure." Election by members adequately balanced the mean between tyranny and chaotic liberty.[87]

The nineteenth-century Harvard historian George Bancroft was one of many who asserted that Calvin's ideas buttressed liberty's cause. He and others noted the influence of Calvin's thought on the development of various freedoms in Western Europe and America.[88] Bancroft extolled Calvin as "the foremost among the most efficient of modern republican legislators," who was responsible for elevating the culture of Geneva into "the impregnable fortress of popular liberty, the fertile seed-plot of democracy."[89] Bancroft even credited the "free institutions of America" as derived "chiefly from Calvinism through the medium of Puritanism," as Schaff observed.[90]

---

85. Calvin, *Commentary*, on Dan. 6:4.
86. Calvin, *Commentary*, on Mic. 5:5.
87. Calvin, *Commentary*, on Acts 6:3.
88. See Philip Schaff, *History of the Christian Church* (1910; repr., Grand Rapids: Eerdmans, 1979), 8:264.
89. Schaff, *History of the Christian Church*, 8:522.
90. Schaff, *History of the Christian Church*, 8:264.

164 Theology Made Practical

Bancroft esteemed Calvin as one of the premier republican pioneers, at one point writing, "The fanatic for Calvinism was a fanatic for liberty; and, in the moral warfare for freedom, his creed was his most faithful counselor and his never-failing support. The Puritans...planted...the undying principles of democratic liberty."[91]

Calvin is known primarily as a churchman, pastor, and theologian, but he also contributed much to theories of societal governance. Douglas Kelly points out some of the various contributions: "Governmental principles for consent of the governed, and separation and balance of powers are all logical consequences of a most serious and Calvinian view of the biblical doctrine of the fall of man."[92] Although historian Franklin Palm mistakenly classified Calvin as "wholly medieval" and as favoring an "aristocratic theocracy in which he was dictator," nevertheless, he recognized Calvin's contribution as "emphasizing the supremacy of God and the right of resistance to all other authority.... He did much to curb the powers of kings and to increase the authority of the elected representatives of the people."[93] Further, Palm noted Calvin's belief in the "right of the individual to remove the magistrate who disobeys the word of God.... Consequently, he justified many revolutionary leaders in their belief that God gave them the right to oppose tyranny."

Recently, John Witte Jr. has noted, "Calvin developed arresting new teachings on authority and liberty, duties and rights, and church and state that have had an enduring influence on Protestant lands." As a result of its adaptability, this "rendered early modern Calvinism one of the driving engines of Western constitutionalism. A number of our bedrock Western understandings of civil and political rights, social and confessional pluralism, federalism and social contract, and more owe a great deal to Calvinist theological and political reforms."[94]

These examples illustrate both the fullness of Calvin's commentary on political subjects as well as illuminate certain nuances of his theory that extend beyond the *Institutes*. His approach was comprehensive, buttressing reform of governments in all sectors—not only in the state. Calvin's legacy in this area may be one of his most enduring.

---

91. As quoted in Kingdon, *Calvin and Calvinism*, xiii. The original citation is George Bancroft, *History of the United States of America* (Boston, 1853), 1:464.
92. Kelly, *Emergence of Liberty in the Modern World*, 18.
93. Palm, *Calvinism and the Religious Wars*, 32.
94. Witte, *Reformation of Rights*, 2.

—10—

Calvin on Welfare: Diaconal Ministry in Geneva and Beyond

David W. Hall

Calvinism was certainly not hidden under a bushel or confined to a cloister; rather, it irradiated many other sectors outside the church, including the treatment of social ills. A consideration of Protestant church history as a guide to this subject is helpful in a study of methods of poverty relief. In this brief chapter, I will present some of the principles and welfare practices from nearly five centuries ago. One assumption is that over even long periods of time, the human condition and social solutions are surprisingly constant. Therefore, it is wise to benefit from what has worked successfully in other eras. This study highlights some of the best practices of Calvinism. In this survey we concentrate on the contribution of John Calvin and others in the Reformed tradition to the diaconate.

The Bourse Francaise, a diaconal ministry of the Genevan church, was founded sometime between 1536 and 1541, thus marking it as an early contribution by Calvin to social structures. Its initial design was to palliate some of the suffering of French residents who, fleeing sectarian persecution in France, arrived in Geneva in large numbers. It has been estimated that in the single decade of 1550 to 1560 some sixty thousand refugees came through Geneva, a large number to produce significant social stress. The Bourse Francaise became a pillar of societal welfare;[1] indeed, this was one of Calvin's contributions—often ignored—to Western civilization. This diaconal ministry may have had nearly as much influence in Calvin's Europe as his theology did in other areas.

Calvin's welfare program in Geneva was contoured to the theological emphases of the Reformers, providing an early illustration that welfare practice was and is (and still should be) built on definite principles that are

---

1. Jeannine Olson, *Calvin and Social Welfare: Deacons and the Bourse Francaise* (Cranbury, N.J.: Susquehanna University Press, 1989), 11–12.

166   Theology Made Practical

religious or ideological in nature. Moreover, the theology of the Reformation was the guiding force for this welfare, just as the theology of medieval Roman Catholicism had been the guiding principle for almsgiving. Ultimate principles shaped the practice of welfare 450 years ago as they do today, which is to say that at no time is welfare truly divorced from underlying ideological values.

The Genevan model for welfare did not claim uniqueness; rather, it viewed itself as the culmination of a number of factors. Among other precedents, it saw itself built upon the earlier texts of the Old Testament, the narratives from the book of Acts, and earlier canonical precedents (e. g., the Synod of Tours in 567, which assigned the responsibility of caring for the poor to each parish priest) describing the work of the diaconate. Thus the Bourse saw itself as standing on the shoulders of the work of preceding Christians.

The activities of the Bourse were numerous. Its diaconal agents were involved in housing orphans, the elderly, or those who were in any way incapacitated. They sheltered the sick and dealt with orphans and those involved in immoralities. This ecclesiastical institution was a precursor to voluntary societies in the nineteenth and twentieth centuries.

Early on in the *Ecclesiastical Ordinances* first proposed in 1541, Calvin had written a charter for the deacons, distinguishing them as one of the four basic offices of the church. This Reformation church order stipulated that among the fourth biblical office, "there were always two kinds in the ancient Church, the one deputed to receive, dispense, and hold goods for the poor, not only daily alms, but also possessions, rents and pensions; the other to tend and care for the sick and administer allowances to the poor."[2] In addition, the 1542 charter prescribed,

> It will be their duty to watch diligently that the public hospital is well maintained, and that this be so both for the sick and the old people unable to work, widowed women, orphaned children and other poor creatures. The sick are always to be lodged in a set of separate rooms from the other people who are unable to work.... Moreover, besides the hospital for those passing through which must be maintained, there should be some attention given to any recognized as worthy of special charity.[3]

----

2. *Calvin: Theological Treatises*, ed. and trans. J. K. S. Reid (Philadelphia: Westminster, 1954), 64.
3. *Calvin: Theological Treatises*, 65.

Calvin on Welfare

In the conclusion of this section, Calvin advocated "to discourage mendicancy which is contrary to good order, it would be well, and we have so ordered it, that there be one of our officials at the entrance of the churches to remove from the place those who loiter; and if there be any who give offence or offer insolence to bring them to one of the Lords Syndic."[4] Begging without honest work was an affront to the biblical Protestant work ethic. With its sophisticated design for administration and its discrimination between root causes for physical needs, Calvin's model is of more than historic interest.

Calvin was so interested in seeing the diaconate flourish that he left not only an inheritance for his family in his will but also made provision for the boys' school and poor strangers.[5] Yet this Bourse was not an entirely new institution, although its roots were decidedly connected to the theology and the experience of Geneva. The deacons cared for a large range of needs, similar to the strata of welfare needs in our own society.

In the 1541 *Ecclesiastical Ordinances* of Geneva, Calvin recommended a strong role for the diaconate, especially in almsgiving. After two decades, those *Ecclesiastical Ordinances* were revised. A modern translation of the 1561 *Ecclesiastical Ordinances* shows the sophistication and refinement of the diaconate even before Calvin's death. The following sections from the 1561 revision make clear that ministry to the poor was significant and well ordered in Calvin's time. It was neither a low priority nor slipshod in organization. The Swiss and French Reformed churches were agreed on "The Fourth Order of the Ecclesiastical Government, the Deacons," which was chartered as follows in the 1561 revision:

> 56. There were always two kinds in the ancient church: some delegated to receive, dispense and conserve the goods of the poor, daily alms as well as possessions, allowances, and pensions; others to attend to and care for the sick and administer the daily pittance. (It is indeed right for all Christian cities to conform to this, as we have tried to do and intend to continue [doing] in the future.) For we have trustees and hospital administrators; and to avoid confusion, let one of the four trustees of the hospital be the receiver of all the possessions of the above, and let him have funds sufficient to perform his task better.

---

4. *Calvin: Theological Treatises*, 66.

5. Geoffrey Bromiley, "The English Reformers and Diaconate," in *Service in Christ*, ed. James I. McCord, T. H. L. Parker, and Karl Barth (London: Epworth Press, 1966), 113.

Theology Made Practical

57. Let the number of four stewards remain as it has been: one of whom will have charge of receipts, as stated, both that provisions may be laid in more promptly and also that those who wish to give alms to the poor may be more certain that the goods will not be used otherwise than they intended. And if the revenue were not sufficient, or even if it exceeded extraordinary necessity, let the Synod advise adjustment in accordance with the poverty they observe....

60. It will be necessary to watch carefully that the common hospital is well maintained and that it is as much for the sick as for the elderly who are unable to work, such as widows, young orphans, and other poor. However, the sick shall be kept together in a lodging apart and separated from the others.

61. Let the care of the poor who are scattered throughout the city return there as the trustees direct.

62. Besides the hospital for transients, which needs to be retained, there shall be some ward apart from those perceived to be especially deserving of charity; and to accomplish this, there shall be a room reserved for their use....

64. Let the ministers, commissioners or elders with one of the Syndics take the responsibility for inquiring whether in the above-mentioned administration of the poor there be any fault or indigence, in order to beseech and warn the Synod to settle the matter. And to do this, some of their company with the stewards shall visit the hospital quarterly to ascertain whether all is in good order.

65. It will also be necessary for the poor of the hospital as well as those of the city who have no way of helping themselves to have a doctor and a qualified surgeon on the city's payroll who, even if they practice in the city, were nevertheless engaged to care for the hospital and visit the other poor.

66. And because not only the old and sick are taken to our hospital but also young children because of their poverty, we have ordered that there always be a teacher to instruct them in morality, and in the rudiments of the letters and Christian doctrine. For the most part, he shall catechize, teaching the servants of the aforesaid hospital and conduct the children to the college.

Calvin on Welfare 169

67. As to the hospital for infectious diseases, it shall be entirely separate, especially if the city happens to have been visited by some scourge from God.

68. Moreover, to prevent begging, which is contrary to good order, it will be necessary (and so we have ordered) that the Synod station some of its officers at the exits of the churches to remove those who would like to beg, and if they resist or are recalcitrant to take them to one of the Syndics. Similarly for the rest of the time let the leaders of the groups of ten see to it that the prohibition on begging is well observed.[6]

The deacons actively encouraged a productive work ethic. They provided interim subsidy and job training as necessary; on occasion, they even provided the necessary tools or supplies so that an able-bodied person could engage in an honest vocation. They were discriminating as they ascertained the difference between the truly needy and the indigent. If necessary, they would also suspend subsidy. Over time, they developed procedures that would protect the church's resources from being pilfered, even requiring new visitors to declare their craft and list character witnesses to vouch for their honesty.[7] Within a generation of this welfare work, the diaconate of Geneva discovered the need to communicate to recipients the goal that they were to return to work as soon as possible.

In sixteenth-century Geneva, there were cases of abandonment; the Bourse was frequently called upon to raise children. They supported the terminally ill who also left their children to be supported. Special gifts were given to truly needy children. The Bourse also included a ministry to widows who often had dependent children and a variety of needs.

Still, it must be noted that although the Bourse resembled many other contemporary welfare funds, it had its own peculiarities. Naturally there were theological peculiarities, and these theological distinctives led to certain practical commitments. For example, there were no guaranteed food handouts. Furthermore, there were certain prerequisites for receiving care; certain moral deficiencies could mean there would be no assistance from the Bourse.

---

6. Mary Crumpacker, "Ecclesiastical Ordinances, 1561," in *Paradigms in Polity*, ed. David W. Hall and Joseph H. Hall (Grand Rapids: Eerdmans, 1994), 148–49.

7. Olson, *Calvin and Social Welfare*, 39–40.

170   Theology Made Practical

The Bourse was not concerned only with spiritual or internal needs. On many occasions they hired medical doctors to take care of the ill. Their records indicate that the deacons oversaw medical care for the needy, reflecting that the full scope of diaconal ministry was not limited only to evangelism. Those who led the Bourse were also prudent. By January 1581, the Bourse adopted a set of constitutional rules underscoring the need to have a vital and well-thought-out disciplined approach to poverty amelioration.[8]

For our own times it is perhaps instructive to observe that in Calvin's era social welfare was not totally egalitarian. Jeannine Olson notes:

> There was an effort in Geneva to maintain the image of the Bourse Francaise as a fund to help people who were considered worthy, rather than as an institution that indiscriminately aided everyone. The funds were intended for those who were in genuine need, particularly those who were ill or handicapped. The deserving poor were numerous in this age before modern medicine or surgery, when a simple hernia or poorly aligned broken bone could render one unable to work. The limited funds of the Bourse were not intended for derelict poor, those who are considered unwilling to work, lazy and slothful vagrants and vagabonds, to use the popular English terminology of the era. The assumption that welfare recipients should be worthy of aid had long been common in Europe, but the definition of worthiness varied from one milieu to another.[9]

Despite the rigor with which the deacons distinguished between the deserving and undeserving poor, charity motivated them to err on the side of generosity. Still, however, there were times and instances in the records of the Bourse when the deacons would not give assistance to those because of attitudinal or moral blights. Charity did not imply a style of giving that mitigated personal industry and responsibility. A number of instances show that those who behaved immodestly or unchastely would not receive certain aid. Recipients of subsidy were expected to uphold Christian standards of morality; if not, the Bourse might well withhold support until immoral behavior was jettisoned. The deacons attempted to use the Bourse as a means of discipline and encouragement.

---

8. Olson, *Calvin and Social Welfare*, 104–6.

9. Olson, *Calvin and Social Welfare*, 139.

Calvin on Welfare

In his commentaries, Calvin consistently set forth similar principles. On 2 Thessalonians 3:10, he commented, "When, however, the Apostle commanded that such persons should not eat, he does not mean that he gave commandment to those persons, but forbade that the Thessalonians should encourage their indolence by supplying them with food.... Paul censures those lazy drones who lived by the sweat of others, while they contribute no service in common for aiding the human race."[10] In commenting on Psalm 112:9, the Genevan Reformer elaborated,

> By dispersing [to the poor], the prophet intimates, that they did not give sparingly and grudgingly, as some do who imagine that they discharge their duty to the poor when they dole out a small pittance to them, but that they give liberally as necessity requires and their means allow; for it may happen that a liberal heart does not possess a large portion of the wealth of this world.... Next he adds, they give to the poor, meaning that they do not bestow their charity at random, but with prudence and discretion meet the wants of the necessitous. We are aware that unnecessary and superfluous expenditure for the sake of ostentation is frequently lauded by the world; and consequently, a larger quantity of the good things of this life is squandered away in luxury and ambition than is dispensed in charity prudently bestowed. The prophet instructs us that the praise which belongs to liberality does not consist in distributing our goods without any regard to the objects upon whom they are conferred, and the purposes to which they are applied, but in relieving the wants of the really necessitous, and in the money being expended on things proper and lawful.[11]

Thus the experiment in welfare in Geneva offers a clinic in what may happen when welfare is conformed to biblical principles.

It is helpful to remember also that the Bourse Francaise was a transitional institution. Occurring at the consummation of centuries of medieval welfare yet renewed by the Protestant Reformation, the founders of the Bourse did not hold to the utopian notion that poverty would be entirely eliminated. In reference to Jesus's statement in Mark 14:7 ("ye have the poor with you always"), these founders of the Genevan diaconate were realists

---

10. Calvin, *Commentary*, on 2 Thess. 3:10.
11. Calvin, *Commentary*, on Ps. 112:9.

172   Theology Made Practical

who consulted the past as they formed new manifestations of earlier models. As Reformers they were most attracted to the institution of the early church, finding that model most fruitful for their reforms. They lived on the cusp of a reform movement, learning from what had gone before them.

As those who look to the past and to the inadequacies of the present, perhaps we should replicate some of that posture too. We might be better off from this and other studies to see what we can learn from the past rather than looking exclusively to the future. In fact, if we find ourselves advocating practices markedly different from what the Bourse in Geneva did nearly five centuries ago, then it may be that our novel methods should be suspect to the extent that we deviate from earlier sound practice in the area of public welfare.

In summary thus far, we have seen the following as principles of Calvin's welfare reform:

- It was only for the truly disadvantaged.
- Moral prerequisites accompanied assistance.
- Private or religious charity, not state largesse, was the vehicle for aid.
- Ordained officers managed and brought accountability.
- Theological underpinnings were normal.
- Productive work ethic was sought.
- Assistance was temporary.
- History is valuable.

In a sermon on 1 Timothy 3:8–10, Calvin depicted the early church's compassion as the canon to measure our Christianity: "When there were neither lands nor possessions nor what is called property of the church, it was necessary that each give his offering and from that the poor be supplied. If we want to be considered Christians and want it to be believed that there is some church among us, this organization must be demonstrated and maintained." Later in that same sermon he enjoined, "Now when that property has been distributed as it ought, if that still does not meet all needs, let each give alms privately and publicly, so that the poor may be aided as is fitting."[12]

Calvin's testimony is quite full. In one of his sermons on 1 Timothy 3:8–13, he remarked:

---

12. *CO*, 53:297–98, as quoted in Elsie A. McKee, *John Calvin on the Diaconate and Liturgical Almsgiving* (Geneva: Librarie Droz, 1984), 62.

We saw this morning what position St. Paul discusses here, that is, that of those who in the ancient church were ordained to distribute the alms. It is certain that God wants such a rule observed in His church: that is, that there be care for the poor—and not only that each one privately support those who are poor, but that there be a public office, people ordained to have the care of those who are in need so that things may be conducted as they ought. And if that is not done, it is certain that we cannot boast that we have a church well-ordered and according to the gospel, but there is just so much confusion.[13]

Later in the same text, Calvin commented,

And yet the deacons are those ordained to have the care of the poor and to distribute alms, the care not only of distributing what is entrusted to them, but of inquiring where there is need and where the property ought to be used.... We must find people who may govern the property of the poor. These are the sacrifices offered to God today, that is, alms. Therefore it is necessary that they be distributed by those whom God considers suitable for such a position, and that the deacons who are chosen *should be as the hands of God*, and be there in a holy office.[14]

So strong was Calvin's view that he preached,

Inasmuch as it is a question of the spiritual government which God has put among His own, St. Paul wants those who are ordained, whether to proclaim the gospel or to have the care of the poor, to be of irreproachable life.... We must carefully note these passages where it is proclaimed to us what order God has established in His Church, so that we may take care to conform ourselves to it the best we can.... Because if we want to have the Church among us, we must have this government which God has established as inviolable, or at least we must strive to conform ourselves to it.[15]

---

13. As quoted in McKee, *John Calvin on the Diaconate*, 183.
14. As quoted in McKee, *John Calvin on the Diaconate*, 184.
15. As quoted in McKee, *John Calvin on the Diaconate*, 184.

174 Theology Made Practical

Commenting on Romans 12:8, Johannes Oecolampadius, an earlier contemporary of Calvin, echoed this point about deacons and ministry to the poor:

> Sixth, those who show mercy, who differ in this way. For those who give mutually, and from their own means supply the hungry and the naked, are said to impart. And these ought to give simply and freely, without respect for temporal concerns, or friendship, or convenience. Those indeed who visit the sick and captives and are present with the afflicted are called those who show mercy, and their office ought to be done with a cheerful spirit and with promptness. Seventh are those who preside in any congregation; these ought to be courteous and diligent.[16]

Calvin's priorities lived on after his death. Even one of the adversaries of Calvin disciple Theodore Beza, Jean Morely, affirmed the church's strong role in caring for those in poverty. In his 1562 *Treatise on Christian Discipline*, Morely asserted that in some organized manner, the church should "relieve the poor, and property should be set aside for its support. For poverty creates temptations to vice and corruption which few can resist.... In fact many of the arrangements are designed primarily to keep the able-bodied but indolent poor from receiving aid on a regular basis, so that all the church's resources for poor relief can go to those victims of circumstance who are deserving and helpless."[17]

Of all the Reformers, Martin Bucer was considered the "theologian of the diaconate" since he wrote most directly about the function of the church in caring for the poor. Bucer argued in his 1560 *De Regno Christi* that "there must be in the 'Christian Republic' a thorough organization of poor relief and assistance to the sick.... For the fulfillment of these ends discipline is essential, and so there must be a thorough organization of labour and leisure."[18]

Bucer went as far as to say of the diaconate that "without it there can be no true communion of saints,"[19] while simultaneously asserting that "the

---

16. Olson, *Calvin and Social Welfare*, 191.

17. As quoted in Robert M. Kingdon, *Geneva and the Consolidation of the French Protestant Movement, 1564–1572* (Madison: University of Wisconsin Press, 1967), 56.

18. Basil Hall, "Diaconia in Martin Butzer," in *Service in Christ*, ed. James I. McCord, T. H. L. Parker, and Karl Barth (London: Epworth Press, 1966), 94.

19. Hall, "Diaconia in Martin Butzer," 99.

first duty of the deacons is to distinguish between the deserving and undeserving poor, for the former to inquire carefully into their needs; the latter, if they lead disorderly lives at the expense of others, to expel them from the community of the faithful. Care, next, is to be taken for needy widows. The second duty of deacons is to keep a written record of accounts, having sought diligently for the proper collecting of funds from all the parishioners according to their capacity."[20]

In the British Isles, almsgiving was emphasized as one means for poverty relief. King Edward VI would assert that "to relieve the poor is...a true worshiping of God."[21]

Hence the Calvinistic tradition was settled and fairly uniform in its institutionalizing care for the poor. It was an ecclesiological function to be carried out by spiritual officers according to biblical standards and principles. As it was carried out well, it cared for the poor, employed the church's gifts, encouraged a productive work ethic, and relieved governmental stewardship in this area. As Bromiley summarizes, "The able-bodied should work and support themselves.... The answer to poverty was still found in individual benevolence exercised either privately or through the Church."[22]

Zurich also was a model for social welfare. The city began its reform and its diaconal ministry as early as 1520. The same may be said for Strasbourg and other cities in Lutheran territory. For example, in Strasbourg, "preaching of welfare reform began before the Protestant Reformation. Geiler Von Kaysersberg urged a new system of poor relief that included a suggestion that able-bodied people should work. Only those incapable of work, he argued, should receive relief."[23] Since when Calvin was exiled from Geneva he spent two years in the late 1530s in Strasbourg, it is possible that these other Swiss Reformed models could have indeed shaped, in no small part, the welfare relief model of Geneva. Luther, it should also be remembered, was opposed to handouts without responsibility or true demonstration of need. He quipped, "Do not spoonfeed the masses. If we were to support Mr. Everybody, he would turn too wanton and go dancing on the ice."[24] According to Luther, the "poor by their own folly" were not deserving of help.

---

20. Hall, "Diaconia in Martin Butzer," 99.
21. As quoted by Geoffrey Bromiley, in "English Reformers and Diaconate," 120.
22. Bromiley, "English Reformers and Diaconate, 113.
23. Bromiley, "English Reformers and Diaconate," 165.
24. As quoted in Bromiley, "English Reformers and Diaconate," 112.

176 Theology Made Practical

Neither did Luther fail to translate his faith into practice in the area of poverty relief. As early as 1520, in his *Address to the German Nobility*, Luther "strongly disapproved of any and every kind of mendicancy and beggary and advised every town to assume responsibility for its own poor and needy by appointing an official to advise the pastor."[25] Begging was to be eliminated as its erstwhile theological foundation crumbled under Dr. Martin's *sola fide* theology. Begging could no longer be viewed as a monastic ideal, as a meritorious work, or as Christian perfection. Instead, it was to be curtailed as much as possible by a proper theological correction. Begging would be eradicated with the care for the poor assigned to each small unit of governing—the individual city. In his *Babylonian Captivity* (1520), Luther saw the church through its diaconate as the agency to minister to the poor, in contrast to the role of deacons within Roman Catholicism: "The diaconate...is a ministry, not for reading the Gospel and the Epistle, as the practice is nowadays, but for distributing the Church's bounty to the poor, in order that the priests might be relieved of the burden of temporal concerns and give themselves more freely to prayer and the Word."[26] In Strasbourg, "we find as early as 1523 a thorough evangelical organization under the care of a director, four assistant directors, nine church workers with twenty-one helpers. Here it was stipulated that the poor were not only to be helped materially but to be visited as persons at least four times in a year."[27] The church's ministry to the poor was not a later development for the Reformers.

Conclusion

Calvin again was bringing light to a blighted sector. He was not alone in the efforts to supercede darkness. Calvin, whose name is not always and immediately identified with compassionate advocacy of welfare to the poor, even on one occasion rhetorically asserted, "Do we want to show that there is reformation among us? We must begin at this point, that is, there must be pastors who bear purely the doctrine of salvation, and then deacons who have the care of the poor."[28]

---

25. James Atkinson, "Diaconia at the Time of the Reformation," in *Service in Christ*, ed. James I. McCord, T. H. L. Parker, and Karl Barth (London: Epworth Press, 1966), 84.

26. Atkinson, "Diaconia at the Time of the Reformation," 86.

27. Atkinson, "Diaconia at the Time of the Reformation," 86.

28. As quoted in McKee, *John Calvin on the Diaconate*, 184.

—11—

Christian Marriage in the Twenty-First Century: Listening to Calvin on the Purpose of Marriage

Michael A. G. Haykin

In the final decade of the second century, an African Christian by the name of Septimius Florens Tertullianus[1]—we know him simply as Tertullian—penned one of the loveliest descriptions of Christian marriage in the literary corpus of the ancient church.

> How shall we ever be able adequately to describe the happiness of that marriage which the Church arranges,... upon which the blessing sets a seal, at which angels are present as witnesses, and to which the Father gives his consent?... How beautiful, then, the marriage of two Christians, two who are one in hope, one in desire, one in the way of life they follow, one in the religion they practice. They are as brother and sister, both servants of the same Master. Nothing divides them, either in flesh or in spirit. They are, in very truth, two in one flesh; and where there is but one flesh there is also but one spirit. They pray together, they worship together, they fast together; instructing one another, encouraging one another, strengthening one another. Side by side they visit God's church and partake of God's Banquet; side by side they face difficulties and persecution, share their consolations. They have no secrets from one another; they never shun each other's company; they never bring sorrow to each other's hearts. Unembarrassed they visit the sick and assist the needy. They give alms without anxiety;... they perform their daily exercises of piety without hindrance.... Psalms and hymns they sing to one another, striving to see which one of them will chant more

---

1. This is the name given to him by medieval manuscripts. See T. D. Barnes, *Tertullian: A Historical and Literary Study* (Oxford: Clarendon, 1971), 242.

178　　　　　　　　　　　Theology Made Practical

beautifully the praises of their Lord. Hearing and seeing this, Christ rejoices. To such as these he gives his peace.[2]

Building on the biblical given that marriage is a one-flesh union (Gen. 2:24; Matt. 19:4–6; 1 Cor. 6:16–17), Tertullian details what such a union entails with regard to Christian privileges and responsibilities. It is noteworthy that Tertullian assumes that a Christian marriage is one that takes place with the blessing of the church, a perspective that can be traced back at least to Ignatius of Antioch at the beginning of the second century.[3]

Tertullian's high view of marriage is also significant in light of the church's battle at the time with the Gnostics, who despised marriage and rejected it as a legitimate choice for one seeking to lead a spiritual life. In the words of one Gnostic, Saturninus, "Marriage and generation are from Satan."[4] The church's general response to this Gnostic disparagement of marriage was shaped by biblical texts such as 1 Timothy 4:1–4, which stressed that marriage is a good estate and ordained of God. From this key truth subsequent Christian thought has never explicitly departed. As John Chrysostom, one of the leading preachers of the late fourth century, argued: "How foolish are those who belittle marriage! If marriage were something to be condemned, Paul would never call Christ a bridegroom and the church a bride."[5]

The Late Patristic and Medieval Backgrounds

Yet there have been writers within the parameters of Christian orthodoxy whose perspectives on this vital institution of marriage have sounded significantly different notes from those of Tertullian and Chrysostom. The latter's fourth-century contemporary Jerome (d. 420), for instance, who was responsible for the Latin translation of the Bible known as the Vulgate, vigorously defended the view that celibacy was a vastly superior state to marriage, more virtuous and more pleasing to God. Jerome was convinced that all those who were closest to God in the Scriptures were celibate. In fact, Jerome

---

2. Septimius Florens Tertullianus, "To His Wife" 2.8, in *Treatises on Marriage and Remarriage*, trans. William P. LeSaint (1951; repr., New York: Paulist Press, n.d.), 35–36.

3. See Ignatius, *Letter to Polycarp*, ch. 5, in *The Ante-Nicene Fathers*, ed. Alexander Roberts and James Donaldson (New York: Charles Scribner's Sons, 1913), 1:95. Henceforth cited as *ANF*.

4. As quoted in Irenaeus, *Against Heresies*, 1.24.2, in *ANF*, 1:349.

5. John Chrysostom, "Homily 20 on Ephesians 5:22–23," in *On Marriage and Family Life*, trans. Catharine Roth and David Anderson (Crestwood, N.J.: St. Vladimir's Press, 1986), 54–55.

Christian Marriage in the Twenty-First Century

argued, sexual relations between spouses were a distinct obstacle to leading a life devoted to the pursuit of genuine spirituality.[6]

Augustine (354–430), another Latin-speaking theologian from the same era whose thought provided the foundation for much of the thinking of the Middle Ages, similarly maintained that those who devote themselves to Christ to live a celibate lifestyle are like the angels. They experience a foretaste of heaven, for in heaven there is no marriage.[7] Why, then, did God ordain marriage? In Augustine's eyes, it was primarily for the procreation of children. Commenting on Genesis 2, Augustine was convinced that Eve would have been of no use to Adam if she had not been able to bear children. What, then, of the biblical idea, found in this chapter of Genesis, that the woman was made to be a delightful companion to the man, a source of comfort and strength? And what of the man as this for the woman? These ideas receive scant attention in Augustine's theology.[8] Augustine argues that God instituted marriage for basically three reasons: for the sake of fidelity—that is, the avoidance of illicit sex; for the purpose of procreation; and as a symbol of the unity of those who would inherit the heavenly Jerusalem.[9]

These positions of Jerome and Augustine were largely embraced by the medieval Roman Catholic Church, which affirmed the goodness of marriage but at the same time argued that celibacy was a much better option for those wanting to pursue a life of holiness and serve God vocationally.[10] Not surprisingly, by the High Middle Ages—the Second Lateran Council (1139) to be specific—the Roman Catholic Church legislated that only those who were celibate were to be ordained. But it was precisely here that reality collided with theological legislation, for many of those who were technically celibate priests in the High and Late Middle Ages were not able actually to live chastely. As Calvin once noted: "Virginity...is an excellent gift; but it is given

---

6. J. N. D. Kelly, *Jerome: His Life, Writings, and Controversies* (New York: Harper & Row, 1975), 183, 187.

7. James A. Mohler, *Late Have I Loved You: An Interpretation of Saint Augustine on Human and Divine Relationships* (New York: New City, 1991), 71.

8. Edmund Leites, "The Duty to Desire: Love, Friendship, and Sexuality in Some Puritan Theories of Marriage," *Journal of Social History* 15 (1981–1982): 384.

9. Mohler, *Late Have I Loved You*, 68. See also the summary of Augustine's position in John Witte Jr., *From Sacrament to Contract: Marriage, Religion and Law in the Western Tradition* (Louisville: Westminster, 1997), 21–22.

10. Witte Jr., *From Sacrament to Contract*, 24–25.

180   Theology Made Practical

only to a few."[11] One of the major scandals of the late medieval church was thus the household of the parish priest who was celibate but not chaste, his so-called cook or housekeeper actually serving as his concubine.[12] For Calvin, the Roman Catholic requirement of the celibacy of its priests was thus a "diabolical system," "a modern tyranny—in sum, a doctrine of devils."[13] So it was that for many in Western Europe, the Reformation in the sixteenth century was not only a rediscovery of the heart of the gospel and the way of salvation but also a recovery of a fully biblical view of marriage.

After the death of his wife, Idelette, in March of 1549, Calvin wrote to his fellow Reformer and confidant Pierre Viret (1511–1571): "I am deprived of my excellent life companion, who, if misfortune had come, would have been my willing companion not only in exile and sorrow, but even in death."[14] This simple statement from one of the central figures of the Reformation who was normally discreet about his personal feelings reveals a view of marriage poles apart from that of medieval Roman Catholicism. For the Reformers and those who followed in their stead—like the Puritans of the seventeenth century and the Evangelicals of the eighteenth and nineteenth centuries— marriage has an innate excellence, is vital for the development of Christian affection and friendship, and is one of God's major means for developing Christian character and spiritual maturity. In what follows, this perspective on Christian marriage is explored through John Calvin's experience of marriage, interweaving with this narrative some theological reflection from Calvin on the institution of marriage. Please note that while Calvin, drawing upon his legal training, was instrumental in crafting a comprehensive body of law surrounding marriage and divorce, this area of Calvin's thought will not be treated directly here.[15]

---

11. As quoted in J. Graham Miller, *Calvin's Wisdom: An Anthology Arranged Alphabetically by a Grateful Reader* (Edinburgh: Banner of Truth Trust, 1992), 206.

12. Susan C. Karant-Nunn, "Reformation Society, Women and the Family," in *The Reformation World*, ed. Andrew Pettegree (London: Routledge, 2000), 437–38.

13. As quoted in Miller, *Calvin's Wisdom*, 206; and Scott Brown, *Family Reformation: The Legacy of Sola Scriptura in Calvin's Geneva* (Wake Forest, N.C.: Merchant Adventurers, 2009), 114. I am deeply indebted to Scott Brown for sending me a copy of his book and to Dr. Joel Beeke for drawing my attention to it.

14. As quoted in Richard Stauffer, *The Humanness of John Calvin*, trans. George H. Shriver (Nashville: Abingdon, 1971), 45.

15. For details of this transformation, see especially John Witte Jr. and Robert M. Kingdon, *Sex, Marriage, and Family in John Calvin's Geneva*, vol. 1, *Courtship, Engagement, and Marriage* (Grand Rapids: Eerdmans, 2005), 97.

Calvin's Courtships

There is no evidence that Calvin seriously entertained getting married prior to his sojourn in Strasbourg.[16] As he wrote around this time: "I have never married, and I do not know whether I ever will. If I do, it will be in order to be freer from many daily troubles and thus freer for the Lord. Lack of sexual continence would not be the reason I would point to for marrying. No one can charge me with that."[17] It was not that Calvin was opposed to marriage. His embrace of Reformation doctrine certainly entailed a positive approval of marriage. As he noted in his sermon on Ephesians 5:31–33: "Marriage is not a thing ordained by men. We know that God is the author of it, and that it is solemnized in his name."[18] In his commentary on the minor prophet Malachi, Calvin puts it even more succinctly, "God is the founder of marriage."[19]

But it was simply the case that there was no pressing need in his own life pushing him in that direction. As he said on another occasion, "I shall not belong to those who are accused of attacking [the Church of] Rome, like the Greeks fought Troy, only to be able to take a wife."[20] If he did enter into the estate of marriage, he confessed, it would be to secure a context in which he could be freed from the concerns of daily life and thus freer to give himself more wholeheartedly to the work of Christ. But if Calvin was not eager to get married, a number of his friends in Strasbourg were anxious to see him wed, among whom the chief were Martin Bucer (1491–1551) and Guillaume Farel (1489–1565).

Bucer was at the forefront of a sweeping reform of marriage, both institutionally and conceptually, in Strasbourg and in various other cities in Switzerland and Germany. A former Dominican monk who had been converted through the preaching of Martin Luther (1483–1546), Bucer had married his first wife, a former nun by the name of Elisabeth Silbersein, in 1522 and had come to view love as the indispensable qualification of marriage.

---

16. Witte Jr. and Kingdon, *Sex, Marriage, and Family in John Calvin's Geneva*, 87.

17. As quoted in Witte Jr. and Kingdon, *Sex, Marriage, and Family in John Calvin's Geneva*, 97.

18. As quoted in John Witte Jr., "Marriage and Family Life," in *The Calvin Handbook*, ed. Herman J. Selderhuis, trans. Henry J. Baron, Judith J. Guder, Randi H. Lundell, and Gerrit W. Sheeres (Grand Rapids: Eerdmans, 2009), 457.

19. As quoted in Miller, *Calvin's Wisdom*, 204.

20. As quoted in William J. Petersen, "Idelette: John Calvin's Search for the Right Wife," *Christian History* 5, no. 4 (1986): 12.

182   Theology Made Practical

Where love was absent, he even reasoned, there was sufficient grounds for divorce.[21] This was not grounds for divorce that Calvin would later sanction, though; in harmony with other Reformers, he would reject the Roman Catholic doctrine of the indissolubility of marriage as it had been defined in the Middle Ages. Bucer was especially convinced that a gospel minister was rarely able, given the stresses and strains of ministry, to fulfill his calling without a faithful companion. Machiel van den Berg rightly suggests that "Bucer may well be called the founder of the Protestant parsonage."[22]

Only a few months after Calvin arrived in Strasbourg in 1538, Bucer had found a woman for Calvin to consider marrying. Things seemed to be proceeding toward an actual wedding, for in February 1539 Calvin wrote to his close friend Guillaume Farel to ask if he could come to Strasbourg "to solemnize and ask a blessing upon the marriage."[23] Calvin told Farel that he expected the bride to arrive shortly after Easter, and there is a distinct possibility that he would only then meet her for the first time.[24] But as it turned out, the marriage did not take place, and there is no surviving literary evidence to indicate why not.

It was now Farel's turn to play matchmaker. By the following May he had found a woman who might suit his friend. When he wrote to ascertain Calvin's level of interest, Calvin responded with details as to what he was seeking in a wife: "I am not one of those insane kind of lovers who, once smitten by the first sight of a fine figure, cherishes even the faults of his lover. The only beauty that seduces me is of one who is chaste, not too fastidious, modest, thrifty, patient, and hopefully she will be attentive to my health."[25] This is an important text, for in it Calvin lays out what was most vital for him in seeking a potential spouse—namely, character and such inner qualities as modesty, self-control, and patience. In other words, in seeking a wife or in seeking a husband, a Christian must consider genuine piety the thing most needful.[26]

---

21. Witte Jr. and Kingdon, *Sex, Marriage, and Family in John Calvin's Geneva*, 98.

22. Machiel van den Berg, *Friends of Calvin*, trans. Reinder Bruinsma (Grand Rapids: Eerdmans, 2009), 125.

23. John Calvin to Guillaume Farel, February 28, 1539, in *Tracts and Letters*, 4:110. In tracing the various attempts by Calvin's friends to get him married, Witte Jr. and Kingdon, *Sex, Marriage, and Family in John Calvin's Geneva*, 97–100 has been very helpful.

24. Calvin to Guillaume Farel, February 28, 1539, in *Tracts and Letters*, 4:110.

25. John Calvin to Guillaume Farel, May 19, 1539, in *Tracts and Letters*, 4:141, following the amended translation by Witte Jr. and Kingdon, *Sex, Marriage, and Family in John Calvin's Geneva*, 109.

26. Witte Jr., "Marriage and Family Life," 461–62.

Christian Marriage in the Twenty-First Century 183

In other texts, Calvin reveals that he did not altogether discount the place of physical beauty in the choice of a spouse. As he pointed out in 1554 in his commentary on Genesis 6:2, "Moses does not condemn men for regarding beauty in their choice of wives, only lust."[27] And in the same work, when he came to comment on Jacob's love for Rachel, he noted: "A man who is induced to choose a wife because of the elegance of her form will not necessarily sin, provided reason always maintains the ascendancy, and holds the wantonness of passion under control.... For it is a very culpable lack of self-control when any man chooses a wife only for her beauty. Her excellence of disposition ought to be deemed the most important."[28]

Calvin is well aware how a man can be bedazzled by a beautiful woman and forget that "excellence of disposition" is what is all-important; hence his emphasis that "reason...maintain the ascendancy" over the passions set in motion by his eyes.

Farel's potential spouse for his friend, though, soon disappeared, only to be replaced by two more the following year. In February 1540 Calvin wrote to Farel that a woman of considerable wealth had been proposed to the Reformer as a possible wife. Calvin told his friend that he had "the audacity to think of taking a wife." But he had concerns about the woman's suitability. First, the woman was German and apparently could not speak French, and when Calvin asked if she was willing to learn French, she asked for time to think about it—not a good sign. Then, she was very wealthy, and Calvin seems to have been concerned that she might find it difficult living with someone like himself whose standard of living was below what she was accustomed to. At the same time, Calvin had his brother Antoine (d. 1573) approach another woman who was highly regarded about marriage. Again Calvin asked Farel to be ready to come to conduct their wedding, which, he hoped, would be held before March 10 of that year. He would look quite foolish, he added, if this second marriage also failed to transpire.[29]

He must have been embarrassed indeed, for this second courtship also fell through. When it did, the family of the wealthy woman who spoke no French began to try to rekindle Calvin's interest in her. But Calvin told Farel

---

27. Calvin, *Commentary*, on Gen. 6:2, as quoted in Witte Jr. and Kingdon, *Sex, Marriage, and Family in John Calvin's Geneva*, 108.

28. Calvin, *Commentary*, on Gen. 29:18, as quoted in Witte Jr. and Kingdon, *Sex, Marriage, and Family in John Calvin's Geneva*, 108.

29. John Calvin to Guillaume Farel, February 6, 1540, in *Tracts and Letters*, 4:173–74.

184   Theology Made Practical

plainly that the only way he would ever consider marrying her was if the Lord had altogether taken away his wits.[30] That summer he told Farel, "I have not yet found a wife" and painfully admitted that he was on the verge of resigning himself to a life of celibacy.[31] But two months later everything had changed. Calvin had married a widow whom he had known for a number of years, Idelette van Buren (d. 1549).[32]

Marriage to Idelette

Idelette van Buren's roots were in the Netherlands. Machiel van den Berg suggests that she may have come from the province of Gelderland, where there is the town of Buren.[33] Be this as it may, her first husband, Jean Stordeur, was a Walloon from Liège, today in Belgium. For a time Jean and his wife Idelette were convinced Anabaptists. And it was as a prominent Anabaptist that Jean had first met Calvin in Geneva in March 1537, when Jean came to the city for a discussion between the Anabaptists and the Reformed pastors. Two years later, now in Strasbourg, Calvin had succeeded in showing Jean and Idelette the error of their distinct Anabaptist views, and they became members of the French congregation that Calvin was pastoring there.

It was not long after this that Jean died of the plague in the spring of 1540. Calvin had obviously gotten to know Idelette initially through the discussions she and her husband had had with him about the Reformed faith. Then, when Jean was dying, Calvin would have seen more of Idelette when he made pastoral visits to their home. What he saw of her made such a deep impression on him that by August 17, 1540, Calvin had married her. Idelette had two children from her first marriage, a boy and a girl, and thus Calvin inherited a ready-made family, as it were. And although Calvin had rightly emphasized that external beauty was not to be a key determinant in marriage, she was, according to Farel, very pretty.[34]

---

30. John Calvin to Guillaume Farel, March 29, 1540, in *Tracts and Letters*, 4:175.

31. John Calvin to Guillaume Farel, June 21, 1540, in *Tracts and Letters*, 4:191.

32. For studies of Idelette, who is often referred to by the French version of her surname "de Bure," see especially Willem Balke, *Calvin and the Anabaptist Radicals*, trans. William Heynen (Grand Rapids: Eerdmans, 1981), 133–38; Petersen, "Idelette: John Calvin's Search for the Right Wife," 12–15; and Van den Berg, *Friends of Calvin*, 123–33. For further studies, see the articles and books listed by Balke, *Calvin and the Anabaptist Radicals*, 133–34n46; and Van den Berg, *Friends of Calvin*, 124n1.

33. Van den Berg, *Friends of Calvin*, 128.

34. Van den Berg, *Friends of Calvin*, 129.

Christian Marriage in the Twenty-First Century 185

We know little about Calvin's marriage to Idelette compared to the marriages of other famous Reformers. Martin Luther's famous marriage to Katharina von Bora, for example, became something of a public exemplar for Protestants. Not so Calvin's marriage, which was very much in line with Calvin's habitual reticence to go public about his personal affairs. Yet in the year following Idelette's death in 1549, he stated in his little tract *Concerning Scandals* (1550) that Idelette was "a rare woman" (*singularis exempli femina*; literally, a woman of matchless type[35]).

And this briefest of statements matches what we learn about Idelette from a letter that Calvin wrote to Pierre Viret after her death on March 29, 1549. In it Calvin stated:

Although the death of my wife has been exceedingly painful to me, yet I subdue my grief as well as I can.... You know well enough how tender, or rather soft, my mind is. Had not a powerful self-control, therefore, been vouchsafed to me, I could not have borne up so long. And truly mine is no common source of grief. I have been bereaved of the best possible companion of my life, of one, who, had it been so ordered, would not only have been the willing sharer of my indigence, but even of my death. During her life she was my faithful co-labourer in my ministry.[36]

Here, in the space of a few lines from his sorrowing heart, Calvin sums up the Reformed understanding of marriage: it is a union of intimate allies. Idelette had been the "best possible companion" of his life (*optima socio vitae*), one who had been a "faithful co-labourer" in his ministry (*fida ministerii me iadjutrix*).

Behind this understanding of marriage lies Genesis 2:18–24, where we are told that Adam's being alone is not "good," which is striking because everything else God had made to that point is said to have been good. So we read in this passage that God made Adam a "helper" (*ezer*), a word, according to Calvin's commentary on this text, that goes to the heart of his understanding of marriage. As he comments on this passage in Genesis:

Now, since God assigns the woman as a help to the man, he…pronounces that marriage will really prove to men the best support of

---

35. Balke, *Calvin and the Anabaptist Radicals*, 136.
36. John Calvin to Pierre Viret, April 7, 1549, in *Tracts and Letters*, 5:216, alt.

186 Theology Made Practical

life.... The vulgar proverb, indeed, is, that she is a necessary evil; but the voice of God is rather to be heard, which declares that woman is given as a companion and an associate to the man, to assist him to live well.[37]

But the fallenness of humanity—which, in Calvin's day, had issued in the unbiblical perspectives on marriage, celibacy, and sexuality promoted by Roman Catholic theologians—has deeply disfigured God's intentions for the holy estate of marriage. As Calvin went on to delineate:

I confess, indeed, that in this corrupt state of mankind, the blessing of God, which is here described, is neither perceived nor flourishes; but the cause of the evil must be considered, namely, that the order of nature, which God had appointed, has been inverted by us. For if the integrity of man had remained to this day such as it was from the beginning, that divine institution would be clearly discerned, and the sweetest harmony would reign in marriage; because the husband would look up with reverence to God; the woman in this would be a faithful assistant to him; and both, with one consent, would cultivate a holy, as well as friendly and peaceful intercourse.[38]

And it was this conviction about marriage, rooted as it was in solid reflection on Scripture, that led Calvin to make such wide-ranging statements about marriage as that it is "the sacred bond," "a holy fellowship," "a divine partnership," "a loving association," "the best support of life," and "the holiest kind of company in all the world."[39]

Having Children

For Calvin, a second purpose of marriage was having children. Thus, Calvin argued that those who were incapable of having sexual relations should not marry, for such marriages "completely obviate the nature and purpose of marriage."[40] In July 1542, during the Calvins' first summer back in Geneva,

---

37. As quoted in Brown, *Family Reformation*, 131–32. On companionship as the central purpose of marriage, see Rousas J. Rushdoony, "The Doctrine of Marriage," in *Toward a Christian Marriage: A Chalcedon Study*, ed. Elizabeth Fellersen, 2nd ed. (Vallecito, Calif.: Ross House Books, 1994), 12.

38. As quoted in Brown, *Family Reformation*, 132.

39. These phrases are quoted in Witte Jr., *From Sacrament to Contract*, 109; and Brown, *Family Reformation*, 97–114, 131–32.

40. As quoted in Witte Jr., "Marriage and Family Life," 462.

Christian Marriage in the Twenty-First Century

Idelette gave premature birth to a boy, whom they named Jacques.[41] By mid-August, though, the young child had died. Pierre Viret's wife wrote a consolatory letter to Idelette, for which Calvin thanked her on behalf of his wife. He pointed out that Idelette was so overcome with grief that she could not even dictate a letter in reply. "The Lord," he told Viret, "has indeed inflicted a severe and bitter wound in the death of our infant son. But he is himself a Father, and knows best what is good for his children."[42] Calvin drew strength from his conviction that God always acts out of goodness with regard to His children. In 1544 Idelette became pregnant again and this time bore a daughter, who also soon succumbed to death.[43] Yet a third child would be born to Calvin and his wife, but this child would also be taken away soon after birth.

A few years before Calvin's death, one of Calvin's former coworkers, François Bauduin, who had become estranged from Calvin and penned a bitter biography of him, stated that God had punished Calvin for his misdeeds by not giving him any children. Calvin tersely replied, "I have myriads of sons throughout the Christian world," as was indeed the case.[44]

We do have a picture of what Calvin would have been like as a father from a letter that he wrote to a Dutch couple who were among his closest friends, Jacques de Bourgogne (d. 1556) and Yolande van Brederode.[45] In 1547 he wrote to them shortly after the birth of one of their children: "I am sorry that I cannot at least spend half a day there with you to laugh together with you, trying to make the little child laugh also, at the risk of having to experience how it would start to weep or cry."[46] Here is a rarely seen side of the Reformer, one that reveals a man who delighted in the joys of family life and who recognized that children were an essential reason for the institution of marriage.

But procreation was not the sole reason for marriage; thus Calvin refused to countenance divorce on the grounds of sterility or barrenness. Nor did he agree with surrogate motherhood, as found in the story of Abraham,

---

41. John Calvin to Pierre Viret, July 1542, in *Tracts and Letters*, 4:335.

42. John Calvin to Pierre Viret, August 19, 1542, in *Tracts and Letters*, 4:344.

43. Calvin mentions an illness of his daughter in a letter to Guillaume Farel on May 30, 1544, in *Tracts and Letters*, 4:420.

44. *Tracts and Letters*, 4:344n3.

45. On Calvin's friendship with this couple as well as the rift that developed between them, see Van den Berg, *Friends of Calvin*, 185–95.

46. As quoted in Van den Berg, *Friends of Calvin*, 193.

188 Theology Made Practical

Sarah, and Hagar and their children. Those who cannot have children, Calvin emphasized, need to recognize first that, in his words, "we are fruitful or barren as God imparts his power."[47] Here we see a concrete display of the theological conviction that undergirded all Calvin's theology—namely, the sovereignty of God. Second, when a couple could not have children, a door was opened to adopt orphans and nurture and care for relatives such as nephews and nieces.[48] Above all, the couple was to continue to be devoted to each other in mutual companionship and continue to engage in marital relations as an aspect of that companionship.[49]

It is noteworthy that Calvin encouraged husbands and wives to continue to enjoy one another sexually, even after child-bearing years were past. "Satan dazzles us," he preached in one of his sermons on Deuteronomy, "to imagine that we are polluted by intercourse," referring to a common Roman Catholic belief. But, he continued, "when the marital bed is dedicated to the name of the Lord, that is, when parties are joined together in his name, and live honourably, it is something of an holy estate."[50] Apart from the Pauline recognition in 1 Corinthians 7 that there may be certain seasons when a husband and wife forego sexual intimacy for spiritual reasons, Calvin emphasizes in two of his sermons that a husband and wife should not withhold sexual intimacy from one another.[51]

Speaking to the Twenty-First Century

The depth and profundity of Calvin's theology of marriage exercised an enormous influence for good on his contemporaries and successors. In the words of John Witte, "Calvin's covenant theology of marriage proved to be a powerful Protestant model for marriage that exercised an enormous and enduring influence on the Western tradition."[52]

But we live in a world that is rapidly retreating from this rigorously biblical vision of the married estate. Ours is a day of sexual chaos when there is massive confusion about what marriage and gender are and why sexuality

---

47. As quoted in Witte Jr., "Marriage and Family Life," 463.
48. Witte Jr., "Marriage and Family Life," 463.
49. Witte Jr., "Marriage and Family Life," 463.
50. As quoted in Witte Jr., "Marriage and Family Life," 463.
51. Witte Jr., "Marriage and Family Life," 463.
52. Witte Jr., *From Sacrament to Contract*, 109.

exists.[53] As the political philosopher Slavoj Žižek has rightly summed it up, ours is a day of "ordained transgression, in which the marital commitment is perceived as ridiculously out of step."[54] But Calvin's day was also a time of confusion, with competing visions of marriage and unbiblical views of sexuality. If we listen to him, his wisdom can help guide our footsteps into ways pleasing to the One who designed marriage in the first place.

1. Christian marriage is an institution ordained and sealed by God.
2. It is an exclusive heterosexual union between one man and one woman.
3. It is not to be entered into lightly, for a critical determining factor in choosing a spouse has to be the spouse's character—is he/she godly, and will he/she help me grow in Christ, will our temperaments complement one another? While external attractiveness is not to be ignored, our culture's preoccupation with it has proven to be utterly foolish.
4. At its heart, marriage is an intimate alliance and companionship of two glorious bearers of the image of God, which finds expression in sexual intimacy.
5. Such a marriage is *the* divinely sanctioned context for the procreation and raising of children.

One final perspective of Calvin on the purpose of marriage, though, remains to be mentioned—that all-important Christological dimension of marriage. The Lord Jesus Christ designed Christian marriages—and here Calvin is surely thinking about Ephesians 5:25–32—to be "an image of his sacred union with the Church. What greater eulogy could be pronounced on the dignity of marriage?"[55]

---

53. Mark Noll, "Calvin's Battle for Marriage," *CT*, April 1, 2006, http://www.ctlibrary .com/ct/2006/april/20.104.html.

54. As quoted by James K. A. Smith, "The Radicality of Marriage," *Fors Clavigera* (blog), October 31, 2008, http://forsclavigera.blogspot.ca/2008/10/radicality-of-marriage.html.

55. As quoted in Brown, *Family Reformation*, 106.

PART 4:
Calvin's Legacy

—12—

Calvin's Circle of Friends:
Propelling an Enduring Movement

David W. Hall

From a distant historical perspective, it is prudent to ask, how does one sustain a movement of ideas over time? And is something as noncognitive as social friendship a factor? One historian of the Swiss Reformation noted that it would be impossible for Calvin to be so dearly loved at his death if he had been a monster all his life. Calvin was not merely praised at his death; his many friends embraced his ideas and sought to cultivate them. This chapter reviews his friendships in different locales; during his student days; while in exile in Strasbourg, as evidenced among Genevan institutions; and at his death.[1] Its goal is to consider the propulsion effect of friendships to cultivate longevity for an ideological movement.[2]

Initially Rehabilitating an Image

Even a cursory study of Calvin's letters reveals a pattern of friendship and collegiality.[3] As Van den Berg observes, without Calvin's wide circle of friends providing a colorful palette for the canvas, students would not be acquainted with his finer points embedded within his extensive correspondence. To be sure, Calvin did not view himself as the only individual involved in these matters of reform. For the side of the story that depicts Calvin diffently from how he is frequently portrayed as cold and unfeeling,

---

1. This chapter is a slightly revised version of an earlier essay and is used with permission. See David W. Hall, "Calvin's Circle of Friends: Propelling an Enduring Movement," in *Reformation Faith: Exegesis and Theology in the Protestant Reformation*, ed. M. Parsons, Studies in Christian History and Thought (Milton Keynes, England: Paternoster, 2014), 190–204.

2. The 1997 Calvin Studies Society Colloquium featured essays on Calvin's friendship with Viret, Farel, Bullinger, Bucer, Melanchthon, and the Budé family. For more on this, see the work by Machiel A. van den Berg, *Friends of Calvin*, trans. Reinder Bruinsma (Grand Rapids: Eerdmans, 2009), which includes vignettes of twenty-four friendships.

3. See Herman Selderhuis's observations regarding these in *John Calvin: A Pilgrim's Life* (Wheaton, Ill.: IVP, 2009).

194 Theology Made Practical

consult *The Humanness of John Calvin* by Richard Stauffer.[4] In the foreword, leading Calvin scholar J. T. McNeill chronicles how he had been led to question the hearsay about Calvin, which depicted him as largely inhumane. As he perused Calvin's letters, he found, to the contrary, that Calvin was vividly humane, was associated with rich and poor alike, and exhibited a sturdy loyalty to friends. He attributed to Calvin the following traits: gentle, warm, tender, generous, hospitable, and other well attested virtues.[5]

Stauffer describes the "calumny" that Calvin has received from his enemies and also how he has "been misunderstood and misinterpreted by his great-grandchildren."[6] Another historian noted that no other Reformer generated more personal loyalty than Calvin. Emile Doumergue put it this way: "There were few men who developed as many friendships as he and who knew how to retain not only the admiration, but also the personal affection of these friends."[7] Abel Lefranc expressed the same sentiment: "The friendships which he inspired...among his teachers as well as among his colleagues, are strong enough testimonies to the fact that he knew how to combine with his serious and intense commitment to work, an affability and graciousness which won everyone over to him."[8]

Whether he was in a university setting or whether he drew on the experience of his teachers to assist him, Calvin was a more sociable man than it is usually thought. He was a prolific letter writer, corresponding with jurists, governors, common people, and many ministers. These letters provide glimpses into the real Calvin. In these letters, he could refer to the affection he had for his teacher Melchior Wolmar and at the same time could mourn the passing of a ministerial friend as so staggering that he was burdened with grief.

The character and impulse of Calvinism (and Lutheranism as well) impacted the world through a fraternity of devoted and committed friends.

---

4. Richard Stauffer, *The Humanness of John Calvin* (New York: Abingdon, 1971).

5. J. T. McNeill, foreword to *The Humanness of John Calvin*, by Richard Stauffer (New York: Abingdon, 1971), 9.

6. Stauffer, *Humanness of John Calvin*, 19.

7. As quoted in Stauffer, *Humanness of John Calvin*, 47. Emile Doumergue wrote (originally in French) *The Character of Calvin: The Man, His System, the Church, the State* (1923; repr., Neuilly: La Cause, 1931). He highlighted the following as distinguishing attributes, among others, of Calvin's character: vivacity, joyfulness, affection (in French, *mignardise*, meaning preciousness), nobility, and a concern to pitch his written style for common understanding.

8. As quoted in Stauffer, *Humanness of John Calvin*, 51.

Calvin's Circle of Friends

No individual could sow so many seeds; these victories were scored by a team of colleagues.

In the area of political formulation, for example, Calvin was the premier but certainly not the only Protestant theorist; indeed, he absorbed much from his comrades. Other Reformers who were in his circle of friendship briskly articulated theologies of the state, for example, with the following seminal works appearing in rapid succession in less than thirty years:

- Martin Bucer, *De Regno Christi* (1551)
- John Ponet, *A Short Treatise of Political Power* (1556)
- Christopher Goodman, *How Superior Powers ought to be obeyed of their subjects; and wherein they may lawfully by God's word be disobeyed and resisted* (1558)
- Peter Viret, *The World and the Empire* (1561)
- Francois Hotman, *Francogallia* (1573)
- Theodore Beza, *De Jure Magisterium* (1574)
- George Buchanan, *De Jure Regni Apud Scotos* (1579)
- Languet, *Vindiciae Contra Tyrannos* (1579).

Each of these works legitimized the idea of citizen resistance against governmental expansion that exceeded proper limits. Interestingly, this corpus of political thought emanated from a tight circle of friends, most of whom were in direct contact with Calvin. Other topics were collegially addressed as well. It is hard to attribute such robust similarity of thought either to accident or to independent discovery.

Calvin's companionship with Theodore Beza is a model of friendship, and with all the heady intellectual issues of the day, what greatly impressed Beza was Calvin's personal support and friendship. Thus Beza (and others) wrote about the camaraderie that Calvin shared with those around him. Calvin epitomized the modern notion of collegiality, and he was prudent enough to attract brilliant friends if at all possible. Once when Beza was ill, Calvin wrote about the "fresh fear" that "overwhelmed him with deep sorrow" upon learning of Beza's sickness. He was "staggered...already weeping for him...grieved" and afraid of the loss that might come to the church and to him personally.[9] Fortunately, Beza recovered.

---

9. *CO*, 14:144–45, as quoted in Stauffer, *Humanness of John Calvin*, 69.

Theology Made Practical

There were many other friends besides Beza. The consensual strains of thought that flowed through the literary veins of Bullinger, Bucer, Viret, and Calvin—soon to be supplemented by Knox, Beza, Hotman, and Junius Brutus—formed an intellectual tradition with Geneva at its epicenter and Calvin its architect. His friendship with these scholars would prove to be the glue that held the movement together in its delicate infancy.[10] J. H. Merle D'Aubigne noted this mutual interchange of ideas:

> The catholicity of the Reformation is a noble feature in its character. The Germans pass into Switzerland; the French into Germany; in latter times men from England and Scotland pass over to the Continent, and doctors from the Continent into Great Britain. The reformers in the different countries spring up almost independently of one another, but no sooner are they born than they hold out the hand of fellowship.... It has been an error, in our opinion, to write as hitherto, the history of the Reformation for a single country; the work is one.[11]

Calvin's associates served to stabilize and standardize an international movement. Their collective effort certainly led to its expansion.

Calvin, Farel, and Peter Viret were called "the tripod" or "three patriarchs," so widely known was their friendship. In Calvin's commentary on Titus, he wrote that he did "not believe that there have ever been such friends who have lived together in such a deep friendship in their everyday style of life in this world as we have in our ministry."[12] In that preface, Calvin referred to their "friendship and holy union" and affirmed that even though the three of them were from different places, their friendship aided the unity of the church. Even when there were strong disagreements, Calvin was a paragon of friendship. When these Reformers experienced family struggles or joys, Calvin shared these things in his letters. His letters to various Reformers are full of sympathy and are quick to illustrate a healthy loyalty. Moreover, his correspondence with refugees exhibits his great compassion as well. He even built bridges to Luther's disciples after Luther denounced him.

---

10. Aurelio Garcia, "Bullinger's Friendship with Calvin: Loving One Another and Edifying the Churches," in *Calvin Studies Society Papers*, 1995, 1997, ed. David Foxgrover (Grand Rapids: CRC Product Services, 1998), 126.

11. J. H. Merle D'Aubigne, *The History of the Reformation of the Sixteenth Century* (New York: American Tract Society, 1848), 3:416.

12. As quoted in Stauffer, *Humanness of John Calvin*, 57.

Calvin's Circle of Friends

Calvin's acquaintance with Melanchthon began with correspondence to Bucer during Calvin's Strasbourg exile. Calvin first met Melanchthon in person, however, at the 1539 Diet of Frankfort. At this early stage of the Reformation, the winds of "ecumenical optimism" blew freely among many Reformers. Calvin thought that Melanchthon agreed with him on a wide range of doctrinal topics, even thinking that perhaps Melanchthon held the key to potential unity with Lutherans.[13] At this early stage of the Reformation, shortly after his arrival in Strasbourg, Calvin advised trying "every remedy" that might affect unity, "persever[ing] even to the last gasp."[14] Despite Calvin and Melanchthon's similarities in personality and scholarly bent—especially contrasted with their mercurial mentors Luther and Farel—the two men never attained the unity first thought possible.

What began in Geneva with a multinational cadre of colleagues, all seeking to extend the "republic of Christ," grew into a movement that featured theology, ideas, and a unique view of history far surpassing the city of Geneva alone.[15] With their confidence in God's providence and divine election, this circle of friends urged civil rulers to adopt their religious views and political practices, "holding that no frontiers, no boundaries, no limits should confine the zeal of pious princes in the matter of God's glory and of the reign of Christ."[16] To some, the theology of resistance maintained by this Genevan circle would appear politically subversive.

At times, as in any historic era, there were also disruptions of friendships. Calvin had to assist church members with broken relationships, and he had to deal with friction among the Protestant Reformers. No realistic

---

13. Randall C. Zachman, "Restoring Access to the Fountain: Melanchthon and Calvin on the Task of Evangelical Theology," in *Calvin Studies Society Papers, 1995, 1997*, ed. David Foxgrover (Grand Rapids: CRC Product Services, 1998), 207. Zachman notes that although their friendship was strained at times—with numerous epistolary rebukes—nevertheless, the friendship lasted until Melanchthon's death. Zachman highlights the difference in methodology between these two Reformers, noting that the mutual admiration, however, remained. Calvin also thought that Melanchthon's differences with Luther on God's decrees might further ecumenical cooperation (211).

14. Zachman, "Restoring Access to the Fountain," 209.

15. A. C. Duke, Gillian Lewis, and Andrew Pettegree, *Calvinism in Europe, 1540–1610: A Collection of Documents* (Manchester: Manchester University Press, 1992), 200. This internationality, to some degree, blunts the suggestion by Hopfl that Geneva was unique in applying Calvinism because it was a relatively small political space in which the laws could be easily enforced. For his discussion, see Harro Hopfl, *The Christian Polity of John Calvin* (Cambridge: Cambridge University Press, 1982), 56–57.

16. Duke, Lewis, and Pettegree, *Calvinism in Europe, 1540–1610*, 200.

198   Theology Made Practical

leader presumes that all will always go smoothly in the area of friendship; Calvin, however, learned to encourage others around him, and he delegated certain responsibilities to his associates.

Richard Stauffer concluded that Calvin was far from "the isolated hero or the lonely genius that has often been pictured. Throughout his career, he had relationships with friends who showed him unfailing affection and indefatigable devotion. If he exerted such charm, it is certainly because he himself had been such an incomparable friend…. For the devotion which one showed him, he paid the tribute of unswerving loyalty."[17] Following Calvin's death, the continuing work of Reformation was entrusted to his colleagues, Beza being the chief.

Calvin's Early Theological Mentors and Peers: Friends in Ideas

Calvin realized that massive change could only occur on strong foundations. He was also modest enough not to claim that all good ideas percolated from his own mind. Calvin's admiration for those excellent theologians who had gone before him reflected his willingness to value the contributions of others—those he viewed as literary friends. He frequently referred to classic writings, and he drew upon wisdom from the past. He did not believe that all new insights were necessarily correct or that he or his generation would be superior in wisdom to others. He was also happy to associate with other peers. Calvin knew better than to seek to re-create all parts of the wheel. He happily drew upon Augustine and built on him.[18] A host of other intellectual mentors to Calvin also laid the foundation for his work.

While at the University of Paris in 1521, Calvin studied rhetoric, logic, and arts—common topics for the day—and received a classical education. He was also influenced by the work of the leading Roman Catholic progressive

---

17. Stauffer, *Humanness of John Calvin*, 71.

18. One scholar found that of the sources Calvin quoted in the *Institutes*, Augustine is in a class of his own, being cited 228 times. The next most frequently cited authorities were Gregory I (thirty-nine times); Chrysostom (twenty-seven times); Bernard (twenty-three times); Ambrose (eighteen times); and Cyprian (fourteen times). The number of citations from Augustine compares to nine from Cicero, seven from Plato, five from Aristotle, and three from Seneca. See Philip Schaff, *History of the Christian Church* (1910; repr., Grand Rapids: Eerdmans, 1979), 8:539. The Reformation was, in the main, a return to Augustinianism, and Calvin's thought can hardly be seen as an imitation of previous, secular models. Arthur Custance, *The Sovereignty of Grace* (Philipsburg, N.J.: Presbyterian and Reformed, 1979), 27.

Calvin's Circle of Friends

John Major[19]—a towering intellect—and Peter of Spain.[20] He also could not avoid the deluge of intellectual currents swirling through Paris at the time. Protestant professors and students alike, originally called Lutherans, huddled together for protection against persecution, forming bonds of friendship that would endure. Calvin counted both Nicholas and Michael Cop as friends in early Protestant Paris, with one study inferring, "Such friendships testify both to the worth and the attractiveness of his character, and contradict the old legend that he was an unsociable misanthrope."[21]

Calvin, like Melanchthon, was trained in three classic languages. Calvin's method was also likely shaped by exposure to Melanchthon's *Elementorum Rhetorices Libri Duo*, frequently used during his Paris student days.[22] Calvin's humanist education[23] included enrollments at key educational institutions at Paris,[24] Orléans, Bourges, Basel, and familiarization with other learning centers of the day. He was exposed to the thought of Erasmus, Le Fevre, Wolmar, and Francois Rabelais, a veritable "Who's Who" of Western European education for his day.

Prior to taking up residence in Geneva in 1536, Calvin enjoyed a friendship with the neighboring Lausanne Reformer Peter Viret, extending back almost a decade to their Paris years. Both studied under the same professors at the College de Montaigu,[25] and both had a common friend and mentor

---

19. Some historians see a common pedagogical strain, insofar as it is likely that Calvin, Knox, and Buchanan were all former students of John Major. John T. McNeill, "Calvinism and European Politics in Historical Perspective," in *Calvinism and the Political Order*, ed. George L. Hunt (Philadelphia: Westminster, 1965), 15. Douglas Kelly sees Major's *History of Great Britain* as especially influential on Knox and Buchanan.

20. Alister McGrath, *A Life of John Calvin* (Cambridge, Mass.: Basil Blackwell, 1990), 34. For an evaluation of the place of Calvin, see also Alister McGrath, "Calvin and the Christian Calling," *First Things* 94 (June/July 1999): 31–35.

21. At Orléans: "His friends here were Melchior Wolmar, a German schoolmaster and a man of exemplary scholarship and character, François Daniel, François de Connam and Nicolas Duchemin; to these his earliest letters were written." "John Calvin," *NNDB*, http://www.nndb.com/people/507/000094225/.

22. Zachman, "Restoring Access to the Fountain," 212–13.

23. The humanism of the day emphasized the classics. *Ad fontes*, or "back to the sources," became the rallying cry of the new educational model.

24. McGrath notes that an inscription on the façade of the Bibliotheque Sainte-Genevieve in Paris lists Calvin, along with Erasmus and others, as an intellectual leader. McGrath, *Life of John Calvin*, 21.

25. Jeannine Olson has noted the friendship with the Budé brothers (Jean, Francois, and Louis) that extends back to Calvin's student days in Paris. She also observes: "Viewing Calvin among his friends puts him, too, in a positive light. It also reveals how he accomplished as much as he did, for the people with whom he associated helped him with his work,

200   Theology Made Practical

in Guillaume Farel.[26] So close were Calvin and Viret that when it came time to return to Geneva from his Strasbourg exile, Calvin asked Viret to prepare the way for his *parousia*.[27] From that point on, whenever mediation was needed in Geneva, Calvin and the leaders often turned to Viret, who eventually settled there in 1559, following his own exile from Lausanne. So close were these friends that both were awarded full citizenship in Geneva on the same day, December 25, 1559.

Among Calvin's correspondents, Viret was one of the most voluminous, with almost four hundred extant letters to him. Calvin and Viret would remain close until death took Calvin. Their shared traits of shyness, determination, sensitivity to sufferers, and tireless labor are reflected in their correspondence. Their epistolary database indicates that they were close enough to give blunt rebukes and correction while also "commiserating with each other in their mutual grief over the loss of spouses whom they described as beloved partners and companions."[28] In terms of impact, Viret may even have wielded an influence far greater than previously known in terms of politics; he supported the right to resist magistrates more than any other of Calvin's friends early on and likely persuaded Calvin (if not his disciples) of that radical idea.[29] Indeed, Robert Linder assessed the friendship to be so strong that to the four statues of Farel, Calvin, Beza, and Knox in Geneva's Parc de Bastions a statue of Viret should be added "symbolically just behind his good friend John Calvin's left shoulder."[30]

---

especially his publications. Together they collectively shaped the Reformation from Geneva." "The Friends of John Calvin: The Budé Family," in *Calvin Studies Society Papers*, 1995, 1997, ed. David Foxgrover (Grand Rapids: CRC Product Services, 1998), 160.

26. Robert D. Linder, "Brothers in Christ: Pierre Viret and John Calvin as Soul-Mates and Co-Laborers in the Work of the Reformation," in *Calvin Studies Society Papers*, 1995, 1997, ed. David Foxgrover (Grand Rapids: CRC Product Services, 1998), 141. Linder also notes that Calvin broke with Farel after his mentor's marriage to a lady half his age in 1558.

27. The well-chosen term is from Linder, "Brothers in Christ," 155. David N. Wiley believes that Calvin wanted Viret to assume the pastorate in Geneva so that he could stay in Strasbourg. "Calvin's Friendship with Guillaume Farel," in *Calvin Studies Society Papers*, 1995, 1997, ed. David Foxgrover (Grand Rapids: CRC Product Services, 1998), 192.

28. Linder, "Brothers in Christ," 150. And they were also close enough to differ on the selection of a new wife after Elizabeth Viret's death (152).

29. Linder terms Viret's view "more advanced and generous" toward the right of resistance than Calvin's. "Brothers in Christ," 154. For more on this, see Robert Linder, *The Political Ideas of Pierre Viret*, Travaux d'Humanisme et Renaissance LXIV (Geneva: Librairie Droz, 1964); David W. Hall, *Calvin in the Public Square* (Phillipsburg, N.J.: P&R, 2009), ch. 4.

30. Linder, "Brothers in Christ," 157.

A Circle of Friends in Strasbourg

Beza's biography is perceptive enough to view Calvin's exile to Strasbourg as part of God's providence, enabling Calvin to train for greater effectiveness while employing his gifts to strengthen another city. After this initial brush with defeat in Geneva, his three years in Strasbourg would prove essential for his future.

Calvin's sojourn in Strasbourg from 1538 to 1541 proved providential, as he later claimed. In Strasbourg, a city that had already traveled further down the path of Reformation than had Geneva at the time, Calvin saw the full potential of Reformed religion and politics. Under the powerful example of such leading educators of the Reformation as Johann Sturm (1507–1589) and Martin Bucer, Calvin received sound mentoring there—not to mention fellowship. He accompanied Bucer on diplomatic missions, taught in Sturm's freshly minted academy that became a model for the one in Geneva, and observed a harmonious relationship between church and state.[31] Calvin also pastored four to five hundred French Protestant refugees in Strasbourg.[32]

Willem van 't Spijker has explored the impact of Bucer's friendship on Calvin during and after his time in Strasbourg. Van 't Spijker reports that Calvin had rebuked Bucer only about three months prior to his April 1538 exile. Despite this, Bucer's magnanimity is seen in his encouragement to young Calvin to seek shelter in Strasbourg· From that time, Bucer was a larger influence over Calvin than Farel. Van 't Spijker states: "A deep friendship developed between them, which continued as long as they lived and which made Calvin always talk about Bucer with deep appreciation, even after Bucer's death. When Calvin was called to return to Geneva in 1541, he consented only on the condition that Bucer was to accompany him to reform the Geneva church together." At least through his commentary on Romans (1536), Bucer wielded a friendly and lasting influence over Calvin and his *Institutes*.[33]

Just prior to returning to Geneva, Calvin became a citizen of Strasbourg and met a widow, Idelette de Bure, who became his wife. He also inherited Idelette's two children by a previous marriage, becoming solely responsible

---

31. McGrath, *Life of John Calvin*, 101.
32. Schaff, *History of the Christian Church*, 8:368.
33. Willem van 't Spijker, "Calvin's Friendship with Martin Bucer: Did It Make Calvin a Calvinist?," in *Calvin Studies Society Papers*, 1995, 1997, ed. David Foxgrover (Grand Rapids: CRC Product Services, 1998), 170–71.

202   Theology Made Practical

to care for them after her death in 1549. When Idelette died in 1549, Calvin faced an unparalleled grief. His letters to Farel and Viret reveal both his faith in God and his love for his wife. In this grief observed, those watching developed admiration. He paid high tribute to Idelette after her death, as one who was an excellent companion in exile, sorrow, or death.

Calvin's exile ended in 1541 when he returned to Geneva, "contrary to [his] desire and inclination." What motivated him to return to the place where he had been so rudely treated only a few years earlier? "The welfare of this church...lay so near my heart," he stated, "that for its sake I would not have hesitated to lay down my life." Competing with his natural diffidence, the weight of "solemn and conscientious duty" was greater than his personal comfort. Still, it was with considerable grief, tears, anxiety, and distress—not to mention "a remarkable act of social pragmatism and religious realism"[34]—that he returned to Geneva.

The Company of Pastors

The venerable Company of Pastors formed a circle of friends during Calvin's second Geneva residence.[35] One of the things that Calvin insisted on upon returning to Geneva was that a presbyterate be formed. Rather than wishing for dictatorial rule, Calvin opted for collegiality in his fraternity of ministers. His Ecclesiastical Ordinances called for the establishment of a circle of ministers who would labor together and meet frequently. Later, when the academy was formed, this added another set of affinity relationships.

Calvin was prudent enough to draw on others and his past experiences— even his painful exile—for inspiration for the educational developments in Geneva. There were three dominant influences on Calvin as he established an enduring university; various leaders from different parts of Protestant Switzerland each made distinct contributions. First, Calvin profited from his friend Peter Viret's previously established Lausanne Academy, which actually had been founded two decades before Calvin's. In the 1540s the Lausanne Academy (approximately forty miles east of Geneva) was the leading French-speaking educational institution, featuring an outstanding faculty. The Lausanne influence on the Genevan academy increased when some of those professors (Theodore Beza, Francois Hotman, and Peter Viret)

---

34. McGrath, *Life of John Calvin*, 86.
35. See Scott Manetsch, *Calvin's Company of Pastors: Pastoral Care and the Emerging Reformed Church, 1536–1609* (Oxford: Oxford University Press, 2015).

Calvin's Circle of Friends 203

came to teach in Geneva after 1559.[36] Rival leaders in Bern accused Calvin of conspiring to steal an excellent faculty, but all this happened because of institutional disruption in Lausanne. Second, during his exile from 1538 to 1541, Calvin witnessed another excellent model in Johann Sturm's academy at Strasbourg. Third, Calvin emphasized the Bible-centered, expository method of Zwingli, elevating the original texts of Scripture to the most authoritative platform possible. Most of the leading voices of the Reformation became leaders in educational reform in Strasbourg, Zurich, Lausanne, and Geneva—surely a local lesson with global implications for a perceptive leader. After its inception in 1558, however, Calvin's academy soon far outpaced these other centers and subsequently remained at the forefront of Protestant educational ventures for over two centuries.[37]

Following the St. Bartholomew's Day massacre (1572), Francois Hotman—one of the leading constitutional lawyers on the Continent—arrived to teach at the Genevan law school and served from 1573 to 1578. In addition to him, Denis Godefroy, who influenced Johannes Althusius, was on the law faculty and was one of two academy professors to become First Syndic (akin to a mayor) in Geneva while teaching. The presence of the legal giants Hotman and Godefroy gave Calvin's academy one of the earliest Swiss legal faculties. The medical school, attempted shortly after Calvin's death, was not successfully established until the 1700s.[38] After an education at Calvin's academy, Thomas Bodley returned to Oxford and established the Bodleian Library, perhaps the finest research library in the world. His action followed Calvin's educational mission. These bonds expanded the reach of the Reformed movement. The whole was greater than the sum of its parts.

After its founding, the Academy also helped nourish alternative power structures. As early as 1555, Geneva was unique in Switzerland for entrusting the power of excommunication to the consistory (comprised of local ministers and elders) rather than the civil magistrate.[39] This policy was both progressive and restrictive of the civil power. Wherever Calvinism spread, other venerable companies of pastors cropped up, for example in Poitiers

---

36. See Marco Marcacci, *Historie de L'Universite de Geneve 1558–1986* (Geneva: University of Geneva, 1987), 20.

37. Under Beza, Geneva was known as a Christian state or a "bibliocentric Republic." Marcacci, *Historie de L'Universite de Geneve 1558–1986*, 23. The pastors and the students played a large role in supporting the city and liberty.

38. Henry Martyn Baird, *Theodore Beza* (n.p., 1899), 106, 113.

39. Monter, *Calvin's Geneva*, 138.

204   Theology Made Practical

(1555), Orléans (1557), La Rochelle (1558), and Nimes (1561).[40] These ecclesiastical governing authorities precluded civil magistrates from acting as the only lawfully ordained governors; power had to be shared with the private sphere. In contrast to other municipalities, one thing that contributed to Geneva's unique adherence to a consistent Reformation was the creation of an institution that was rare for her day: the consistory. The collegial religious body assumed numerous roles, such as moral correction, corporate guidance, and censorship, which had once been the prerogatives of princely courts.[41] It is doubtful, however, that Calvin's ideas would have been exported as quickly or in as sustained a fashion without his groundbreaking work in the Genevan academy.

Calvin even enjoyed amicable relationships with many rulers. The amount of concerted interaction among Calvin, his Company of Pastors, and the Genevan city council may unsettle modern readers a bit. Although there was a purposeful separation of jurisdictions, these Reformers did not think it was healthy for the leading spheres of influence, church and state, to operate in strict isolation. The Genevan Senate and the Council of Two Hundred frequently consulted with the Genevan pastors. At times, the pastors suggested legislation or due processes that were approved by the civil council. While each power was to have "autonomy of function, the relationship envisaged was one of harmony in which church and state cooperated fruitfully with each other to the glory of God."[42]

Friends in Correspondence and via Dedications

It is customary to acknowledge friends in book dedications. It is also true that such dedications can, at times, be aspirational (more than accomplished) for friendships. Calvin, however, dedicated the following volumes of his commentaries to these friends in politics or ministry:

- Henry (IV), Duke of Navarre, at the age of ten (Genesis)
- Edward, the 17th Earl of Oxford (Psalms)
- Prince Edward VI and Queen Elizabeth of England (Isaiah)

---

40. McGrath, *Life of John Calvin*, 184.

41. See Ronald S. Wallace, *Calvin, Geneva and the Reformation* (Edinburgh: Scottish Academic Press, 1988), 36.

42. Philip E. Hughes, ed., *The Register of the Company of Pastors in the Time of Calvin* (Grand Rapids: Eerdmans, 1966), 7.

Calvin's Circle of Friends

- Prince Frederick of Palatine (Jeremiah)
- Gaspar Coligny (Ezekiel, posthumously in 1565 by Beza)
- To all pious worshipers in France (Daniel)
- King Gustave of Sweden (the Minor Prophets, ending with prayers for best wishes to Prince Heric and Gustave's brothers)
- The Noblemen and Council of Frankfort (the Harmony of the Gospels)
- The Syndics and Council of Geneva (gospel of John, in which he praises these civic leaders for their hospitality
- Prince Nicolas Radziwill, Duke of Lithuania (Acts; he is commended for withstanding public opposition for his faith)
- Simon Grynaeus (Romans; Calvin acknowledges that he writes this commentary after Melanchthon and Bucer, not mentioning Luther and Peter Martyr)
- James of Burgundy (1 Corinthians)
- Melchior Wolmar (2 Corinthians, as an apology for not writing in over five years)
- Prince Christopher, Duke of Wirtemberg (Galatians)
- Edward, Duke of Somerset (1 Timothy)
- Farel and Viret (Titus)
- Edward VI, king of England (the Catholic Epistles)

It may be debated how well Calvin knew each of these people. In most of these dedications, however, his familiarity with their situations seems obvious, indicating some level of intimacy. Moreover, the international affinities, at the very least, must be acknowledged.

Earlier, Calvin had dedicated his 1543 *Bondage and Liberation of the Will* to Melanchthon, hoping to underscore the unity among Reformers on this locus. Calvin's reasons for this dedication were numerous, including Melanchthon's professed love for Calvin and Calvin's commendation for Melanchthon's similar teaching, referring to Melanchthon in these halcyon years as a "most zealous supporter" and "a distinguished and very brave champion."[43] Calvin, known for his love for brevity, clarity, and simplicity

---

43. Zachman, "Restoring Access to the Fountain," 211. As early as 1539, Calvin also interpreted Melanchthon's differences with Luther on matters of the eternal decree as a point of contact. See Zachman, "Restoring Access to the Fountain," 215.

206 Theology Made Practical

(perhaps going back to Melanchthon's text on rhetoric used in Paris during Calvin's student days), commended Melanchthon similarly for his sharpness, perspicuity, and simplicity.

Calvin's friends also included childhood friends who were publishers. One recent study states, "No description of the international efforts of the Reform can omit to mention the contributions of the printer and scholar Robert Estienne, the printer and martyrologist Jean Crespin…or for that matter the lifelong and deliberate use of publication as a weapon on the part of Calvin and Theodore de Beze."[44] From Geneva Robert Estienne printed French editions by Calvin's disciples Beza, Hotman, and Viret. Jean Crespin, a groomsman at Beza's secret marriage,[45] published popular devotional material; moreover, a wide array of educational material was produced for the burgeoning academy. Bibles and theological texts flew off Genevan printing presses.

Friends to the End: A Vignette from Calvin's Death

Before concluding our survey of Calvin's life of friendship, we should note the accolades given to him by contemporaries at his death. Calvin was revered by many during and at the end of his life. The plaudits of his peers are an impressive correction to a faulty image.

On April 25, 1564, sensing the nearness of death, Calvin filed his final will. In it he pled his unworthiness ("Woe is me; my ardor and zeal have been so careless and languid, that I confess I have failed innumerable times"[46]) and thanked God for mercy. He appointed his brother Anthony (whose reputation for divorcing a wife for adultery had been maliciously used to malign Calvin himself) to be his heir, and in his will he bequeathed equal amounts to the boys' school, the poor refugees, and his stepchildren. He also left part of his meager estate to his nephews and their children. To vindicate Calvin against charges of greed, Beza reiterated what Calvin had stated earlier: "If some will not be persuaded while I am alive, my death, at all events will show that I have not been a money-making man."[47] When his

---

44. Duke, Lewis, and Pettegree, *Calvinism in Europe, 1540–1610*, 201.
45. Schaff, *History of the Christian Church*, 8:851.
46. Beza, *Life of John Calvin*, in *Tracts and Letters*, 1:cxxv.
47. Beza, *Life of John Calvin*, in *Tracts and Letters*, 1:cxxxviii.

Calvin's Circle of Friends

will was notarized and brought to the attention of the Senate,[48] members of that council visited the declining Calvin to hear his final farewell personally. Calvin was not viewed as a foe to be shunned by his contemporaries.

Calvin's concluding relationship to the city leaders may be gleaned from his "Farewell Address to the Members of the Little Council."[49] The members of this council had gone to his home to hear his advice and to express their appreciation for the "services he has performed for the Seigneurie and for that of which he has faithfully acquitted himself in his duty." A contemporary recorded his sentiments from April 27, 1564. In that chronicle, the dying Calvin first thanked these leaders for their support, cooperation, and friendship. Although they had engaged in numerous struggles, still their relationship was cordial.

He concluded by encouraging each one to "walk according to his station and use faithfully that which God gave him in order to uphold this Republic. Regarding civil or criminal trials, one should reject all favor, hate, errors, commendations." He also advised leaders not to aspire to privilege as if rank was a benefit for governors. "And if one is tempted to deviate from this," Calvin added, "one should resist and be constant, considering the One who established us, asking him to conduct us by his Holy Spirit, and he will not desert us."

Calvin's farewell to these political leaders was followed by his "Farewell Address to the Ministers" on April 28, 1564.[50] From his chamber, Calvin reminded them poignantly: "When I first arrived in this church there was almost nothing. They were preaching and that's all. They were good at seeking out idols and burning them, but there was no Reformation. Everything was in turmoil.... Here have I lived through wondrous battles. I have been saluted in derision outside my door in the evening by fifty or sixty arquebus [gun] shots. You may well imagine how this could astonish a poor, timid scholar such as I am and always have been, I confess."[51] The farewell address continued to review his Strasbourg exile, the tensions he faced upon return, and some of his experiences with various councils. Calvin concluded by predicting that the battles would not lessen in the days ahead, warning, "You

---

48. Beza refers to this Little Council as the "senate." See Beza, *Life of John Calvin*, in *Tracts and Letters*, 1:cxxii.

49. *CO*, 9:887–91. I am using the unpublished translation of the farewell address by Kim McMahon Isbell. For a summary, see Monter, *Calvin's Geneva*, 93–95.

50. *CO*, 9:891–94. English translation available in Monter, *Calvin's Geneva*, 95–97.

51. As quoted in Monter, *Calvin's Geneva*, 95.

208   Theology Made Practical

will have your hands full after God has taken me away. For even though I am as nothing, I know that I have prevented three thousand tumults that might have taken place in Geneva. But take courage and fortify yourselves, for God will use this Church and will uphold it; I assure you that He will preserve it."[52]

Calvin humbly confessed:

> I have had many infirmities which had to be borne and yet, all that I have done is worth nothing. Evil men will seize upon that word; but still I say that all I have done is worthy of nothing and that I am a miserable creature. But I can say that I meant well, that my vices have always displeased me, and that the root of the fear of God has been in my heart. And you can say that my intention has been good. I beg you to pardon me the bad; but if there be some good, may you confirm it and follow it.[53]

He denied that he had written hateful things about others, and he confirmed that the pastors had elected Beza to be his successor. "Take care to help him, for his burden is heavy and so difficult that he must necessarily be overcome by it. Take care to support him. As for him, I know that he has a good will and will do what he can," exhorted the dying Calvin. Further, he urged them "to make no innovations, for novelty is often requested." He said, "It is not that I desire from personal ambition that what is mine remain and that it be kept without seeking anything better, but because all changes are dangerous."[54] The advice from this leader is filled with layer upon layer of wisdom.

When Calvin passed away almost a month after making these comments on May 27, 1564, the city mourned the death of its wisest citizen and spiritual father. He was interred in a common cemetery at Plein Palais, finally finding the anonymity he craved. That humility, one historian wrote, was characteristic of Calvin in life as in death.[55] The widespread notice and sadness at his death should serve to correct any faulty view that his contemporaries either despised him or underestimated his importance. He was mourned, and his large number of friends would keep his memory alive

---

52. As quoted in Monter, *Calvin's Geneva*, 96.
53. As quoted in Monter, *Calvin's Geneva*, 96.
54. As quoted in Monter, *Calvin's Geneva*, 96–97.
55. Doumergue, *Character of Calvin*, 173.

far more than contemporaries would have predicted. This leader's successes were recognized and celebrated by others.

Conclusion

These kinds of friendships show how Reformers strove for unity; at the same time, they did not withhold rebukes. Calvin could severely accuse Melanchthon of being timid, too quick to concede matters that were not adiaphoric, and as unwilling to draw orthodox lines at some loci. At the same time, Calvin wrote that, merely due to his reproofs, which Melanchthon had given him full liberty to issue, any construal that he and Luther's lieutenant were "in opposition greatly wrongs both the one and the other, as well as the whole Church of God."[56] Yes, these Reforming friends defended one another's reputations and sought to build bridges based on common belief, but no, they were not always affirming. Still, as late as December 1558, Calvin would write to Melanchthon, urging him to let his zeal burn more brightly (noting that even "pious friends" were criticizing his timidity) while cheering: "Whatever happens, let us cultivate with sincerity a fraternal affection towards each other, of which no wiles of Satan shall ever burst asunder the ties."[57]

Few (if any) social or theological movements will endure if led by only an individual. For lasting impact, a set of ideas must be attractive to more than one or a few. It is not accidental, then, that faculties or schools often have more longevity than even the finest individual thinkers of a generation. Barth would have little influence if there were no Barthians; the same is true for Luther and Lutherans. Interestingly, few identify themselves as generic Protestants; most of the living strands of Protestantism that thrive and survive anchor themselves in a Luther, a Calvin, or a Zwingli. Those same enduring Protestant traditions each seem to have radiating circles of friendship at their fonts.

---

56. Zachman, "Restoring Access to the Fountain," 224.

57. Zachman, "Restoring Access to the Fountain," 227. Nevertheless, Zachman also notes the deterioration of ecumenicity after Melanchthon's 1560 death, showing that Calvin began to view Lutheranism more negatively ("I am carefully on the watch that Lutheranism gain no ground, not be introduced into France") until his death (228).

Calvin as a Calvinist

Joel R. Beeke

Was Calvin a Calvinist? The question may seem odd. Yet it is a question that has been asked numerous times throughout the past half century. Remarkably, for decades it has often been answered by scholars in the negative: "Calvin was not a Calvinist." So said men such as Ernst Bizer, Basil Hall, Walter Kickel, Thomas F. Torrance, and Philip Holtrop.[1]

The term "Calvinist" had not fully developed in Calvin's day, so the question is in some sense anachronistic. In addition, any answer to the question depends entirely on how one defines the term "Calvinist." This probably seems, at first, to be a dry academic debate. While some of the literature written about the question certainly is dry, the question has some tangible and practical implications for our Christian lives. The question of Calvin and the Calvinists is not simply one of historical curiosity; it is one that intersects with everyday Christian life today. So let's explore the question and see how doing so can help sharpen our theology and warm our souls.

Preliminary Questions: Developing the Issues at Stake

Was Calvin a Calvinist is virtually identical to asking the question, was Calvin Reformed? To ask this question in many ways is to answer it. To be Reformed is to hold firmly to the five *solas* of the Reformation: Scripture alone (*sola Scriptura*), grace alone (*sola gratia*), faith alone (*sola fide*), Christ alone (*solus Christus*), and the glory of God alone (*soli Deo gloria*). Certainly no reputable scholar today would hesitate to affirm that Calvin strongly adhered to each of these *solas* in both his theology and practice. If we were to begin a search of all the doctrinal areas in which Calvin and the Calvinists

---

1. For example, see Basil Hall, "Calvin against the Calvinists," in *John Calvin*, ed. G.E. Duffield (Appleford: Sutton Courtenay Press, 1966), 19–37. The chapter was first delivered as an address at a Reformation Conference organized by Jon Payne.

212   Theology Made Practical

are unquestionably in full harmony, we would soon, no doubt, be numbering in the hundreds.

But this simply begs the nearly synonymous question, What is a Calvinist? It won't do to simply answer by saying, "Someone who believes in the doctrines that John Calvin taught," for that only begs the question, What did Calvin and the Calvinists teach? This, then, must be the first issue we might raise: What is the central dogma of Calvin and the Calvinists?

Another way of answering the question of what Calvin and the Calvinists taught would be to turn to the historic, confessional Reformed creeds, such as the Heidelberg Catechism, and then confess: Calvin was a Calvinist because before he died he read the Heidelberg Catechism, which is a solidly Calvinist confession, and thoroughly agreed with its contents, only desiring that it would include a question that rejected the Roman Catholic Mass.

But that doesn't answer all the questions about the development of confessional theology. Many more Reformed confessions were written both during and after Calvin's lifetime. How do these relate to Calvin? Can we use Calvin as a benchmark for judging all these confessions? That, then, is the second issue we need to address—the issue of Calvin vis-à-vis Reformed confessional theology in general.

But there are still several issues to address. Another way of answering the question of what Calvin and the Calvinists taught would be to turn to the historical question of the methodology in their theology—that is, *how* Calvin actually thought in contrast to how his followers thought. This raises the whole question of scholasticism, which does need to be answered, so this is the third area we will need to address.

But that, too, doesn't answer all the questions. Since the Heidelberg Catechism does cover nearly every major doctrine of the Reformed faith, it is at least comforting for those of us who want to view Calvin as a Calvinist to know that Calvin approved of this classic confession. More issues arose, however, after the Heidelberg Catechism was written and after Calvin's death that could not be fully resolved by the Catechism, as they were not adequately addressed there—issues surrounding man's depravity, election, atonement, the irresistibility of grace, and the perseverance of the saints. The Great Synod of Dordrecht (1618–1619) answered those issues definitively in the so-called Canons of Dort, which became even better known in the form of the acronym TULIP given to it much later, probably in the nineteenth century. TULIP stands for

Calvin as a Calvinist

- Total depravity
- Unconditonal election
- Limited atonement
- Irresistible grace
- Perseverance of the saints

These also came to be nicknamed the five points of Calvinism. Here we reach more turbulent water, since though nearly all scholars would agree that Calvin certainly adhered to—strongly—the first two and the last two of these points, the matter concerning limited atonement is not easily resolved. Scholars have offered many different opinions on this. Even though it is commonplace today to recognize that the five points of Calvinism by no means embrace all of Calvinism and that Calvinism embraces many more points or teachings, if it is true that Calvin and the Calvinists diverge on the question of whom Christ died for, that is a major difference indeed. So this is the fourth and biggest issue we need to consider—the whole question of the objects and extent of Christ's atonement.

But neither is this the only remaining issue. Perhaps the strongest Calvinists of subsequent generations were the Puritans. Nearly all the Puritans openly confessed that they were solid Calvinists. They were not interested in changing Calvin's doctrines in any substantial way as much as they were interested in applying those doctrines to every area of the lives of both believers and unbelievers. The Puritans codified their views in the Westminster Standards. Though reputable scholars agree that Calvin and the Westminster Standards are in full harmony on the vast majority of doctrines that the standards address, there are several issues that need further investigation. The biggest of these issues, or at least the issue over which the most ink has been spilled, is that of assurance of faith. Some scholars think that Calvin simply taught that all believers have full assurance of faith at all times, and therefore that the Puritans, in their constant search for assurance, departed far from Calvin. So that is the fifth issue we must address.

Then, too, the Westminster Standards present a much more developed covenant theology than did Calvin. Was that difference due to Calvin's limited understanding of covenant theology, which the Puritans would later build on and develop, or is there really a fundamental difference between them on this subject? Here, then, is a sixth issue we must touch on.

So was Calvin a Calvinist? Let's look at it this way. Nearly every Calvin or Calvinist scholar would agree that Calvin and the Calvinists after him would

214 Theology Made Practical

have agreed on scores of major doctrines, so if we can show that they were also fundamentally harmonious on the six matters just mentioned—that is, on the areas of supposedly greatest divergence—we can then confidently conclude that Calvin was a Calvinist. That is the task before me now, and I invite you to accompany me on this journey. So let's turn to the first area— the question of a central dogma.

What Calvin and Calvinists Taught—Different Central Dogmas

Over the centuries, many scholars have sought to identify a controlling, single concept that governs Calvin's theology and that of his successors. Scholars from the Calvin versus Calvinist school have, at times, concluded that warm, comforting doctrines like union and communion with Christ have been dominant in Calvin's theology and cold, causal, and supposedly rigid doctrines like sovereignty and predestination (including supralapsarianism) lay at the center of the theology of Calvin's successor, Theodore Beza (1519–1605), as evidenced by his chart of salvation contained in his *Tabula Praedestinationis*. These scholars say that Beza deduced and restructured the whole scheme of salvation by using supralapsarian predestination as a starting point. Further, they assert that Beza's most illustrious supralapsarian pupil, William Perkins (1558–1602), the so-called father of Puritanism, then modified Beza's chart in his own work, *A Golden Chaine*, thereby moving Puritanism into a kind of decretal, Bezan way of thinking, which in turn, "ensured Beza's influence in English and, given the significance of the Anglo-Dutch book trade, in Dutch Reformed circles."[2]

In recent decades, however, this argument has been proven wrong for several reasons: first, neither Calvin's theology nor that of his successors, including both Beza and the Puritans, can be subsumed under one central, overarching dogma. Calvin, Beza, Perkins, and the Puritans all present far too biblical of a theology to have their theological teachings brought under one head. Since the Bible doesn't do this, and they are all preeminently biblical theologians, neither do they. Second, while some scholars say predestination is the core Calvinistic truth, Calvin and Beza and the Calvinists of the next century asserted that it can be misleading to assume that everything proceeds from absolute predestination in such a way that what transpires in

---

2. Carl Trueman, "Calvin and Reformed Orthodoxy," in *The Calvin Handbook*, ed. Herman J. Selderhuis (Grand Rapids: Eerdmans, 2009), 473.

Calvin as a Calvinist 215

time matters little. Third, Richard Muller has shown definitively that neither Beza nor Perkins uses predestination as a governing principle of his theology. Actually, the kind of diagrams used in their writings were not to be read from the top down in the sixteenth century but from the bottom up, "and thus cannot be taken as evidence of theology becoming an exercise in logical deduction from a single axiom" of supralapsarian, double predestination.[3] Fourth, since Beza wrote his *Tabula* in 1555 and shared his writings with Calvin before he published them, we can assume that this treatise also met with his approval. Fifth, though holding a supralapsarian position in terms of decretal theology, Beza and Perkins are warm and pastoral in their writings, and anyone who bothers to actually read them will soon discover this.

The idea of the fatherly sovereignty of God rather than the idea of a cold, capriciously sovereign God comes closest to the heart of the theology of both Calvin and Calvinism. Sovereignty means "rule"; hence, God's sovereignty means that God rules. God's sovereignty is His supremacy, His kingship, and His deity. His sovereignty declares Him to be God, the knowable yet incomprehensible Trinity. Both Calvin and the Calvinist believe that God is the Lord of life and Sovereign of the universe whose will is the key to history. Both believe that God is free and independent of any force outside Himself to accomplish His purposes; that He knows the end from the beginning; that He creates, sustains, governs, and directs all things; and that His marvelous design will be fully and perfectly manifest at the end of the ages.[4]

Though not the overarching doctrine, God's fatherly sovereignty, which is not arbitrary and capricious but is rooted in the loving fatherhood of the God and Father of our Lord Jesus Christ, lies at the heart of Calvin's theology and that of nearly all the Reformers and Calvinists, including the Reformed orthodox, the Puritans, the Dutch Further Reformation divines, and the German Pietists. B. B. Warfield wrote in his essay on predestination, "The Biblical writers find their comfort continually in the assurance that it is the righteous, holy, faithful, loving God in whose hands rests the determination of the sequence of events and all their issues.... The roots of the divine election are planted in His unsearchable love, by which it appears as the supreme act of grace."[5]

---

3. Trueman, "Calvin and Reformed Orthodoxy," 473.

4. G. C. Berkouwer, *The Providence of God* (Grand Rapids: Eerdmans, 1952), 7–10.

5. B. B. Warfield, *Biblical and Theological Studies* (Philadelphia: Presbyterian and Reformed, 1952), 301, 323–24.

216 Theology Made Practical

This is balanced, genuine, defensible Calvinism. It is the Calvinism expressed in Isaiah 9:6, which says that the government, or sovereignty, is upon the shoulders of Him who is "Wonderful, Counsellor, The mighty God, The everlasting Father, The Prince of Peace." God's fatherly sovereignty in Christ is the essence of who God is. Thus, if we had to summarize Calvin and Calvinism's theology into one concept, we might be safest to echo B. B. Warfield, who said that to be Calvinistic means to be theocentric. The primary interest of Calvinistic theology is the triune God, for the transcendent-immanent fatherly God in Jesus Christ is God Himself. Calvinists are people whose theology is dominated by the idea of God. As one person said, "Just as the Methodist places in the foreground the idea of the salvation of sinners; the Baptist, the mystery of regeneration; the Lutheran, justification by faith; the Moravian, the wounds of Christ; the Greek Catholic, the mysticism of the Holy Spirit; and the Romanist, the catholicity of the church, so the Calvinist is always placing in the foreground the thought of God."[6]

To be Calvinistic is to stress the comprehensive, sovereign, fatherly lordship of God over everything: every area of creation, every creature's endeavor, and every aspect of the believer's life. Here Calvin, Beza, Perkins, and the Puritans are wonderfully united. The ruling motif in Calvinism is, "In the beginning God" (Gen. 1:1). To be Calvinistic is to view all of life religiously, to experience all of life *coram Deo*—that is, lived before the face of God. As B. B. Warfield wrote:

> The Calvinist is the man who sees God: God in nature, God in history, God in grace. Everywhere he sees God in His mighty stepping, everywhere he feels the working of His mighty arm, the throbbing of His mighty heart. The Calvinist is the man who sees God behind all phenomena and in all that occurs recognizes the hand of God, working out His will. [The Calvinist] makes the attitude of the soul to God in prayer its permanent attitude in all its life activities; [he] casts himself on the grace of God alone, excluding every trace of dependence on self from the whole work of his salvation.[7]

---

6. Mason Pressly, quoted in H. Henry Meeter, *The Basic Ideas of Calvinism*, 6th ed., rev. Paul A. Marshall (Grand Rapids: Baker, 1990), 17.

7. B. B. Warfield, *Calvin as a Theologian and Calvinism Today* (London: Evangelical Press, 1969), 23–24.

The doctrine of God—a fatherly, sovereign God in Christ Jesus—is therefore the closest we can come to finding a center for Reformed theology. Here Calvin, the Calvinists (think only of Stephen Charnock's massive *Existence and Attributes of God*), and, I trust, you and I are also so obviously one that the matter need not be debated further. As Calvinists we are unitedly enamored with God. We are overwhelmed by His majesty, His beauty, His holiness, His grace. We seek His glory, desire His presence, and yearn to model our lives after Him.

Calvin as the Measuring Stick of Reformed Confessional Theology and Later Calvinists

One of the major problems in the Calvin-versus-the-Calvinist debate is that Calvin is often held up as the ideal—a kind of be-all and end-all of pristine Reformed theology, with the result that anyone or any doctrinal exposition that departs from Calvin's teaching in any area to the slightest degree is rendered second-rate at best or is suspect of being non-Calvinistic and perhaps un-Reformed or even heretical at worst. In this scenario, Calvin is held to be on par with Reformed confessional theology or, in some cases, even standing above it. Thus, for example, when the Puritans support a slightly different emphasis than Calvin on how believers should gain assurance and codify their teaching in the Westminster Confession of Faith (chap. 18), advocates of the Calvin-versus-Calvinism motif decry the confessional statement as a radical departure from Calvin's view.[8]

Much of this idolization of Calvin has been rectified, however, in recent decades as scholars have come to realize that Calvin cannot be used as an unequivocal measuring stick for assessing his contemporary theologians, the Reformed confessions, and later Calvinists. Scholars like Richard Muller have relativized Calvin's status within the Reformed tradition by showing that though Calvin was one of the greatest Reformed theologians, there were many others in his own day, such as Peter Martyr Vermigli, Martin Bucer, and Henry Bullinger, who were regarded as being on par with him in the quality of their work and, in some cases, surpassing him in their influence. For example, did you know that Bullinger's *Decades* easily outsold Calvin's *Institutes* in England for decades? Recognizing that the Reformation itself is

---

8. See Beeke, *The Quest for Full Assurance*, 111–64. Cf. Joel R. Beeke, *Knowing and Growing in Assurance of Faith* (Rosshire, Scotland: Christian Focus, 2017).

218   Theology Made Practical

an eclectic movement of remarkable agreement on all the essential doctrines but with considerable variations on nonessentials rather than a monolithic movement with only trivial differences between leading Reformers in various countries, a notable Reformation scholar such as Carter Lindberg can now title his textbook *The European Reformations*. In the generation that succeeded Calvin, theologians such as John Knox, Zacharias Ursinus, Franciscus Junius, Jean Taffin, and William Perkins continued this eclecticism.

The effect of recent scholarship is to show that the various shades of doctrinal emphases found in the sixteenth-century Reformers and their confessional statements underscore their continuity within their diversity. Consider only the fundamental unity within the diversity of the major national confessional standards of the 1560s: the Scots Confession, the Belgic Confession, the Heidelberg Catechism, and the Second Helvetic Confession. Calvin's influence upon these confessional statements as well as other Reformed doctrinal standards up to the Canons of Dort in 1619 is considerable, but his influence is still of one among many, unlike Luther and Melanchthon's dominant influence on the Lutheran Book of Concord.[9]

By extension, the various shades of doctrinal emphases found between Calvin and his sixteenth-century colleagues in comparison to the seventeenth-century Calvinistic Puritans are now also being increasingly judged to underscore their continuity within their diversity. Scott Clark summarizes this well when he writes:

> By focusing on issues of exegesis and doctrinal continuity set within the much broader and variegated contexts of the development of Western theology as a whole, a new picture has emerged that not only relativizes Calvin's status within the Reformed tradition, but that also demonstrates the exegetical, methodological, and theological complexity of the Reformed tradition of which Calvin is a part and the substantial continuities in these areas between Reformation and post-Reformation Reformed dogmatics.[10]

This more recent rectification of setting Calvin as a notable leader in his own context rather than placing him as king of the hill with all the other Reformers as epigones coincides more realistically with Calvin's own day in two ways. First, as already hinted at, men like Bullinger and Beza were as

---

9. Trueman, "Calvin and Reformed Orthodoxy," 476.
10. Trueman, "Calvin and Reformed Orthodoxy," 472.

well known as Calvin. Interestingly, there are more extant letters of Bullinger answering concerns related to the Reformation than there are of Luther and Calvin combined.[11] Second, many later Calvinistic writers, representing Reformed orthodoxy, Puritanism, the Dutch Further Reformation, and German Pietism, often quote Calvin's colleagues as much as or more than Calvin. The evidence of recent scholarship shows that the continuities between Calvin and the Calvinists are much greater and the discontinuities much smaller than liberal scholars suggested in much of the latter half of the twentieth century.

How Calvin and Calvinists Thought—Scholasticism and Methodology

The Calvin versus Calvinist debate is fueled as much by the whole question of *how* Calvin actually thought as by *what* he thought. This historical question is argued on a number of different levels. The most fundamental level is that of how Calvin actually thought in contrast to how his followers thought.

You may have heard of scholasticism and scholastics. For many historians and theologians, those are dismissive terms. You've heard of the medieval debates about how many angels can dance on the head of a pin. That sort of thing is often derided and dismissed as "scholastic." Few seem to know precisely what "scholastic" means, but they are quite sure it's bad. There are two periods that are often characterized as scholastic. The first is the medieval scholastic period, and the second is the Protestant scholastic period, which dates from several decades after the Reformation. The Reformed scholastic theologians are often placed under the rubric of Reformed orthodoxy. The theologians of both these periods are caricatured as nit-picking, petty, argumentative men who loved nothing better than to endlessly debate pointless questions in Aristotelian terms. And standing between these two periods, his majestic head and shoulders rising above such worthless debates, stands John Calvin, paragon of clear thinking and Christological piety.

According to this understanding, Calvin got just about everything right and held it all in a near perfect balance, while his followers who missed the woods for the trees messed everything up and then labeled their disastrous theology "Calvinism." Calvin would have been appalled at their beliefs,

---

11. George Ella, "Henry Bullinger (1504–1575): Shepherd of the Churches," in *The Decades of Henry Bullinger*, ed. Thomas Harding, intro. George Ella and Joel R. Beeke (Grand Rapids: Reformation Heritage Books, 2004), 1:xlix.

220 Theology Made Practical

but unfortunately, being dead and buried, he is unable to communicate his disapproval.

This charge has massive implications for those of us who call ourselves Calvinists and who derive our theology first of all from the Scriptures and then from a long line of Calvinists, many of whom were scholastics. Have we been led horribly astray, almost since the time of Calvin's death? Many scholars would argue that we have. I believe the evidence clearly shows that we have not.

We won't go into the details of the debates about Protestant scholasticism. Suffice it to say that most of what has been said about scholasticism has risen from a shallow understanding of the term and from a general distaste for precision in religious matters. Many have also confused content and method. Scholasticism is really just a method of reasoning and teaching. The content of that teaching is almost totally independent from the method, but few recognized this until recent years. Richard Muller has done a lot of work in this area to revive study in Protestant scholasticism from a less antagonistic point of view. So when someone dismisses predestination or definite atonement as "scholastic," you can kindly inform them that they are confused. The scholastic method is a method of teaching and reasoning, not the content of that teaching.

So that is one level of the debate. Calvin is good because he is exegetical, Christocentric, and warm in his theology; the Reformed orthodox scholastics that followed him are bad because they are more predestinarian, more rigidly logical. Scholars and people who say such things are usually making one of two errors: first, they are forgetting that due to the effective, detailed Roman Catholic response—especially from the Jesuits—to the theology of the Reformers, Calvinists following Calvin had to sharpen their pencils and respond to charges in much more detail than Calvin ever had to. As Carl Trueman writes: "With the Holy Roman Empire being convulsed by wars and the Catholic Church engaging in major theological retrenchment at the Council of Trent, it was inevitable that the generation of theologians after Calvin would need both to formulate their theological positions more clearly and to engage in more thorough and widespread polemics as the ecclesiastical politics of Europe became both more complicated and more clearly defined."[12]

---

12. Trueman, "Calvin and Reformed Orthodoxy," 476.

The scholastic method was an effective way to help them do just that. Yes, they were more logical, but they were more logical in order to defend the faith more powerfully. It is a mythical objection to assert that Reformed orthodoxy dealt with such matters as how many angels could dance on the head of a pin. Those were the medieval Roman Catholic scholastics, not the post-Reformed Orthodox scholastics.

Second, those who make such charges against the Reformed scholastics appear to have seldom read their works. A classic example of this is all the criticism that has been heaped upon Beza's chart of salvation. The chart lacks a Christological emphasis, which has repeatedly been decried by many liberals as a just cause for condemning the scholastic approach, but those same liberals have not read the book that explains the chart, which, as Muller has convincingly shown, is quite Christological throughout.[13]

Limited Atonement and the Offer of Grace

Here lies the crux of the debate. Before we enter into it, let me stress an issue behind the issue. It would be possible to discuss Calvin's Calvinism as if it were simply a historical question. While many participants have asserted that their interest in the debate is merely historical, at least some of them enter this debate more to justify their own beliefs than to settle a historical conundrum. This isn't merely a historical question for them; it has real implications for their own life. The question of whether Calvin was a Calvinist is a search for justification. Many throughout Protestant Christianity see Calvin as a great fountainhead of true theology, and to appeal to him is to appeal to a great authority. Those who want to solidify their position and confirm their ideals find it a great help to "discover" that Calvin's teaching harmonizes with their own. Few people are under the impression that Calvin is infallible, but we should recognize the great gifts that God gave Calvin and the great insight into His Word contained in his writings. It is because we recognize that Calvin was a greater theologian than we are that an appeal to him lends authority to our ideas.

So when scholars argue that Calvin was actually not a Calvinist, they are appealing to Calvin in opposition to those followers of Calvin who call themselves Calvinists. An example will help clarify what I am talking about.

---

13. Richard A. Muller, *Christ and the Decree: Christology and Predestination in Reformed Theology from Calvin to Perkins* (Durham, N.C.: Labyrinth, 1986), 79–83.

Imagine that I, as a theologian, am convinced that Christ died for all men. If I want to argue that position, it would be good if I could find some great theologians of the past who agree with me. Of course Calvinists will disagree with me. They have their five points of Calvinism, one of which is limited or definite atonement, which states that Christ did not die for all men but for the elect only. Imagine that in my search for great men of the past who share my belief, I find that John Calvin agrees with me that Christ died for all men! What a discovery that would be! John Calvin, to whom nearly all Calvinists appeal (and from whom they derive their name), agrees with me and disagrees with them! So if Calvinism can be summarized by those five points, one of which is definite atonement, then Calvin himself would not be an authentic Calvinist!

Did Calvin actually believe in definite atonement? This debate usually takes the form of arguing about various quotations from Calvin's extensive writings. Many quotes are offered as proof of the idea that Calvin believed that Christ died for all men.

The surprising thing is that, at first glance, many of these quotations do indeed seem to show that Calvin wasn't a Calvinist after all. Many have embraced this view, but I believe that it can be clearly shown that Calvin was a Calvinist with regard to this question.

Before looking at some representative quotes from Calvin, we must note two issues that frequently hamper our ability to understand Calvin on this point. In the first place, Calvin writes his *Institutes* in the first person plural; that is, he often uses words like "we" and "us." Paul Helm notes that the increase in warmth derived from this language is welcome, but it comes at the cost of precision. When Calvin says that Christ died for us, what does he mean? Who are the "us"? It's clear that Calvin most often uses "us" and "we" to refer to believers, though some have wrongly asserted that he means "us" to refer to all of humanity.

The second issue is that of historical context. Because of the constant debate between Calvinists and Arminians that has surrounded us since the seventeenth century, we are so sensitive to language about the extent of the atonement that we have learned to choose our words carefully when speaking about this subject. Calvin did not live in such a context. Technically speaking, there were no Arminians in Calvin's day, so he exercised far less care in how he spoke about the extent of the atonement. He didn't have to worry about someone thinking he was teaching Arminianism. Thus, Calvin makes some statements that the typical Calvinist would be hesitant to make, worried that they could be interpreted as being Arminian. If we keep these two factors in mind: the imprecision of "us" and "we," and the historical context of Calvin, we will be well equipped to properly interpret his writings.

One of Calvin's most debated passages with regard to the extent of the atonement is his comments on 1 Timothy 2:1–5, particularly the words, "God our Saviour; who will have all men to be saved, and to come unto the knowledge of the truth" (vv. 3b–4). You'll notice the key word "all" in verse 4. Calvin comments about that verse: "The universal term 'all' must always be referred to classes of men but never to individuals. It is as if he had said, 'Not only Jews, but also Greeks, not only people of humble rank, but also princes have been redeemed by the death of Christ.' Since therefore he intends the benefit of his death to be common to all, those who hold a view that would exclude any from the hope of salvation do him an injury."[14]

It is easy to see, especially when we read the last line, why someone would use such a passage to show that Calvin believed in universal atonement. But it is not fair to remove that sentence from the context of its paragraph. The paragraph makes clear that Calvin sees "all" as referring to all classes of people, not every person who has ever lived. Besides this, Calvin clearly believes that Christ's work actually saves those it is for, and so he cannot believe that His work is for all. As I mentioned before, a Calvinist today would be careful about using the word "all" without a disclaimer, but Calvin has no such inhibitions. That he employs the word "all" here proves nothing. We could look at many more passages, but this gives an idea of how the debate runs.

Another method of demonstrating that Calvin was supposedly not a Calvinist is to appeal to his clear teaching on indiscriminately offering salvation to all, now usually referred to as the free offer of grace. Calvin cannot have believed in definite atonement, so the argument runs, if he so clearly championed the free offer of grace. This debate still rages in some circles. It has massive implications for preaching and spiritual life. But it is simply not true that one must believe in universal atonement to freely offer the gospel to all. Roger Nicole is helpful here.

Nicole says our major problem in understanding definite atonement is that we think that a coextensive provision is necessary for a sincere offer of any kind; that is, Christ has to have died for every person in order for

---

14. Calvin, *Commentary*, on 1 Tim. 2:4.

Theology Made Practical

every person to be offered salvation in Him. Nicole says this premise is false even in mundane human affairs: "For instance, advertisers who offer some objects on the pages of a newspaper do not feel that honesty in any way demands of them to have a stock coextensive with the circulation figures of the newspaper. Really, the only requisite for a sincere invitation is this—that if the conditions be fulfilled, that which is offered will actually be granted."[15] Jesus says, "Him that cometh to me I will in no wise cast out" (John 6:37). Unlike stores with limited stock, Jesus's stock is never exhausted.

William Symington argues likewise:

> We hold that the sacrifice of the Lord Jesus possessed an intrinsic value sufficient for the salvation of the whole world. In this sense it was adequate to the redemption of every human being.... The worth of Christ's atonement we hold to be, in the strictest sense of the term, infinite, absolute, all-sufficient.... This all-sufficiency is what lays the foundation for the unrestricted universality of the gospel call.... Such is my impression of the sufficiency of the atonement, that were all the guilt of all mankind concentrated in my own person, I should see no reason, relying on that blood which cleanseth from all sin, to indulge despair.[16]

Symington concludes: "Let sinners everywhere know that if they perish it is not because there is not merit in Christ sufficient to meet all the demands of law and justice against them. Let them all turn and embrace the kind, the sincere, the urgent call to life and salvation by mere gratuity on the part of God: 'Whosoever will, let him take the water of life freely.'"[17]

What Calvin and the Calvinists are saying is this: If, by grace, you take this water of life, you will be saved. No one has ever perished who has truly believed in the Lord Jesus Christ alone for salvation. The message of the gospel is this: The bridge of salvation between God and the sinner is finished in and through Jesus Christ and His sacrifice from one end (God) to the other (the sinner). Christ will enable you to put your weight on that bridge, and He will carry you all the way across. He welcomes all who come. Trust Him.

---

15. Roger Nicole, *Evangelical Theological Society Bulletin* (Fall 1967): 207.

16. William Symington, *The Atonement and Intercession of Christ* (Grand Rapids: Reformation Heritage Books, 2006), 185–86.

17. Symington, *Atonement and Intercession of Christ*, 185–86.

Without faith, Christ's atonement does us no good. We experience the benefits of Christ's accomplishment only when we, with our empty hands, embrace Christ. The good news is that the atonement has been achieved before we exercise faith (Rom. 5:5–11). The reconciliation is there to be received, and by grace we receive it when Christ, by the Holy Spirit, draws us to Himself.

As Calvinists who hold to the doctrine of definite atonement, we can be assured that we may and must offer the gospel indiscriminately to all people. The argument that Calvin could do this on the basis of a universal atonement but that his followers, with their definite atonement, cannot is false.

There are other ways in which proponents of this view attempt to demonstrate that Calvin was not a Calvinist, but none of them are conclusive. They are arguments from silence and rise from statements often taken out of context. Having addressed the arguments of those who assert that Calvin was not a Calvinist, we will now conclude with some summary evidence that favors viewing Calvin as being a Calvinist.

First, Calvin's entire theology is the study of a sovereign God who has a specific plan, which He is working out by His almighty power. A critical component of this plan is God's elective purpose toward a part of humankind whom He will redeem and make His own. A merely hypothetical and uncertain atonement sits so awkwardly within this framework that to argue Calvin holds such a view is simply preposterous. It just doesn't fit everything else we know about Calvin's theology.

Second, the various instances where Calvin's language is unclear are often cited as evidence that he believed in universal atonement. But these passages can just as easily (and more convincingly) be read as evidence for a definite atonement view, as we saw in the example already cited from 1 Timothy 2:3b–4.

Third, in his expositions of numerous texts that use inclusive language, Calvin never runs with them in a universal direction. Rather, he argues that they refer to all classes of people or that they militate against an exclusively Jewish soteriology. Are we to believe that a theologian who promotes a universal atonement refrains from employing the most likely texts in a defense of that position? Certainly not, since Calvin would then be blithely passing over the texts that purportedly support universal atonement. In his exposition of those texts that form the foundation of the argument for universal redemption, Calvin offers no real support to that argument.

226 Theology Made Practical

Finally, we should note that though many of Calvin's statements related to the atonement, when taken in isolation, can be read either way, there are some statements that seem to foil all attempts at a universal atonement reading. One of these appears in a discussion of unbelievers participating in the Lord's Supper. Calvin states, "I should like to know how the wicked can eat the flesh of Christ which was not crucified for them, and how they can drink the blood which was not shed to expiate their sins."[18]

This quotation, in conjunction with the points already made, demonstrates that Calvin was a Calvinist. The position that he was misinterpreted by nearly every Calvinist until the twentieth century is untenable. Rather, his theology was inherited by following generations who developed it further and articulated it in new ways but did not substantially change its core. We may consider ourselves yet another generation that has been given custody of this great treasure, and we may feel confident that our Calvinism (which is nothing more than biblically faithful Christianity, in my opinion) is such that Calvin would have no trouble at all subscribing to it.

So Calvin was a Calvinist. But what are the practical conclusions of this? Recall the observation that appeals to Calvin are often attempts to justify one's own beliefs. The arguments are historical in the sense that they have to do with the theology of historical figures, but these historical arguments are often in the service of establishing what we should believe today. This isn't just about Calvin; it is about us and our theology today. It is about the truth of the gospel and about properly and correctly understanding it. And so there are serious and practical implications. Let's look at one of these that arise from this discussion—namely, assurance of faith.

Assurance of Faith

How can people know if they are Christians or not? How can they be assured that they are right with God? One of the most popular and well-known books arguing that Calvin was not a Calvinist—R. T. Kendall's *Calvin and English Calvinism to 1649*—propounds that Calvin believed in a universal atonement and that he *must* have believed this since there could be no basis of assurance without it.[19] According to this book, if men and women don't know that Christ died for them—which they cannot know unless Christ

---

18. Calvin, *Tracts and Letters*, 2:527.
19. R. T. Kendall, *Calvin and English Calvinism to 1649* (Carlisle, England: Paternoster, 1997).

died for all people—they can never have assurance. Calvin thus provided a basis for assurance with his universal atonement, but his misguided followers with their doctrine of definite, particular, or personal atonement (all three words work) removed the foundation of assurance. They said that assurance was based on the observation of fruit in the life of the believer, and thus they turned Calvinism into a religion of works righteousness. One has to work for assurance. Whereas Calvin wanted the believer to look to Christ and His death for all people, Calvin's followers—most particularly the Puritans—directed believers to look at themselves for assurance. No believer is perfect, and thus no one can have perfect assurance based on the fruit in their lives. The only possible basis for assurance is a universal atonement, so that every person may know for certain that Christ died for him or her. Consequently, Kendall regards Theodore Beza and William Perkins as the culprits who pushed the post-Reformation doctrine of assurance down the slope of experimental subjectivity until it resulted in the Westminster Assembly's betrayal of Calvinism through an "apparently unquestioned acceptance of a distinction between faith and assurance, for 'Faith' was one heading in the Confession, and 'Certainty of Salvation' another."[20]

At first glance, this may seem like a logical conclusion. But it fails at two points. First, it contains the historically erroneous claim that Calvin taught universal atonement. Second, it fails in its argumentation, as Roger Nicole points out:

> Universal atonement is neither necessary nor sufficient for assurance. It is not necessary since my understanding of how the work of Christ affects others is not essential for a perception of how it affects me. It is not sufficient, since on Kendall's showing all covered by the atonement will not be saved; assurance, if it is to be reliable, needs to be grounded in something that actually makes a difference between the saved and the lost.[21]

In other words, the idea of universal atonement does *not* provide assurance. Unless you carry universal atonement over into universal salvation (which Kendall would not do), there can be no assurance on that basis. If

---

20. R. T. Kendall, "The Puritan Modification of Calvin's Theology," in *John Calvin*, ed. W. Stanford Reid (Grand Rapids: Zondervan, 1982), 214.

21. Roger Nicole, "John Calvin's View of the Extent of the Atonement," in *Standing Forth: Collected Writings of Roger Nicole* (Fearn, Ross-shire, Scotland: Mentor, 2002), 283–312.

228 Theology Made Practical

Christ died for everyone but not everyone is saved, the knowledge that He died for me does not provide assurance, since I may be one of those for whom He died but will not be saved.

Kendall both misstates and oversimplifies his case. Carl Trueman says:

The question of development on this issue [of assurance] is complicated and must be understood as more than simply a theological problem. It has been demonstrated by scholars such as Joel R. Beeke and Paul Helm that the issue is much more complex in Calvin than had been thought. While the *Institutes* do seem to make assurance of the essence of faith, the commentaries and sermons indicate clearly that Calvin was aware that the pastoral reality was far more complex and that both lack of assurance and presumption on God's grace were, even in the early Reformation, key pastoral issues. Further, it seems clear that Calvin and the earlier reformers, in their reaction against the medieval church's virtual denial of any assurance, tended to emphasize this point somewhat in their rhetoric of faith. Thus, Reformation theology itself changed the pastoral landscape, emphasizing the normativity of assurance, and this was at precisely the same time as dramatic social, economic, cultural, and ecclesiastical changes were taking hold in Europe, a wider context designed, if anything to exacerbate problems of assurance. As a result, the theology of the earlier Reformation itself generated new pastoral problems to which later generations had to respond.[22]

So this debate has a personal and practical application. How do we know that we are one of God's children? Both Calvin and the Calvinists would say: We know primarily from trusting in the promises of God, and secondarily from the fruits of salvation evident in our hearts and lives, and finally from the testimony of the Holy Spirit witnessing with our spirits that we are the children of God. The differences between Calvin and the Puritans in expounding these three ways of knowing that we are believers are quantitative, not qualitative. Those quantitative differences are largely twofold: first, Calvin put more emphasis than the Puritans did on the promises of God and less on the fruits of salvation; second, Calvin emphasized more the ideal in his definition of faith, underscoring that faith contains no doubt. The effect

---

22. Trueman, "Calvin and Reformed Orthodoxy," 474. Actually, the *Institutes* demonstrate the same sensitivity in a number of places.

of that emphasis is that he seemed to be teaching more than did the Puritans that assurance was of the essence of faith. But that, too, was only a matter of emphasis, since the Puritans also recognized repeatedly that the seeds of assurance lie in the smallest exercise of true faith. Calvin, on the other hand, also stressed that unbelief dies hard. He emphasized the difference between the ideal definition of faith and the practical reality of the believer's experience, in which doubt is always present and even eclipses assurance at times. He acknowledged the daily tension in faith in the spiritual warfare of flesh versus spirit. And he distinguished between the germ of faith and the consciousness of faith. Ultimately, the seeds of the more pastorally nuanced doctrine of assurance of faith carefully developed by the Puritans were actually sown by Calvin. Calvin is the forerunner, not the antagonist, of the Puritans on assurance.[23]

Covenant and Covenant Theology

Some have said that covenant is the central idea of Calvin's theology in contrast to the Puritans. That is patently false. Actually, the Puritans developed Calvin's idea of covenant much further than Calvin ever did. While the covenantal relationship between God and humanity is emphasized in Calvinistic theology, it is not the overruling concept. All people are indeed either in covenant with God or are covenant breakers, but neither Calvin nor the Calvinistic Puritans structured all doctrines under this important concept.

Much of the debate on Calvin versus the Calvinists in this area focuses on the covenant of works. Carl Trueman summarizes this well:

> The issue of Calvin's relationship to [Puritan] covenant theology has proved controversial. Scholars such as T. F. and J. B. Torrance see the development of the concept of the covenant of works in the later sixteenth century as a clear shift in Reformed theology toward a legalistic view of Christianity linked to a notion of God that prioritizes law and justice over grace. This view has, however, been seriously challenged by, among others, Richard A. Muller, Willem van Asselt, and Peter A. Lillback. Lillback in particular has demonstrated that many of the later elements that are essential to the concept of the covenant of works are already present in Calvin, specifically, the federally representative nature of Adam, the existence

---

23. Beeke, *Quest for Full Assurance*, 37–72, 111–64.

230   Theology Made Practical

of a promise in the garden, and the basis of the God-Adam arrangement on grounds that avoid any notion of strict merit.[24]

Much like with the doctrine of assurance, Puritan covenant theology is not opposing Calvin but is developing his thinking.

Conclusion

We wish to make four points in concluding: first, though other issues could also be addressed that are anachronistic to Calvin, such as the imputation of Christ's active obedience to the believer,[25] the issue of Amyraldianism,[26] the morphology of conversion,[27] and the role of works in salvation,[28] enough has been written to show that Calvin was essentially a Calvinist. Though some of his followers were scholastic and articulated the Reformed faith in ways that differed slightly from Calvin or developed his thinking further, those who remained confessionally Reformed did not substantially differ from Calvin. Nor did their scholastic method corrupt the content of the gospel but helped make it more precisely nuanced.

Second, it should also be pointed out that Calvin and Beza as well as most of the Calvinists of succeeding generations never sensed any substantial differences between Calvin and their own teachings. They recognized that in the throes of developing church history, certain doctrines, such as covenant theology, assurance, and adoption, received further development, but in no case did the Calvinistic Puritans and the Dutch Further Reformation divines feel that they had developed doctrines that differed essentially from those of Calvin. Happily, we've seen that recent scholarship is increasingly recognizing this, so that Trueman concludes his helpful article by saying: "Calvin now emerges not so much as the culmination of a pristine tradition that is perverted by his successors and more as the theological *primus inter pares* of his generation of Reformed theologians whose work stimulated many of the later developments in Reformed Orthodoxy."[29]

Third, we've also seen that our conclusions in this debate have real consequences for how we understand key aspects of the Christian life. The

---

24. Trueman, "Calvin and Reformed Orthodoxy," 474.
25. Trueman, "Calvin and Reformed Orthodoxy," 475.
26. Trueman, "Calvin and Reformed Orthodoxy," 477–78.
27. Paul Helm, *Calvin and the Calvinists* (Edinburgh: Banner of Truth Trust, 1982), 51–70.
28. Helm, *Calvin and the Calvinists*, 71–81.
29. Trueman, "Calvin and Reformed Orthodoxy," 479.

question, then, that remains is a personal one: Are you a Calvinist? Am I a Calvinist? Do we have the kind of passion and zeal for God and His glory that Calvin and the Calvinists had?

It seems that the genuine God-centered passion of Calvin and the Calvinists has mostly been lost due to our backsliding and the theological errors of our day. In many so-called evangelical churches, the fear of God has been largely lost and thus, in a real measure, so has a biblical understanding of the love of God in Christ Jesus. Evangelicalism has become man-centered and, as a result, promotes a view of God that is far less than the reality set forth in Holy Scripture, Calvin, and the first- and second-century Calvinists.

But even many who delight in Reformed truth seem to have lost their sense of the awe of God. As in the broader evangelical culture, God-centeredness has given way to man-centeredness in many Calvinist churches. We aim too often at giving people what they want instead of following the example of the great Calvinistic evangelists, whose first objective was to confront men and women with God's greatness and majesty.

Too many of us today present God as more user-friendly than His own Word does. We want to make people feel comfortable, so we avoid telling them anything that will make them uneasy. We are so concerned about losing our young people that we never ask them to gaze on the holiness of God or challenge them to live out that holiness in the childlike fear of God. We condone materialism, worldliness, and triviality because we have so little sense of an ever-present, infinitely holy God.

Our lives seldom testify that we are willing, at any price, to "buy the truth, and sell it not" (Prov. 23:23). Dangerous compromises, subtle backsliding, Ephesian coldness, and Laodicean indifference multiply the "un-Reformedness" of our lives. How often we esteem ourselves and our reputation above the name of God and His reputation!

But once the Holy Spirit shows us the Father's divine generosity to us in His Son, together with the absolute freeness of His grace, we, like Calvin and the Calvinists, will wholeheartedly yearn to glorify our worthy, fatherly triune God with all that is within us. As Maurice Roberts writes:

> The realization that God has chosen an individual to life and glory, though he was not a whit better than others, leads the mature Christian to cherish the most ecstatic feelings of gratitude to our heavenly Father. With an upturned face the adoring believer confesses to heaven that, apart from eternally given grace, he would never have

believed in Christ, nor even have wished to believe. Then, lowering his gaze and covering his streaming eyes, the grateful Christian exclaims: "My Father and my God! To Thee alone be everlasting glory for such unmerited grace!"[30]

Are we true sons and daughters of the Calvinistic Reformation who are enamored with God and with honoring and obeying Him? If so, let us pray with the psalmist:

> By all whom Thou hast made
> Be praise and worship paid
> Thro' earth abroad;
> Thy Name be glorified,
> There is none great beside,
> Matchless Thy works abide,
> For Thou art God.
>
> Help me Thy will to do,
> Thy truth I will pursue,
> Teach me to fear;
> Give me the single eye
> Thy Name to glorify,
> O Lord, my God Most High,
> With heart sincere.[31]

---

30. Maurice Roberts, "Before the Omnipotent's Throne," *Tabletalk*, 16, no. 11 (November 1992): 17.

31. *The Psalter* (Grand Rapids: Reformation Heritage Books, 2003), no. 236, stanzas 1–2.

—14—

Calvinism and Revival

Michael A. G. Haykin

One of the key means by which God has brought about a renewal of interest in Reformed teaching and doctrine over the past forty years has been the British Westminster Conference (formerly known as the Puritan Conference). Organized in the 1950s by, among others, D. Martyn Lloyd-Jones and J. I. Packer, this conference, which still meets annually in December, has played a vital role in awakening evangelicals to the riches of Puritan and Reformed theology. For many years it was customary for Lloyd-Jones to give the final address of the conference. The first of such addresses was the one that he gave in 1959 titled "Revival: An Historical and Theological Survey."[1] Lloyd-Jones began his address by defining revival as "an experience in the life of the church when the Holy Spirit does an unusual work." These extraordinary movements of the Spirit consist first of all, he stated, in the "enlivening and quickening and awakening of lethargic, sleeping, almost moribund church members" and then in "the conversion of masses of people who hitherto have been outside in indifference and in sin."[2] Lloyd-Jones went on to illustrate his definition of revival from the history of the church and from Scripture and to show that "the history of the progress and development of the church is largely a history of revivals,... these mighty exceptional effusions of the Spirit of God." What is so striking about Lloyd-Jones's survey of revival from the history of the church is how large a place revivals have occupied in the Reformed tradition. Lloyd-Jones asserted that one of the main reasons revivals have not been prominent in the last century is because the final half of the nineteenth century witnessed a widespread

---

1. For the full address, see D. Martyn Lloyd-Jones, *The Puritans: Their Origins and Successors: Addresses Delivered at the Puritan and Westminster Conferences 1959–1978* (Edinburgh: Banner of Truth Trust, 1987), 1–23.

2. Lloyd-Jones, *Puritans: Their Origins and Successors*, 1–2.

234 Theology Made Practical

turning away from Reformed theology, which continued unabated until the late 1940s.[3]

In what follows in this essay, two examples of Calvinist revival are briefly examined—the awakening at Kirk of Shotts and William Williams as a Calvinist proponent of revival—and then the bulk of the essay looks at revival among a quintessential Calvinist body, the English Particular Baptists.

Kirk of Shotts, June 1630

In the seventeenth century, a number of Calvin's spiritual heirs, the Puritans, also knew revival firsthand.[4] For instance, a celebration of the Lord's Supper at Shotts near Glasgow on Sunday, June 20, 1630, was attended by such a rich sense of the presence of God that at the end of the services, instead of retiring to bed, the people continued together in prayer and devotion throughout the night. Evidently it was not the custom at that time to have a further service on the Monday following Communion. Yet God had so presenced Himself with them that they were unable to part without further thanksgiving and praise. A Monday preaching service was therefore arranged, and a young man named John Livingstone (1603–1672), chaplain to the Countess of Wigton, was persuaded to be the preacher.

He too had spent the previous night in prayer. Alone in the fields, at eight or nine in the morning he was so overcome with a sense of his unworthiness (particularly as so many choice ministers and experienced Christians were present) that he thought he would slip away quietly. He had actually gone some way and was almost out of sight of the church when the words "Was I ever a barren wilderness or a land of darkness?" were so impressed upon his heart that he felt bound to return and preach. What was to ensue was a most remarkable demonstration of the power and the grace of God under the preaching of His Word.

Livingstone preached for about an hour and a half on Ezekiel 36:25–26: "Then will I sprinkle clean water upon you, and ye shall be clean: from all your filthiness, and from all your idols, will I cleanse you. A new heart also

---

3. Lloyd-Jones, *Puritans: Their Origins and Successors*, 4–5.

4. For good discussions of revival during the Puritan era, see Iain Murray, "The Puritans and Revival Christianity," *Banner of Truth* 72 (September 1969): 9–19; J. I. Packer, "Puritanism as a Movement of Revival," in *A Quest for Godliness: The Puritan Vision of the Christian Life* (Wheaton, Ill.: Crossway, 1994), 35–48; and R. E. Davies, *I Will Pour Out My Spirit: A History and Theology of Revivals and Evangelical Awakenings* (Tunbridge Wells, Kent: Monarch, 1992), 63–68.

Calvinism and Revival

will I give you, and a new spirit will I put within you: and I will take away the stony heart out of your flesh, and I will give you an heart of flesh." He was about to finish when a heavy rain shower caused people in the churchyard to cover themselves hastily with their cloaks. This prompted the preacher to continue:

> If a few drops of rain so discompose you, how discomposed would you be, how full of horror and despair, if God should deal with you as you deserve? And God will deal thus with all the finally impenitent. God might justly rain fire and brimstone upon you, as he did upon Sodom and Gomorrah, and the other cities of the plain. But, for ever blessed be his name! the door of mercy still stands open for such as you are. The Son of God, by tabernacling in our nature, and obeying and suffering in it, is the only refuge and covert from the storm of divine wrath due to us for sin. His merits and mediation alone are the screen from that storm, and none but those who come to Christ just as they are, empty of everything, and take the offered mercy at his hand, will have the benefit of this shelter.[5]

Livingstone continued preaching in such a manner for another hour, experiencing, in his own words, "such liberty and melting of heart, as I never had the like in public all my lifetime." The impact of this rich outpouring of the Spirit of God was close to five hundred individuals were converted that day.[6]

William Williams and the Welsh Revival

In the following century, in 1738, a twenty-one-year-old medical student named William Williams (1717–1791) was returning home to Carmarthenshire when he happened to pass through a little village called Talgarth in Breconshire.[7] It was Sunday and the village church bell was calling the village parishioners to worship, and Williams joined them. But the service that morning was spiritually cold and lifeless. As he came out of the church, however, he was amazed to see another young man standing on top of a table tomb, the evangelist Howell Harris (1714–1773). Harris had been prevented

---

5. As quoted in "Revival Snapshots: Kirk of Shotts," *Evangelical Times* 31, no. 6 (June 1997): 16.

6. Michael J. Crawford, *Seasons of Grace: Colonial New England's Revival Tradition in Its British Context* (New York: Oxford University Press, 1991), 24–25.

7. For a life of Williams, see Eifion Evans, *Bread of Heaven: The Life and Work of William Williams, Pantycelyn* (Bryntirion, Bridgend: Bryntirion Press, 2010).

236   Theology Made Practical

from preaching within the church and thus had resorted to the graveyard. It was a sermon, Williams would later recall, that was "unusually terrifying." Around him the words of the evangelist were being driven home by the Spirit of God to sinful hearts and sinners were coming to Christ.

Unlike the revival at Kirk O'Shotts, though, this incident was part of a nationwide revival. Known as the Great Awakening in Wales, Harris described it in the early days to the English preacher George Whitefield (1714–1770) thus:

> The outpouring of the Blessed Spirit is now so plentiful and common, that I think it was our deliberate observation that not one sent by Him opens his mouth without some remarkable showers. He comes either as a Spirit of wisdom to enlighten the soul, to teach and build up, and set out the works of light and darkness, or else a Spirit of tenderness and love, sweetly melting the souls like the dew, and watering the graces; or as the Spirit of hot burning zeal, setting their hearts in a flame, so that their eyes sparkle with fire, love, and joy; or also such a Spirit of uncommon power that the heavens seem to be rent, and hell to tremble.[8]

Not surprisingly, Williams never forgot the day he heard Harris preach. "It was a morning," he wrote many years later, "which I shall always remember, for it was then that I heard the voice of heaven."[9] Henceforth Williams regarded himself as a pilgrim on his way to the celestial city.[10]

When William Williams, Pantycelyn,[11] died in 1791, he had written some 860 hymns and over ninety books and had traveled nearly 112,000 miles as an itinerant preacher during this revival.[12] Lloyd-Jones considered Williams to be "the theologian of Welsh Calvinistic Methodism," which was

---

8. As quoted in Eifion Evans, *Daniel Rowland and the Great Evangelical Awakening in Wales* (Edinburgh: Banner of Truth Trust, 1985), 243.

9. As quoted in Tim Shenton, *Christmas Evans: The Life and Times of the One-Eyed Preacher of Wales* (Darlington, U. K.: Evangelical Press, 2001), 34.

10. Eifion Evans, "'A Most Gifted, Respected and Useful Man': Part 1: A Survey of Williams' Life," in William Williams, *Pursued by God*, trans. Eifion Evans (Bryntirion, Bridgend: Evangelical Press of Wales, 1996), 17.

11. "Pantycelyn" was the name of his mother's old home, which he inhabited from 1748 onward after his marriage.

12. Evans, *Daniel Rowland and the Great Evangelical Awakening in Wales*, 63.

Calvinism and Revival 237

born in that Welsh revival.[13] His great contribution to that revival was in the realm of "experimental hymnody and revival apologetic."[14] His hymns were a central vehicle in the extension of the revival and also in creating a hunger for literacy.[15] Thomas Charles of Bala later said of him: "He was one of the most gifted, respected and useful men of his age. His gift of poetry was naturally and abundantly given him by the Lord.... His hymns wrought a remarkable change in the religious aspect of Wales, and in public worship. Some verses in his hymns are like coals of fire, warming and firing every passion when sung."[16]

Of Williams's hymns, Lloyd-Jones commented: "The hymns of William Williams are packed with theology and experience.... William Williams was the greatest hymn-writer of them all. You get greatness, and bigness, and largeness in Isaac Watts; you get the experimental side wonderfully in Charles Wesley. But in William Williams you get both at the same time."[17] Regretfully, only a very few of his hymns have been translated into English; among them are "Guide Me, O Thou Great Jehovah" and "O'er the Gloomy Hills of Darkness."

The Revival of the Calvinistic Baptists

In the seventeenth century, one of the most spiritually alive denominations in the British Isles was the Calvinistic Baptists. From the early 1640s, when there were only seven churches in England, they grew to the point where, by 1689, there were close to three hundred congregations. It is important to remember that Baptist growth during this period came in the midst of persecution. In the 1660s and early 1670s, a series of laws were passed which made it illegal to worship in any setting other than the Established Church and which basically reduced any but Church of England members to second-class citizens. Between 1660 and 1688, Baptists who refused to go along with these laws often ended up paying substantial fines or experiencing life-threatening imprisonment.

---

13. D. Martyn Lloyd-Jones, "William Williams and Welsh Calvinistic Methodism," in *The Puritans: Their Origins and Successors* (Edinburgh: Banner of Truth Trust, 1987), 192.

14. Evans, *Daniel Rowland and the Great Evangelical Awakening in Wales*, 63.

15. W. Glanffrwd Thomas, "Welsh Hymnody," in *Dictionary of Hymnology*, ed. John Julian (1907; repr., Grand Rapids: Kregel, 1985), 2:1251.

16. As quoted in Evans, *Daniel Rowland and the Great Evangelical Awakening in Wales*, 63.

17. As quoted in Evans, *Daniel Rowland and the Great Evangelical Awakening in Wales*, 296.

238 Theology Made Practical

Religious toleration finally came in 1689. The Baptists were now free to plant and build congregations, though it was still illegal for them to evangelize outside their church buildings. Yet despite the advent of toleration, the denomination as a whole began to plateau in its growth, and, in some parts of England, it actually went into decline. In 1715 there were around 220 Calvinistic Baptist churches in England and Wales; by 1750 that number had dwindled to about 150.

The Baptists did not emerge from this spiritual "winter" until the last two or three decades of the century. There was a variety of reasons for what amounts to a profound revival among their ranks. There was theological reformation, in which the hyper-Calvinism of the past that had dominated far too many congregations was largely rejected in favor of a truly evangelical Calvinism. Then there were calls for repentance. For instance, in his *Causes of Declension in Religion, and Means of Revival* (1785), Andrew Fuller outlined the spiritual apathy then reigning among many Baptists of his day:

> It is to be feared the old puritanical way of devoting ourselves wholly to be the Lord's, resigning up our bodies, souls, gifts, time, property, with all we have and are to serve him, and frequently renewing these covenants before him, is now awfully neglected. This was to make a business of religion, a life's work, and not merely an accidental affair, occurring but now and then, and what must be attended to only when we can spare time from other arrangements. Few seem to aim, pray, and strive after eminent love to God and one other. Many appear to be contented if they can but remember the time when they had such love in exercise, and then, tacking to it the notion of perseverance without the thing, they go on and on, satisfied, it seems, if they do but make shift just to get to heaven at last, without much caring how. If we were in a proper spirit, the question with us would not so much be What must I do for God? as, What can I do for God? A servant that heartily loves his master counts it a privilege to be employed by him, yea, an honour to be entrusted with any of his concerns.[18]

Many, Fuller noted, were merely content to get to heaven without concerning themselves overly about *how* they get there. The practice of giving oneself wholly to God that had been common among the seventeenth-century

---

18. *The Complete Works of the Rev. Andrew Fuller*, ed. Joseph Belcher (Harrisonburg, Va.: Sprinkle Publications, 1988), 3:320.

Calvinism and Revival

239

Puritans had generally ceased to be part of late eighteenth-century Baptist piety. This apathy was well revealed in the question, "What I must do for God?" In other words, they were asking what is the minimum they must do to get to heaven.

Seeking to change this dire situation, Fuller suggested:

> If it is required "What then is to be done? Wherein in particular can we glorify God more than we have done?," we answer by asking: Is there no room for amendment? Have we been sufficiently earnest and constant in private prayer? Are there none of us that have opportunities to set apart particular times to pray for the effusion of the Holy Spirit? Can we do more than we have done in instructing our families? Are there none of our dependents, workmen, or neighbours that we might speak to, at least so far as to ask them to go and hear the gospel? Can we rectify nothing in our tempers and behaviour in the world so as better to recommend religion? Cannot we watch more? Cannot we save a little more of our substance to give to the poor? In a word, is there no room or possibility left for our being more meek, loving, and resembling the blessed Jesus than we have been?[19]

Here, Fuller listed five ways in which his fellow Baptists could prepare themselves for renewal. At the top of the list is (1) prayer; then (2) the cultivation of Christianity in the home; (3) witnessing to unbelievers; (4) honest examination of what needs to be changed in one's character and purposefully seeking to change it; and finally, (5) the development of a spirit of generosity to those in need.

Fuller went on to stress, however, that one's heart attitude was also important: "Think it not sufficient that we lament and mourn over our departures from God. We must return to him with full purpose of heart." As Fuller reflected on this matter of heart renewal, he urged his readers to "cherish a greater love to the truths of God; pay an invariable regard to the discipline of his house; cultivate love to one another, frequently mingle souls by frequently assembling yourselves together; encourage a meek, humble, and savoury spirit."[20]

Above all, Fuller emphasized, there must be prayer.

---

19. *Complete Works of the Rev. Andrew Fuller*, 3:320.
20. *Complete Works of the Rev. Andrew Fuller*, 3:324.

240 Theology Made Practical

> Finally, brethren, let us not forget to intermingle prayer with all we do. Our need of God's Holy Spirit to enable us to do any thing, and every thing, truly good should excite us to this. Without his blessing all means are without efficacy and every effort for revival will be in vain. Constantly and earnestly, therefore, let us approach his throne. Take all occasions especially for closet prayer; here, if anywhere, we shall get fresh strength and maintain a life of communion with God. Our Lord Jesus used frequently to retire into a mountain alone for prayer; he, therefore, that is a follower of Christ, must follow him in this important duty.[21]

The year before Fuller wrote these words, regular meetings for prayer had begun to pray for one specific object: biblical revival.

The Prayer Call of 1784

The origin of these prayer meetings can be traced back to 1784 to the town of Nottingham, in the heart of England, where in June of that year the pastors of the Baptist churches belonging to the Northamptonshire Association were meeting. Earlier that year a treatise on corporate prayer for revival by Jonathan Edwards (1703–1758), the New England divine, had come into the hands of John Sutcliff (1752–1814), the Baptist pastor of Olney, Buckinghamshire, and a close friend of Andrew Fuller. Deeply impressed and moved by this treatise, Sutcliff proposed to his fellow pastors that a monthly prayer meeting be established to pray for the outpouring of God's Spirit not only upon the Baptist churches of England but also upon all those churches that loved the Lord Jesus. This proposal ran as follows:

> Upon a motion being made to the ministers and messengers of the associate Baptist churches assembled at Nottingham, respecting meetings for prayer, to bewail the low estate of religion, and earnestly implore a revival of our churches, and of the general cause of our Redeemer, and for that end to wrestle with God for the effusion of his Holy Spirit, which alone can produce the blessed effect, it was unanimously RESOLVED, to recommend to all our churches and congregations, the spending of one hour in this important exercise, on the first Monday in every calendar month.

---

21. *Complete Works of the Rev. Andrew Fuller*, 3:324.

We hereby solemnly exhort all the churches in our connection, to engage heartily and perseveringly in the prosecution of this plan. And as it may be well to endeavour to keep the same hour, as a token of our unity herein, it is supposed the following scheme may suit many congregations, viz. to meet on the first Monday evening in May, June, and July, from 8 to 9. In Aug. from 7 to 8. Sept. and Oct. from 6 to 7. Nov. Dec. Jan. and Feb. from 5 to 6. March, from 6 to 7; and April, from 7 to 8. Nevertheless if this hour, or even the particular evening, should not suit in particular places, we wish our brethren to fix on one more convenient to themselves.

We hope also, that as many of our brethren who live at a distance from our places of worship may not be able to attend there, that as many as are conveniently situated in a village or neighbourhood, will unite in small societies at the same time. And if any single individual should be so situated as not to be able to attend to this duty in society with others, let him retire at the appointed hour, to unite the breath of prayer in private with those who are thus engaged in a more public manner.

The grand object of prayer is to be that the Holy Spirit may be poured down on our ministers and churches, that sinners may be converted, the saints edified, the interest of religion revived, and the name of God glorified. At the same time, remember, we trust you will not confine your requests to your own societies [i.e. churches]; or to your own immediate connection [i.e. denomination]; let the whole interest of the Redeemer be affectionately remembered, and the spread of the gospel to the most distant parts of the habitable globe be the object of your most fervent requests. We shall rejoice if *any other Christian societies* of our own or other denominations will unite with us, and do now *invite them* most cordially to join heart and hand in the attempt.

Who can tell what the consequences of such an united effort in prayer may be! Let us plead with God the many gracious promises of His Word, which relate to the future success of His gospel. He has said, "I will yet for this be enquired of by the house of Israel, to do it for them; I will increase them with men like a flock" Ezek. xxxvi.37.

242   Theology Made Practical

Surely we have love enough for Zion to set apart *one hour* at a time, twelve times in a year, to seek her welfare.[22]

The focus of this momentous call to prayer was the "revival of our churches, and of the general cause of our Redeemer." How was this to be achieved? By "the effusion of [God's] Holy Spirit, which alone can produce [this] blessed effect." There is, in these words, a distinct recognition that the revival of the denomination lay ultimately in the hands of God the Holy Spirit, and all of their labors without His blessing would come to nought. Yet those who issued this statement were not high Calvinists who expected results without the use of means. And thus they encouraged their congregations to gather for prayer for one hour on the first Monday of the month.

The heart of the prayer call is to be found in the fourth and fifth paragraphs. The conviction that reversing the downward trend of Calvinistic Baptists could not be accomplished by mere human zeal is mentioned again. It must be effected by an outpouring of God's Holy Spirit: "The grand object of prayer is to be that the Holy Spirit may be poured down on our ministers and churches, that sinners may be converted, the interest of religion revived, and the name of God glorified." Without the Spirit all of the church's best efforts to bring men and women to Christ will fail; all of her noblest attempts to edify God's people and bring glory to God's name fall short of success. The Spirit is the true agent of renewal and revival. Thus, there was a desperate need for prayer.

Then, there is the inclusive nature of the praying. As the Calvinistic Baptists of this association came together for prayer, they were urged not to pray solely for their own churches or even for their own denomination but to embrace in prayer other Baptist churches throughout the length and breadth of England, and even churches of other denominational bodies.

Third, there is a definite missionary focus: the readers of this call to prayer are encouraged to pray that there would be a spread of the gospel "to the most distant parts of the habitable globe." It is important to note that it was out of this group of praying Baptists that William Carey (1761–1834) came, the so-called father of the modern missionary movement. All great missionary ventures are born in the cradle of prayer.

---

22. "The Prayer Call of 1784," in John Ryland Jr., *The Nature, Evidences, and Advantages, of Humility* (Northamptonshire Association, 1784), 12. For a detailed discussion of this call to prayer and its historical context, see Michael A. G. Haykin, *One Heart and One Soul: John Sutcliff of Olney, His Friends and His Times* (Darlington, U.K.: Evangelical Press, 1994), 153–71.

Calvinism and Revival 243

Fourth, there is the scriptural foundation for the call to pray for revival. Only one text is cited—Ezekiel 36:37—but those who drew up this document were well aware that there are other biblical texts that could be cited. One of Sutcliff's friends, Thomas Blundel (c. 1752–1824), says the following regarding this verse from Ezekiel: "It is chiefly in answer to prayer that God has carried on his cause in the world: he could work without such means; but he does not, neither will he.… He loves that his people should feel interested in his cause, and labour to promote it, though he himself worketh all in all."[23]

The Record of Revival

There is little doubt from the record of history that God heard the prayers of Sutcliff and Fuller and their fellow Calvinistic Baptists. As they prayed, the Calvinistic Baptists in England began to experience the blessing of revival, though, it should be noted, a great change was not immediately evident. For instance, in 1785, Sutcliff's close friend Andrew Fuller reported about their meetings for prayer:

> It affords us no little satisfaction to hear in what manner the monthly prayer meetings which were proposed in our letter of last year have been carried on, and how God has been evidently present in those meetings, stirring up the hearts of his people to wrestle hard with him for the revival of his blessed cause. Though as to the number of members there is no increase this year, but something of the contrary; yet a spirit of prayer in some measure being poured out more than balances in our account for this defect. We cannot but hope, wherever we see a spirit of earnest prayer generally and perseveringly prevail, that God has some good in reserve, which in his own time he will graciously bestow.[24]

The stirring up of many to wrestle in prayer for revival was considered by Fuller as more than balancing the failure to increase the membership of the

---

23. Thomas Blundel, *The River of Life Impeded*, in *Sermons on Various Subjects* (London, 1806), 183, 184.

24. *Complete Works of the Rev. Andrew Fuller*, 3:318.

244 Theology Made Practical

churches. And so it was resolved "without any hesitation, to continue the meetings of prayer on the first Monday evening in every calendar month."[25]

By 1798 there were close to 361 Calvinistic Baptist churches in England and Wales. This number had risen to 532 by 1812, and in 1851 it stood at over 1,370. We can observe the revival that was taking place from a more personal angle in the following extracts from the letters of Andrew Fuller.[26]

In 1810 Fuller noted in a letter to William Carey: "I preached a sermon to the youth last Lord's Day from 1 Thess 2:19. I think we must have had nearly one thousand. They came from all quarters. My heart's desire and prayer for them is that they may be saved." Fuller was still rejoicing when he wrote to a fellow Baptist pastor, John Ryland, on December 28: "I hope the Lord is at work among our young people. Our Monday and Friday night meetings are much thronged." A couple of months later he told Ryland: "The Friday evening discourses are now, and have been for nearly a year, much thronged, because they have been mostly addressed to persons under some concern about their salvation." And what was happening in Fuller's church was happening in Baptist causes throughout the length and breadth of England and Wales.

A second fruit of the revival was the formation of the Baptist Missionary Society in 1792 with Andrew Fuller as the first secretary. The following year William Carey was sent out as the Society's first missionary. Carey had been converted in the late 1770s and had eventually become a member of the church that John Sutcliff pastored in Olney. Not long after his conversion, Carey was gripped by the responsibility that the church had been given by the risen Christ in the Great Commission (Matt. 28:18–20) to spread the good news to the ends of the earth. It needs to be recalled that part of the Prayer Call of 1784 had urged prayer for "the spread of the gospel to the most distant parts of the habitable globe." The formation of this society was a direct result of prayer for revival.

Carey labored in India until his death in 1834. The impact of his missionary labors can be well seen in the following extract from a letter by an Anglican evangelical named Thomas Scott, who had known Carey in his

---

25. As quoted in Arthur Fawcett, *The Cambuslang Revival* (London: Banner of Truth Trust, 1971), 230.

26. The following extracts from the letters of Andrew Fuller are all quoted in Doyle L. Young, "The Place of Andrew Fuller in the Developing Modern Missions Movement" (PhD thesis, Southwestern Baptist Theological Seminary, 1981), 232.

Calvinism and Revival 245

early years. Writing on December 3, 1814, to John Ryland Jr. (1753–1825), a close friend of both Carey and Fuller, Scott stated:

> I do most heartily rejoice in what your missionaries are doing in India. Their's is the most regular and best conducted plan against the kingdom of darkness that modern times have shewn; and I augur the most extensive success. More genuine Christian wisdom, fortitude, and disinterested assiduity, perseverance, and patience appear, than I elsewhere read of. May God protect and prosper! May all India be peopled with true Christians!—even though they be all baptists.... The Lord is doing great things, and answering prayer every where.[27]

Concluding Words

When Sutcliff was dying in 1814, among the things he said, one statement in particular stuck in the minds of his family and friends: "I wish I had prayed more." It was an amazing statement for Sutcliff to make, for he had been a key figure in a movement of prayer, which was definitely owned by God to bring revival to the English Calvinistic Baptists. When Andrew Fuller heard what his dear friend Sutcliff had said, he reflected on it thus:

> I wish that I had prayed more. I do not suppose that brother Sutcliffe meant that he wished he had prayed more frequently, but more *spiritually*. I wish I had prayed more for the influences of the Holy Spirit, I might have enjoyed more of the power of vital godliness. I wish I had prayed more for the assistance of the Holy Spirit, in studying and preaching my sermons: I might have seen more of the blessing of God attending my ministry. I wish I had prayed more for the outpouring of the Holy Spirit to attend the labours of our friends in India; I might have witnessed more of the effects of their efforts in the conversion of the heathen.[28]

Fuller used Sutcliff's dying statement as a test of his own prayer life, and he found it wanting. Yet seen in the light of all we have looked at, Sutcliff's

---

27. John Scott, *Letters and Papers of the Rev. Thomas Scott* (London: L. B. Seeley and Son, 1824), 254.

28. As quoted in John W. Morris, *Memoirs of the Life and Writings of the Rev Andrew Fuller* (London, 1816), 443.

statement as he lay dying and Fuller's reflection on it also reveal something else: a profound awareness that the Spirit's blessing and empowerment in personal and corporate revival is *the* most important aspect of the believer's and the church's life.

Afterword

The Reformation has proven to be the most significant event in the history of Christianity in the past millennium. And within that "event" that took close to a century to play out, the life of John Calvin is arguably the most influential, apart from that of Martin Luther. In the decades after Calvin's death and through the seventeenth century, Calvinism became a distinct ethos and body of thought that crossed national and denominational boundaries, shaping church life from Eastern Europe in places like Lithuania and Poland to the Celtic nations of the British Isles, Scotland and Wales, and even in the New World with the British colonies of New England. Whole denominations developed that identified themselves with the shape of his thought, from the Reformed churches in Germany for which the Heidelberg Catechism was first developed to the Reformed congregations in Holland that defended their Calvinist heritage at the Synod of Dort. But as the essays in this book have demonstrated, his legacy also embraces politics—it is hard to imagine the American Revolution without Calvin's thinking about the right of the lesser magistrates to resist oppressive rulers[1]—marriage legislation, and profound social issues like the alleviation of poverty. In fact, scarcely is there an area of life in modern history and Western civilization that is not permeated by Calvin's influence. As the English statesman John Morley declared well over a hundred years ago, "To omit Calvin from the forces of Western evolution is to read history with one eye shut."[2]

But if Calvin were asked what he would most desire to be remembered for—though it is hard to envision him even responding to such a question,

---

1. See the detailed argument of Gary Lee Steward, "Justifying Revolution: The American Clergy's Argument for Political Resistance, 1763–1783" (PhD diss.,n, The Southern Baptist Theological Seminary, 2017).

2. As quoted in Richard Taylor Stevenson, *John Calvin, the Statesman* (Cincinnati: Jennings and Graham; New York: Eaton and Mains, 1907), 5.

as he deliberately sought not to speak about himself—he would probably cite the realms of preaching and piety. In his mind, preaching and teaching the flawless Word of God lay at the center of his calling to the city of Geneva, which, through the publication of his sermons and commentaries, has given him a worldwide congregation. His systematic theology, the *Institutes*, is above all things a treatise of piety. Calvin's theological explication of knowing God through His peerless revelation in His Word, the nature of the human condition and the fall, the necessity of justification and its profoundly forensic nature, the Christocentric shape of salvation and union with Christ, the work of the Spirit in the church, and God's wrapping up of time in the last days has this grand focus: how to live this earthly life to the glory of God.

It is not given to every life lived in this world to so impact contemporaries and posterity that it can be said nothing was the same after their passing from this earthly scene. But Calvin—in his life and thought—was such a gift.